NORTHWEST ANGLING

by
ENOS BRADNER

Black and White Drawings by the Author
and
Color Plates by Alan Pratt

BINFORDS & MORT, *Publishers*
Portland   •   Oregon   •   97242

Northwest Angling

LIBRARY OF CONGRESS CATALOG CARD NUMBER: 70-81629
T-395M

Printed in the United States of America

SECOND EDITION

To my many fishing partners
who have helped
to write this book.

It is, indeed, an interesting study in human nature to observe how quickly and with what instant forgetfulness of self and selfishness men descend from their high horses to speak of certain streams and certain fishes, of baits and lures and riffles and lurking places and shallows and windfalls. They are touched by a spell that is unfailing in its strength and candor and which brushes aside all artificiality as easily as a freshet clears the stream of impediments. The talk is brisk, animated, sincere, and the eyes are likewise. The demeanor of men of all races is identical when they speak of fishing.

—*from* How Could I Be Forgetting

by Ben Hur Lampman

INTRODUCTION

The Pacific Northwest, which embraces the Province of British Columbia, and the states of Washington, Oregon, and northern California, is bountifully blessed with all the resources that make a year-round playground for the sportsman-angler.

It is a country of contrasts. There is the coastal plain reaching down to the inner passage off British Columbia, and to the waters of Puget Sound and the broad Pacific off Oregon and California. Here a temperate climate permits fishing every month of the year. Away from the coast, in the more or less arid plateau of the eastern section, there are inland lakes and rivers that attract anglers all summer and fall. And throughout the Cascades and the Sierras there exists some of the best mountain lake fishing in the United States.

Except for minor differences due mainly to climate, waters and species of fish are the same throughout this wide-spreading section. And fishing methods vary little. An angler who knows how to take trout in a Washington lake will do equally well in the high Sierras and up the Cariboo in British Columbia. The methods of taking migratory trout, the steelhead or the sea-run cutthroats are also more or less uniform from Vancouver Island to the Eel.

Many of the techniques for taking the two varieties of Pacific salmon—the chinook and the silver—were developed in Puget Sound. The lures and other new refinements for salt water trolling developed by the active sport anglers of the Northwest have spread north to Alaska and south into Oregon and the Columbia River areas.

Although the bulk of the fishing experiences described in the following chapters deal with Washington, most of them could be duplicated at any other spot in this vast Northwest. The author finds that he can take steelhead, rainbow or cutthroat by the same methods throughout this territory. For example, when he participated in a salmon derby at Juneau, Alaska, in August of 1947, he found anglers there using the same lures and methods that are commonly used in Puget Sound.

The newly arrived sportsman to the coast often has difficulty adjusting himself to the alluring piscatorial menu that is offered him the year round. The die-hard resident sportsman, on the other hand, has become so accustomed to at least one fishing trip for every one of the fifty-two weeks of the year that he finds it hard to realize that for half the year the rest of the trout sections of the United States are frozen tight in the icy grip of winter.

The types of angling in the Northwest are so varied that very few sportsmen attempt them all but tend to specialize in the one that appeals to them most, especially since each type may be practiced every month of the year. If you happen to be a trout fisherman there are thousands of mountain lakes for summer sport, and tens of thousands of lowland lakes for the rest of the year. These lakes are everywhere—some even in the midst of our largest cities. In these lakes the angler can find the type of trout fishing best suited to his temperament or his age. He can still-fish ten feet off a trunk highway or he can hike in twenty miles back from the jumping-off place.

Those who pursue the migratory trout—the steelhead and the sea-run cutthroat—can find them the year round. They can chase steelhead all winter long and then mix steelhead and sea-runs all during the summer. The winter fish run from December until April; the summer-run steelhead enter streams from May to September. Then through the fall and winter the ocean cutthroats make their migratory runs and provide a fine sport for a new lot of specialists.

The Pacific salmon as a sport fish has become nationally famous within the past decade. Once taken only on heavy trolling gear, the chinook or the cohoe is now boated on light sporty tackle with lures ranging from plugs to flies. Most of the mature salmon are caught when they approach the estuaries lying off their parent rivers. The main runs of the chinooks come within the reach of the sportsman angler during the period from June through September. The cohoes enter the same waters about a month later and will be found even into November.

The water of Puget Sound, when the runs of migratory fish are over, provide a winter fishery for salmon the equal of which is not found anywhere else along the Pacific Coast. For at this time, when the nearly matured salmon are far out at sea building up weight for their life's climax—the spawning run—there are thousands of immature kings or blackmouth salmon to be found within Puget Sound itself. Anglers follow these young salmon from one fishing ground to another and take fish all winter long.

CONTENTS

PART ONE

Chapter One

"OPENING DAY"

"The Opening Day of Trout Season"—these magic words strike a responsive chord in the hearts of millions of Americans. It is unlikely that there is any other outdoor event that appeals to more sportsmen than this first try at trout fishing each spring. For from Maine to Washington, throughout the length and breadth of our northern trout country, anglers rarely miss spending this annual date on a favored lake or stream.

Opening day, no matter in which section of the country it occurs, usually coincides with the advent of spring. By the tag end of winter

3

the idle trout anglers start planning, and as the day approaches they begin working themselves into a lather of anticipation. For by this time the sap is running freely in tree and human alike. Like a shrub sending forth buds of green, the fisherman blossoms out in new boots, a fancy jacket or a hat with its brim stuck full of trout flies.

There seems to be a sort of inherent love of fishing, bred into every-one of us, that after being suppressed all winter long, breaks out in an urge that cannot be denied. A disciple of Izaak Walton just "hasta" go fishing and neither late snow storm, high water nor impassable roads will hold him back, when opening day rolls around.

Most sportsmen started their angling careers as youngsters messing around a resort lake for perch, bullhead or maybe a trout or two. Later they graduated into the trout class, where they usually remain in various stages of development until the end of their days. Many of them how-ever get sidetracked in some specialized field such as steelheading, bass casting or occasionally even backsliding into the status of salt-chuck (salt-water) enthusiasts. But they all retain a sneaking fondness for their first love and many of them wet a line for trout on opening day whether they ever go out a second time or not.

Opening Dates. Trout fishing in the Northwest, because of the variety of conditions inherent in the topography, presents special problems that have caused a rather complicated series of opening dates. The lowland lakes of the Pacific coast do not freeze up in winter and could be fished the year round. The same holds true for the rivers. Consequently in these areas, trout conservation and management principles dictate the opening dates.

But as we travel up to the foothills of the Olympics, the Cascades and the Sierras the lakes become colder and good fishing must await warmer days. As for the mountain lakes, many are frozen over until July, and Nature herself takes care of the fishing seasons.

The latest fish laws indicate that the trout seasons open in British Columbia, Washington and Oregon sometime in the month of April. There are exceptions in special areas but the angler can count on don-ning his hip boots and limbering up his fly rod around the middle of April each year. This applies whether he lives in the Okanogan district of British Columbia, the Puget Sound country of Washington, or in the lake country near Bend, Oregon. California holds up its season a bit, usu-ally not permitting a trout angler to wet his line until around the first of May.

Throughout the Northwest the trout fishing season extends into October. Oregon usually closes the season by October 15, and California by the end of October. But both Washington and British Columbia permit fishing in the lowland lakes into November. The two northern sections have varying exceptions: some that permit fishing until December and others that keep waters open all winter, a boon to really enthusiastic fishermen.

The Low Lakes of Washington. There are so many lowland lakes scattered throughout this Northwest country that no one angler could ever hope to fish them all. However they possess characteristics in common as to species of trout and the methods of taking them. They may vary as to setting or size, and the insect hatch and underwater food may not be uniform, but the experienced western angler should be able to catch himself a creel of trout wherever he goes, providing the trout are in a hitting mood. The fly fisherman will have success in all but the largest and deepest lakes, the trollers should do well in all but the small ponds, and the still fisherman will take trout wherever he can anchor his boat.

Having had a close acquaintance with the lakes of Washington for twenty years I shall deal here with the waters that I know the best, hoping that the reader will realize that most of the techniques described will apply all throughout our northcoast waters.

In Washington State, the trout season usually opens the third Sunday in April, but fishing at that time is confined to the lowland lakes. All of the lakes in the following nine counties will have the uniform April opening: Adams, Franklin, Grant, Island, Kitsap, Spokane, Thurston and Whitman. In the remaining counties of the state, the lakes opening on this date will all be named in the State Game Department, *Fishery Regulation Pamphlet.* This list of waters is an imposing one, and although it is restricted to lakes, it offers a wide variety of fishing fare for various species of trout as well as for bass.

All of the waters not named in the *Fishery Regulation Pamphlet*—mostly altitude or mountain lakes—will not be open for fishing until the last Sunday in May. Many of these lakes are either snow-bound or ice-covered until June and could not possibly be fished until after that time in any case.

Except for a few streams that are open the year round, the rivers of the state are not open to the trout angler until the same date as the mountain lakes. This late opening for the streams which has been in effect since 1941 was instituted in order to protect the immature migratory trout of the coastal streams—the steelhead and cutthroats—which are on their way to the ocean during the late spring.

Washington is especially blessed in the number and variety of its fishing spots. There are 948 named lakes in the State and almost all of these contain fish. However only about 30% of them are producing up to their capacity, with the remainder turning out less than half of their potential.

There are lakes of every size from beaver ponds that you can spit across (if you happen to be proficient in that art) to imposing bodies of water such as Lakes Chelan or Crescent. Chelan, one of the least publicized lakes in the Northwest, is at the same time one of the most beautiful. It winds for 52 miles deep into the heart of the Cascade Mountains and offers rainbow, cutthroat, Dolly Varden and silver trout fishing.

Crescent is another lake of superlative beauty, its aquamarine blue depths reflecting the tree-clad peaks of the Olympics. This lake, too, is little fished. Although its trout population is not large its crystal clear waters hold the Beardsley and the Crescenti trout, two species not found anywhere else in the world.

The Crescenti are derived from cutthroat stock, are quite silvery in appearance with few spots and grow to medium size. The Beardsley's ancestors were rainbows or steelhead and these trout sometimes attain fifteen to twenty pounds in weight. They are dark green on the back, heavily spotted and white on the belly. The smaller sizes may be taken on fly outfits in the shallows along shore. The larger specimens must be taken on a deep troll, and as the lake is reported to be 900 feet deep in spots, one must use weight to get down to them.

However, many of the lowland lakes lie in thickly populated districts, their shores lined with houses. Often where there are resorts, boats may be rented. A number of these attract large crowds on opening day and every year there are several that turn out exceedingly good catches of trout in both number and size.

But the smaller lakes also get a big play. You will find these everywhere, alongside the highways, set down in pasture lands or nestled in groups among the foothills. They are scattered like bright coins thrown from the fists of a Paul Bunyan over the cutover timber lands along the coast. Some of these are reached only over skid roads or dim trails and in these spots the angler must usually provide his own water transportation. Sometimes there are unwieldly rafts hidden along the brushy shore that will furnish a slippery vehicle for getting out onto the open water. These backwoods lakes usually offer a better brand of fishing than the resort lakes and occasionally one is classed as a "hot spot."

Native Cutthroats. Back in the good old days before the first tourists started driving their steaming jalopies over the passes in the Rockies and the Cascades, most of the lakes in this section held native cutthroat trout. From the Pend Oreille country of the east side with its Yellowstone variety to the lakes of the Olympics with their coastal strain, the cutthroat trout was the dominant species of fish in lakes, large or small. They spawned efficiently in the small tributary creeks and in some of the larger lakes containing adequate food supplies they grew to large size. On the coast where the majority of the "cuts" made a salt water migration, they would come back into the rivers and penetrate up the

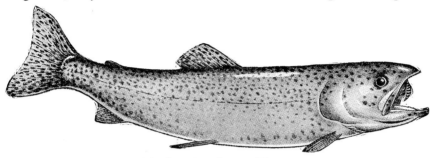

Native Cutthroat Trout

small creeks in the back country. In the valleys back in the hills, where beaver dammed the small streams, the cutthroats often lost their migratory tendencies and took up residence in the ponds, where they colored up as if they had never seen the ocean.

But as the cities along the coast grew in size and ranchers settled in the fertile cutover land, the cutthroats started to lose ground. Plantings of other species of trout and spiny rays in many lakes started an intense competition for the available food and the native "cuts" declined in numbers. They were surface feeders and hit lures readily so that in time fish of good size and virile stock became scarce. The "cuts" were hard to raise in the hatcheries, their eggs were often infertile or the young trout died, and artificial plantings of these natives could not keep up with the rate of depletion. Fortunately, Dr. L. R. Donaldson of the Washington University School of Fisheries developed a hardy strain of these trout: a mixture of native and sea-run varieties that could be hatched successfully and reared quickly in hatchery ponds. The Game Department has now taken over the rearing of this strain, and increased its planting from 745,350 fish in 1941 to 2,124,000 in the fiscal year ending April, 1948. The bulk of these are fry with only 250,000 raised to fingerling size.

Just for the record, the plantings of the Washington Game Department for the same period on the other species of trout were as follows: rainbows, 13,275,000, of which about ten million were fingerlings, which represents approximately the number and proportion planted each year; 945,000 eastern brook, most of them advanced fry, which represents an increase over the past few years; and 43,200,000 silver trout fry representing a small decrease due over past years to a drop in the taking of spawn.

But while the cutthroat population was steadily losing ground the rainbows were taking their place. These trout were easy to raise and their eggs could be purchased on the open market. Although they could spawn successfully in only a few of the lowland lakes, the Game Department adopted the policy of planting large numbers of legal-sized rainbows, expecting to have the bulk of the plant caught each season. This proved out well in the resort lakes, where thousands of these trout were caught each day in the first month of each new season. Nevertheless in many of the Eastern Washington lakes and in others on the coast near large cities, these planted rainbows grew to good size and proved hard to take. Most of these lunkers were bottom feeders and did not appear too often in anglers' creels.

Brook trout have never been popular with Washington anglers but in the right spots they have shown themselves to be a fine sport fish. They have not done too well in the lowland lakes or the streams, but in the mountain lakes or in the ponds at an elevation of 1,000 feet or more they will grow up to three pounds or so, and can be taken on flies during the spring or fall.

The mountain lakes which are clear cold bodies of water will grow almost any species of trout. But these lakes have been planted in recent years mainly with rainbows and cutthroats. In the past, many brook trout and Montana black spotted cutthroat were planted and did well. A few of the lakes in the Copper Lake chain were planted with golden trout some years ago, and although some of these grew to good size, their continued existence must depend on natural spawning as no new plants have been made since then. During the past two years, grayling trout eggs have been obtained from the Montana strain and these were planted in lakes in Whatcom and Skagit Counties and up the Middle Fork of the Snoqualmie River. One of these lakes produced grayling this past summer, but it is too early to know how the balance will develop.

A third native species called a silver trout, although it is in reality a landlocked variety of the sockeye, is now planted in vast numbers in the coastal lakes and affords fine family fishing during the spring months.

Most of the foregoing species will be found in the rest of the Northwest although in varying proportions. In British Columbia the rainbow's place has been taken by its cousin, the Kamloops, which predominates in the majority of British Columbian lakes. Kokanee and large lake trout are found in numbers, but there are few good cutthroat lakes in this region. In Oregon, the rainbows and cutthroats dominate, with some native kokanees. In a few of the lakes brook trout have done remarkably well. In California, the lakes are full of rainbows, some cutthroats and brown trout. In the Sierras the world famed golden trout is native.

A Day at "Cutthroat Meadows." Many sportsmen know of lakes that because they are fished infrequently, always seem to turn out limit catches to those fortunate "anglers-in-the-know." Some of these lakes are difficult to find, others are a long hike in, and some have apparently just been forgotten. These forgotten lakes or ponds are intriguing spots. They have been neglected because they have the reputation of being fished out. But a few of them have paid surprising dividends to inquisitive anglers who have patiently explored their possibilities.

I know of such a spot, fondly called "Cutthroat Meadows," that so far remains in this forgotten category. Every winter I keep my fingers crossed in the hope that it will be in the same status come another trout season. It is in the background of my mind all through the winter steelhead season, and as soon as possible after opening day I make my first trip into this long cherished "trout pool."

As is the case with most of our backswoods lakes it is a long hike into Cutthroat Meadows. The trail meanders off from the highway, through open glades heavy with the pungent odor from the pink blossoms of the flowering currant. You walk silently over thick moss through heavy stands of timber so thick that the trail is always shaded. You come into the open where you scuff through salal brush whose deep green leaves cover the path like a deep piled rug. You push through second growth fir whose branches across the trail are so firmly meshed that they leave only a narrow tunnel through which to crawl. You hit an old right of way that hugs a steep bank and you glimpse a rushing creek far down in the gully below. Then you edge through a thicket of alder and willow and there is the glint of your beloved lake right at your feet.

It is always good to see familiar waters after a year of absence. Your eyes travel over the well-known surface, seeking the spot where you lost that big cutthroat last spring. You glance up to the sharp cutover ridge at your right and then down to the deep green of the wooded slope along the left shore. You check again on the rounded knob that closes in the valley at the head of the lake. The same old logs still stretch out from the shore. The floating deadheads clutter up one end of the pond. A spatter of rain roughens up the surface this morning as you push out from the alder-shrouded bank.

You start out with a carot nymph. You make short casts along the logs or the underwater clumps of grass, slowly moving your fly along just below the surface. There is the merest touch with no disturbance of the water and a couple of seconds go by before you realize that you have missed your first strike. You then cover a noisy rise and hook a rash ten-inch trout that splashes all over the surface before you bring it to net.

You drift with the riffle up the small pond. As you approach, a kingfisher swoops from a dead stump to glide across the pond, breaking the silence with its hoarse chattering cry. You try a cast alongside that big cedar log. There is another one of those easy touches, but this time you are ready and set the hook. Boy, is that a solid hit! And then a golden dark shape boils the surface as it turns to head under the log. You are hooked fast to a real trout and how those big lunkers fool you when they stop your fly with that velvet touch.

This proves to be one of your lucky days for your trout fails to hook up on the snag-infested bottom, and after much careful nursing and a lot of surface splashing you net a 19-inch native cutthroat. You gaze at its dark green back, the deep yellow sides and belly thickly covered with dark spots that run into the fins and spatter the tail. Dark golden "cuts" are all too rare these days, but they are fish that will test any angler's skill. They will shoot his blood pressure up alarmingly before they are caught, and they look almighty handsome lying on a bed of ferns when you display them that night at home on the kitchen table.

Egg Fishing for Rainbows. The first month of the "lake season" is often a difficult time for the fly angler. April usually brings a succession of cold rainy days, making lakes appear dead and sodden, as calm on the surface as a city reservoir, and apparently as devoid of fish life. Cutthroats, it is true, are "rainy day" trout, and often hit well with rain pelting the water, when it would normally seem foolish to use a fly. In fact, some of my best fishing days on the smaller cutthroat ponds have been on the days when the rain came down steadily and heavily. But the majority of Washington's lowland waters, particularly along Puget Sound's coast line, are planted to rainbows. And these acrobatic trout need a spot of sun to bring them up from the bottom. They are notorious underwater feeders in the early spring and are difficult to take on the fly in that season. They do not start cruising the surface until the weather warms up and brings with the heat an early morning or late evening hatch of insects or nymphs.

Still-fishing with bait or trolling with a small spoon and worm has in the past been the popular fishing method during the inclement April and May weather. Much of the bait fishing in this state is done with salmon eggs. This was once a very killing method of taking trout but since fishing has greatly increased in intensity with every accessible lake covered with anglers, it has lost much of its effectiveness.

However, there are still a number of experts in the use of the single egg and feed eggs who take large rainbows on light tackle. These anglers like a whippy fly rod, usually not longer than eight feet, with a limber tip. They use a multiple reel with 300 yards or more of monofilament nylon line testing six to ten pounds. They attach leaders six feet or longer testing 1¼ to 2 pounds. Their hooks are small—size 10 to 14—and the hook will be buried entirely in the egg. See illustration on page 11. It is preferable to match as closely as possible the color of the single eggs to those that are being used as feed attractors.

After anchoring near a drop-off or at the edge of a hole in the lake, the angler will throw a spoonful of feed eggs over the water he intends

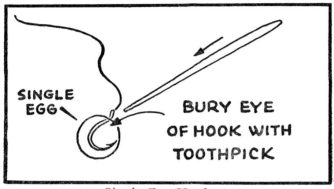

Single Egg Hook-up

to fish. He will then cast his line with his single-egg lure into the same piece of water and allow it to sink slowly. At times no weight is used but usually one buckshot clinched on the leader about two feet from the hook is used to pull the egg down. Care must be taken not to strip the egg off when making the cast. When your line has sunk, the egg may be left on the bottom and the rod rested on the side of the boat. When the rod tip moves with a strike, slack should be taken up, and the trout hooked with a gentle set. The fish, if a large one, must be played with great care. This accounts for the length of line as with so light a leader the trout must be allowed to run without checking.

Trolling for Trout. Multiple-trolling gear—that is a gang troll or a length of spoons a yard or more long—is permitted in most of the rain-bow lakes, but this type of gear has little appeal to the angler who fishes for sport, as it does not give the trout a chance. When the fish do not run over a foot in length they have little chance to fight the pull of the heavy spoons, and as a consequence the angler simply reels in a dead fish. However single jigger spoons, in the small sizes of any one of the local designs devised for salmon, are excellent lures. They do not revolve but weave from side to side in the water and are easy on a fly rod. The F.S.T., one of the most popular types, is used in either the number o or 1 sizes in silver or brass. It may be trolled either without weight or with a single buckshot.

The old reliable Boyle spoon and worm—a revolving spoon in a number four—is used with a single hook attached behind the spoon by a two- or three-inch leader. The worm is impaled on the hook so that it has an end free and is not bunched up. One drawback to this method is that striking trout are hard to hook and the angleworm must be continuously replaced.

Although the majority of the lowland lakes are open to the use of feed eggs and multiple gear one should check the *Game Fish Pamphlet* carefully before using these types of tackle.

Nymphing the Fly and a Few Typical Patterns. Within the past decade more and more "fly flitters" have continued to use their feathered offerings during fair weather and foul and have evolved a well-nigh infallible method of taking trout under almost all kinds of weather conditions. In fact, if the trout—whether they are rainbows, cutthroats or brook trout—are feeding at all, they can be taken on flies by the nymph method, which, simply stated, is merely trolling a fly in the same manner as one would troll a spoon. Some of the fishermen call it nymphing, but in the vernacular, borrowing a term from salt-water fishing, it is called "mooching a fly."

There is no question that an angler gets more thrill and satisfaction out of casting a fly instead of simply dragging it along behind a boat. There is no more exciting sport for an angler than to drop a fly into the ring of a rising trout and then wait for seconds that seem like hours in the expectation of a smashing strike; or to match a hatch on a lake and drop a well-doped dry fly among the cruising rainbows and wait with your heart up among your tonsils as a lunker comes along gulping in natural flies on every side. It is an engrossing pastime to travel along the "trouty" shore line of a lake and cover the water with a wet fly and try to tease a trout from its hiding place in the snags, logs, or lily pads. Every fly angler likes to work his tackle. He enjoys the very act of covering the water with a well-placed fly. He enjoys using the tools of his craft and can spend many happy and profitable hours working the fly even without taking a fish. Personally, I would rather spend an hour or two whipping a fly than a whole day of nymphing from a boat even if the latter method should produce more trout. But in describing our coast-lake fishing I am going to forego, in the main, the pleasure of writing about the proper way to cast a wet or dry fly. This technique has been covered in all its phases by experts for many years past, and except for a variation of insect hatch their methods can and do apply on our western lakes. Northwest anglers, when the occasion permits, take trout— and large ones too—with the floating fly on our lowland lakes.

So in this section I will confine myself mainly to an explanation of the nymphing technique, feeling that its purpose and methods have not had a wide circulation outside of this coastal area.

The months of April and May throughout the Northwest are usually a period of raw days with wet weather the rule rather than the exception. Lakes are inclined to be high and nature usually presents a forbidding frown on the ordinary manner of working the fly. Lowland lakes are prone to appear fishless; their surface may go all day without showing a rise. The trout are apparently way down nosing leisurely along the bottom. At such times a nymphed fly if handled correctly will nearly always take trout.

I have fished a lake on opening day when ice crackled in the car tracks and puddles in the trail were frozen over. There was new snow sprinkled over the firs on the hills sloping up from the lake, and frost upon its banks. The water looked dark and unpromising, but a patient searching through the channels and feed holes with a trolled nymph fly put a few trout into the creel. Usually these were worthwhile trout; not the little playboys, but husky solid meated oldsters, sometimes tipping the scales up to the three-pound mark.

Realizing that not any old pattern will work when trolled, Washington's anglers are gradually evolving a series of nymph-type flies that are especially suited to Northwest waters. The standard fly patterns as well as many of the nymph flies of the East have not been too productive here for cold-weather angling. In fact, until flies adapted to our local waters were devised, early season fly fishing was never too successful.

The development of Northwest nymphs is still in its infancy and new patterns appear and disappear every spring. Many an inventive fly dresser has brought home a queer looking nymph from an early lake trip and by the next week-end has dreamed up an imitation that may or may not be a "taker." But a backlog of tried-and-true lures have already appeared and most of them will be found in local anglers' fly boxes.

Although the Puget Sound lakes are not noted for their insect life there are many types of underwater food on which trout wax fat and large. Trout sometimes gorge themselves on small snails to the point that these crustaceans will drop out of their jaws when the trout happens to hit an artificial fly. Others fill themselves with small fresh water shrimps, or rust-red plankton or the very tiny worm-like larva of water insects. Some of these types may be imitated by the fly maker but others do not lend themselves to facsimiles of fur and feathers.

Among the fly patterns that successfully represent western trout food is the widely used Carey Special, a staple pattern for Northwest and British Columbia lakes. Originated in Canada, it is a suggestive imitation of the dragon fly or damsel fly nymph in various stages of development. As some of these nymphs grow up to 1½ inches long a fat, husky fly is necessary. I have caught trout in April whose stomachs contained several of the ugly dark dragon fly nymphs. The same nymphs appeared in trout's gullets in the month of October. As these flies are regularly found on most lowland lakes all season this fly is a year-round favorite.

Like most nymph flies this pattern should be trolled slowly. The majority of anglers in this section use a 9-foot leader tapered down to 1 or 2x. Most of our lowland lakes are not particularly clear, some showing a brownish cast, and too light a tippet is not necessary. About seventy-five feet of line are played out and the rod should be slanted over the end of the boat at such an angle that the trout will usually hook itself by the spring of the rod tip. The line should not be greased as it must sink to troll properly. If the lake happens to be absolutely calm, the wake of a floating line will often prevent the trout from striking.

A great deal of nymphing is done in comparatively shallow lakes, or in channels where the water runs from 10 to 25 feet in depth. The fly is first cast out, then extra line is released and the fly is allowed to sink. It can be fished either just below the surface, several feet down, or near the bottom. Variation in depth can be obtained by stopping the boat at intervals to allow the fly to drop down or by taking several hurried strokes of the oars to bring it toward the surface.

Very often a fly that is being pulled along on an upward tangent will bring strikes, as the trout apparently think it is a nymph coming up from the bottom. An effective trick is to row the boat in a circular sweep through an especially good spot. The trout will often hit the fly as it comes around in the last arc of the circle.

The proper rowing speed and the varying of this speed from very slow to a medium speed is highly important.

Often trout will hit with tremendous force and if they are rainbows or Kamloops they immediately start a leaping exhibition that will shake the fly loose unless the angler immediately takes a firm grasp of the rod and strips in all the slack line. At other times the trout will merely twitch the rod tip—ticking the lure rapidly without getting hooked. When they are hitting lightly one should still grasp the rod quickly, but strip in the line gently, and be ready to "set" on the trout the second he feels a "touch." It would be nice if the angler could possess a sort of second sight in this type of fishing, permitting him to know what type of trout is ticking on his fly, seventy-five feet out there in the lake. A heavy set on a 12-incher will probably set the barb correctly into the trout's jaws. But if this ticking fish happens to be a fat 20-incher, then too powerful a wrist will not only result in losing the fly but most of the leader as well.

It is well not to set the drag on one's reel too tightly when nymphing. I remember one spring day at Price's Lake when after lunch I started lazily rowing out into the feeding channel. The sun was trying to peep out from under some heavy gray clouds and I wasn't paying much heed to the fly slowly working along back of the boat. Then as the fly passed along one of the sunken logs, I saw the rod tip twitch twice very lightly.

"Ho hum!—just another 10-incher," I thought and didn't care whether it got hooked or not. But only a wink of the eye later, there was a vicious strike, and my entire outfit, line, rod, and reel, disappeared over the stern of the boat into the lake neatly evading my desperately clutching fingers.

I immediately dropped anchor and called my partner over and transferred to his boat. He rigged up (on a heavy cord) a triple hook that he happened to have in his pack as a drag. As the rod had dropped in only about 10 feet of water, by lowering our faces to the surface we could locate the yellow line resting on the bottom. After some scrabbling around we succeeded in getting the line to the top and with it pulled up the rod. As I started to strip in the line there was a sudden run and to my astonishment I found myself playing the trout. It was still full of fight and when it came to net I found I had hooked a one and a half pound brookie.

Creating a New Nymph. The time-tried principle of basing the selection of a fly by learning at first hand what a trout has been having for breakfast holds true when nymphing. So as soon as one nets his first trout one should lose no time in examining the contents of stomach and gullet. Although one occasionally takes a trout that apparently has been on a strict diet, it is a feeding fish that hits a fly; his stomach is a store house of culinary information.

I recall one cold very slow fishing day four years ago, on Price's Lake, when Frank Headrick and myself were well into mid-morning without having set a hook into a single trout. Frank finally netted a fat 14-inch brook.

"Hey, Brad, row over here," he called, "and see what Mr. Brookie has been eating."

I came alongside and found that Frank had spread out on the seat several green nymphs about three quarters of an inch long, all partly digested, and on the blade of his knife was a nearly perfect specimen of the same worm-like nymph. See illustration on page 15. It had a narrow head, its body was divided into segments like that of a caddis-fly worm and its color ranged from a dark green above to a vivid grass green on the under side. It resembled the larva of a river stone fly.

"I found a trout full of these things last spring," said Frank, "and tied me up a sample pair out of green yarn and a gray hackle. Here's my chance to try one."

I pawed through my fly boxes but could find only some dry green sedges dressed for British Columbia fishing that came anywhere matching the green of the appetizing nymph. But after I had trimmed off all but a short section of the wings and most of the gray hackle I had a passable imitation.

In the meantime Frank had been casting his imitation green nymph into a deep channel along a weed bed, allowing it to sink and getting a strike nearly every cast. He netted two brooks and a rainbow before he broke off his last fly on a lunker fish.

I had floated into the center of the weed bed and cast into an open spot, slowly stripping the sunken nymph through the water. This produced six strikes and two brooks before I lost my fly on the weeds.

Needless to say, we both got busy that week over our fly vises and Frank finally evolved the pattern we named the Dandy Green Nymph. As is true with most of the underwater patterns that have proved effective here, fur bodies appear to make the best imitations. We dress it as follows. The hook should be from size 7 to 10. The tail is made of several wisps of gray-green Chinese cock pheasant hackle. The ribs are yellow tying silk. The body may be green yarn, but we prefer a dubbed body of mixed grass-green and yellow polar bear fur (the fuzz next to the hide). The hackle is made from the gray-green small feather found on cock pheasants just back of the rump, tied sparsely and in spider fashion.

This fly has proved to be a good early season pattern and works well on cutthroats, rainbows and brook trout. It may be used in spiny ray lakes and has produced some husky specimens of perch and secondary members of the perch family.

Casting the Nymph for "Cuts" and Rainbows. It is not always necessary to use these nymphs as trolled flies. When the trout are nymphing or taking food just under the surface a cast fly will often prove effective.

Some of the smaller lakes have narrow feeding channels or deep holes surrounded by snags where a trolled nymph is not practical. In such spots when the fish are not rising, a deeply sunken fly will often take some surprisingly large trout. One should cast close up to the shore, brush or logs and allow the fly to sink almost to the bottom. Then strip in slowly in even jerks, taking in about two feet of line at every motion. The rod should be held at about a 45 degree angle. Be sure to strip in the fly until you have pulled the leader out of the water, and then slowly lift the fly out in a final pull. Trout will often follow the fly with their noses almost touching the hook, and not make a pass at it until it is being lifted from the water. If you miss the strike, drop the fly back into the water immediately, without lengthening the cast, and skitter the fly along on the surface or just under it. This will often evoke a second strike from the trout which will sometimes have waited to see what had happened to that tasty morsel that had disappeared so suddenly while it was following it. In this case, fisherman's patience and "thinking like a fish" may get you a nice dinner.

One must be lightning fast to hook the trout when practicing this method of stripping the sunken nymph fly. A large fish is capable of taking the fly with the gentlest of nudges which may seem no heavier than the pull caused by touching a blade of grass with the fly. One must strike without hesitation, and unless one's reflexes are working well the trout will not be hooked. Often the trout will take the fly without causing the slightest disturbance of the water. But just often enough to prevent the angler from becoming complacent, a big trout will take the fly as it nears the surface with a terrific smash, making one feel as if he had lifted a wash tub out of water. This is likely to startle the angler, causing him to set the hook with power enough to break the trout's neck, with the result that he not only loses his fly but puts down a good fish.

Many times I have, by standing up in a boat, seen cutthroats come for a nymph stripped just under the surface that I would not have realized were striking if I had been sitting down. Occasionally they would make a lightning-like dart in from one side, turning away almost at the instant they touched the fly. Possibly they do turn away without touch-

ing it at times, but usually an instant strike at the proper moment should
hook the fish.

When fishing a small lake or pond, I often find a particular pattern
of nymph that is a better taker that day than any other. I may be work-

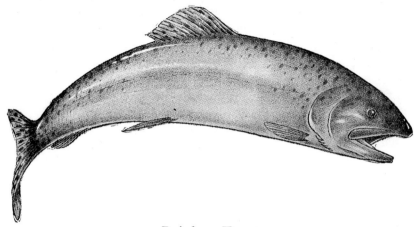

Rainbow Trout

ing the deep pockets under alders along the shore or beneath a log and
raise a trout which boils at the fly but is not hooked. At such times I use
a little stunt which, while it works well for me, may not appeal to anyone
else.

In addition to the leader that I am using I keep two others all soaked
up and tied onto other contrasting but usually effective nymph patterns.
So after missing the trout, I make two or three very careful casts to see
if the fish will come back for the same fly. Usually it won't. I then sit
down in the boat and replace the taking fly and leader with one of the
others and cast into the same spot. Frequently this will produce a second
vicious strike, and if I am again too slow, I rest the fish while tying on
the third leader. This will generally do the trick. For by this time the
trout wants a fly and really takes it.

After fighting the fish I can go back to covering water with the fly
that is good-for-that-day, simply by changing leaders. This method not
only saves time but it saves tippets by avoiding continuously bending on
new patterns.

For the past eight years the State Game Department has been making
heavy plants of rainbow trout in most of the lowland lakes. While most
of these trout are taken during the first month of the season as small
size fish ranging from six to 12 inches, a few of the rainbows live to grow
up to grandaddy size. They can be found in many of the resort lakes

alongside the highways; and lakes even completely surrounded by summer homes may contain rainbows that have grown to lengths from 14 to 20 inches. These large trout are very difficult to take on a fly, for much of the time they are feeding off the bottom, and are finicky at hitting any kind of bait. But during the spring months of May and June and in the fall during September and October, they will take a cast fly. One must be familiar, however, with their habits to catch them successfully on a feathered offering.

Looking over one of these lakes at midday you would swear that it did not hold fish. But if you should row quietly out onto the lake in the dim murk before dawn on a calm June morning you would see a sight that would give you the jitters if you didn't have your fly rod along. For the rainbows would be rising all over the lake, dotting the surface with rings like a heavy rain. At times you will glimpse a lunker cruising on the surface gulping in food with very evident smacks of its jaws. This feeding period will last until the sun hits the water. Usually it will not occur if the water is wind ruffled. The same feeding usually takes place during the couple of hours before dark, providing conditions are similar.

These rainbows are apparently feeding on nymphs or larvae just below the surface. At times the nymphs are hatching and the trout are taking the fly itself. But in the majority of cases they are gulping in nymphs. And although your first thought would be: "Here is the spot for a dry fly," experience has indicated that the sunken fly is best.

Some anglers prefer a nymph made of clear nylon tied over various colors of silk, while others use any of the smaller original nymph patterns that are being developed in the Northwest. But it is the method of presenting the nymph that makes the difference between taking trout or taking a skunking. It is better to be alone in a boat and, rather than chase rises, to row out on the lake to a likely spot and then rest quietly. Should a rise come within range, and it will, cover it. Since under these circumstances the trout are cruising while they are feeding it is very difficult to judge just where they will make their next rise. But if you watch a trout's progress carefully you can often anticipate where it should come up next and cast your fly in its pathway. Or if the rise is close in, by hitting the ring before it has spread out too far you can sometimes catch the trout's attention before it has gone down or turned away.

There are two methods of using the nymph. One is with the sunken line that does not disturb the surface. The angler strips in the fly under the surface without allowing it to sink too deeply. When using this method he must cover a rise quickly and trust to luck that he is stripping ahead of a trout, for if the fish has turned away it of course cannot see the fly. A second method is to grease the line and part of the leader so as to permit the nymph to sink only to the depth at which the rainbows are feeding. The angler casts in front of the trout or covers a rise. Stripping the fly is commonly done quickly just beneath the water. Short casts

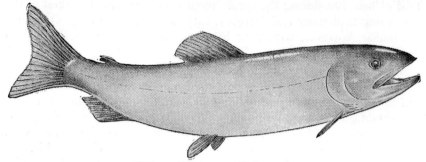

Silver Trout or Kokanee

are preferable as they can be easily controlled and do not tend to put down the trout.

A light tippet is customary (2x or 3x) and, as a fat 18-inch rainbow will weigh over two pounds, a light wrist on the strike is necessary if you want to save your nymph. Most anglers use a tapered nine foot leader, either nylon or gut.

The popular rod used for lake-fishing here on the coast has been a nine footer weighing 5 ounces or a bit over. This rod is capable of handling a long line as well as casting a fly into a fairly stiff wind. In the spring or fall, winds generally arise on the lowland lakes during the middle of the day.

Within recent years many anglers have been turning to an eight or 8½ foot rod weighing 3¾ to 4 ounces. Such a rod will give more sport and action on small trout than the longer one. Its light tip will handle 3x or 4x tippets gently so that one can set on a larger fish without breaking off on every strike. The modern tendency has been toward rods with a fairly stiff action that will cast into the wind and are suitable for use on a river for sea-runs or large trout. Rods under eight feet in length are rarities on the West Coast.

The Silver Trout or Kokanee. Although rainbows and cutthroats form the bulk of the catch made by fly fishermen in our lowland lakes, kokanee or silver trout are caught in great numbers by thousands of anglers during the spring and early summer. This silver trout, which is the native fish of the Washington lakes, is a trout with a fascinating history. In fact it has so many peculiar characteristics in its life cycle that if these were not vouched for by a biologist one would hardly give them credence.

In the first place this native trout, which is found only in the North-

Opening Day Crush at Bay Lake

On the lowland lakes of the Pacific Northwest, opening day of the trout season each spring is a hectic affair. Overflow crowds rush to the popular lakes, boats cover the usually placid surface of the waters, and cars are lined up hub-cap to hub-cap in solid array. The fishermen are happy and helpful. This is their big spring holiday and they are going to enjoy themselves regardless of conditions.

Bay Lake in Southwestern Washington, pictured here, always attracts huge crowds. The opening in 1965 set a record. Parking areas were filled before dawn and cars were backed up half a mile waiting for their occupants to launch their boats. Here, at 8:30 a.m., boats filled with anglers who have already creeled their limits are converging on the narrow launching area waiting to take out and head for home. An estimated 20,000 rainbows were caught, ranging from 11 inches to 3 pounds.

Pearrygin Lake, the Pride of Okanogan County

The lakes of the Okanogan in East Central Washington offer some of the most tempting and exciting trout fishing to be found in the state. They are lowland lakes set down amid the rolling hills of Okanogan and Chelan counties. Most are natural lakes although several of the top waters are man-made reservoirs. Their waters provide excellent angling from opening day into midsummer. After many of the lakes in Western Washington have tapered off, Okanogan lakes are still turning out bulging creels.

Situated about 250 miles east of the dense Seattle population complex, these lakes are not heavily fished except on holiday weekends. About half of them include resorts with over-night accommodations and boats for rent. The others are in the "bring-your-own-boat" class. On many weekends campers and trailers funnel into the Okanogan in such numbers that they create overnight villages amid the pine forests.

Most of the lakes are planted with rainbow. Pearrygin Lake, shown here, ranks year after year as one of the top lakes of the area both as to the number and size of the rainbows taken on sports gear. However, a few of the smaller waters and impoundments hold brook trout or cutthroats. The trout are fat, fine-tasting fish that average 12 inches in length. In some of the waters trout measuring up to 18 inches are commonly taken.

Game Department checks on three of the lakes show how prolific the Okanogan waters are and how they hold up after the opening-day rush. In the 1967 opener (April 17) trout were creeled as follows: at Pearrygin Lake, 1,010 anglers had 9,005 rainbows; at Salmon Lake, 155 anglers had 1,012; and at Alta, 900 anglers had 5,500. On April 24 at Pearrygin, 344 anglers had 1,461 rainbows; at Salmon, 280 anglers had 1,932; and at Alta, 124 anglers had 812.

west, British Columbia and Alaska, is not a trout but a salmon. Like a salmon it dies after spawning but unlike a salmon it does not migrate to salt water. It does not grow to the enormous weight of a salmon but usually runs not more than a foot in length. It is always caught in lakes, and never in rivers or salt water. It is bright silvery blue most of the year, but turns red in the fall before spawning.

Although the kokanee, little red fish, or Kennerly's salmon is usually called a silver trout in Washington it is actually a small variety of the sockeye salmon with the unwieldy monicker of *oncorhynchus nerka kennerli*. It is generally considered to be a landlocked variety of the sockeye but it would probably be more exact to call it a sockeye that has preferred a more or less permanent residence in fresh water. Kokanee were native to Lake Washington long before the white man ever saw the Northwest, but they have resided there by choice and not because they were landlocked, for this lake has an open passageway to the salt chuck. Moreover there is evidence to show that kokanee may become migratory, and on the other hand sockeye salmon may turn resident and evolve into kokanee.

These silver trout as a rule have a three- to four-year life cycle and die after making their spawning migration up a creek or river out of their home lake. In such streams from September to November anglers may observe schools of these red trout traveling up to their spawning beds. The State Game Department strips out millions of kokanee eggs each year, raises them to fry and plants them in lakes throughout the state. The mature fish killed in this stripping are frozen and used as food in the various trout hatcheries.

Silver trout live in compact schools most of their lake existence. They feed on various forms of plankton, filtering these microscopic bits of animal life through their finely meshed gill rakers. They do not compete with other species of trout for food and thrive only in deep lakes where plankton may be found the year round. This type of food is near the surface in the spring and winter, but as the weather warms the plankton descends to the 50° zone of temperature as it can live only at that temperature.

This 50° zone is referred to as the thermocline, and it usually will be found at depths of 30 to 40 feet. The thermocline in Lake Washington for instance during the hot months is generally down about 40 feet.

Silver trout are caught in their greatest numbers when they are found near the surface before the lake has "turned over." They are taken by two methods—still fishing with bait or trolling. Bait anglers will anchor in spots where the trout habitually congregate. At times almost a score of boats will be moored in a line with only a few feet separating each one. The usual bait is a single salmon egg, although any type of bait such as worms or grubs may be used. Baiting the fishing area is lawful in most of the silver trout lakes and anglers scatter feed eggs, corn or similar agents to attract the fish.

The popular baits for trolling are spoons and worms. A gang troll may be used ahead of a worm, attached with a short two-inch leader. At times only two spoons are used or a single Boyle. Trollers generally use an outboard motor and thus are able to cover a large segment of the lake.

These silver trout are highly prized as pan fish. In fact many fishing families feel that spring hasn't come until they sit down to a heaping platter of sizzling brown silvers, which they eat with the greatest of relish from their tails to their heads.

Kokanee are a wonderful source of food for rainbow trout. Wherever there are great numbers of these silver trout and rainbows are introduced the latter will often grow to great size in a short time. A prime example of this will be found at Lake Pend Oreille in Idaho which, not too long ago, was teeming with millions of dwarfed silvers. Eggs of the famous Kamloops were imported from Canada, hatched at the Lake and then planted. In less than a decade, Pend Oreille was producing world-record rainbows and had become a mecca for anglers from all over the country.

The Kamloops Trout of British Columbia. The Kamloops trout, native only to British Columbia, is the Canadian version of an American rainbow. Under proper conditions it provides some of the greatest trout fishing to be found on this continent. Anglers who have never sat out on a British Columbia lake when the Kamloops were rising to a hatch of traveling sedge have yet to encounter one of the biggest thrills of lake fishing.

The Kamloops, when prime, is a landlocked twin of the coastal steelhead. It will hit a fly with a smashing strike and jump repeatedly, one beautiful leap after another. It makes long fast runs, and is extremely active from the time that it is hooked until it is brought to net.

These Kamloops are as outstanding in their size as they are in their fighting prowess. In most of the British Columbian lakes the one- to two-pound trout are as common as the 6- to 10-inch trout in comparable waters in the United States. Fish between two and three pounds are not uncommon and in many a lake the angler should tie onto a lunker or two weighing between four and eight pounds during a week's stay. That is the average every-vacation-trip sort of fishing that the anglers of the west expect when they journey across the border.

The best periods for taking Kamloops on a fly are in the spring from June to the middle of July and in the fall from September into October.

Many of the good lakes lie at high altitudes and weather will be bad before June. Moreover there may be many late spawners at that time and even a six-pound Kamloops is not sporty when it is still wearing its dark spawning uniform.

During the summer months the water warms and the fish are down. The fall is one of the best times of the year to fish in British Columbia and the sportsman can profitably combine a hunting and fishing trip at that time.

There are hundreds of lakes that offer superlative fishing, many of them having resort accommodations with cabins and boats. Most of these can be reached by automobile but a few necessitate a pack trip; a trail or very poor tote road is the only means of access to some of them.

Knouff Lake up the Thompson River and only 28 miles from the town of Kamloops was once world-famous as a dry fly lake and produced lunkers weighing up to 17 pounds. It is still a good dry fly lake, although now a five pounder is a good fish. I spent a week there in the early part of July several years ago after a late spring. The weather was hot and the angler could take fish all day long if he wished to work for them. Canadians seldom go fishing until after a late breakfast, getting out on the water around 10 o'clock. Knouff Lake is long and narrow, dotted with wooded islands. Other islands lurk below the surface. Along one shore there is a shallow shelf which ends in a quick drop off about 75 feet out.

We had luck casting into the islands and along the shore with a Black O'Lindsay during the day. You could anchor over a sunken island in about eight feet of water and strip a wet fly up from the drop off or wait for a hatch to come off the sunken reef.

During the afternoon you could anchor on the shore shelf and float a bushy greased sedge just over the drop off. If you had patience to sit and wait, you might after ten minutes get a rise that sounded like the gulp of a horse, and, if you didn't set your hook at once, you sat there just watching a hole in the water that would hold a kitchen chair.

If you felt like rowing slowly about the lake, a "mooched" Carey Special, dragged about 75 feet back of the boat, would be almost certain to produce results. The trout would hit this nymph fly so hard that your rod had to be grabbed at once or it would go overboard with the strike.

But the most exciting fishing at Knouff occurs whenever there is a hatch of the traveling sedge. This usually takes place in the hour or two before dark. We had three hatches during that week and they more than paid for the trip in thrills. We anchored, Malcolm Newell and myself each in a boat, at the edge of the shallows out from the lodge the night of the first hatch.

The lake was calm and it had turned cool after a hot day. We had each tied on a large dry sedge fly equipped with number 8 hooks, one of us using a green and one a gray body. Then we sat relaxed in the boats to wait. After a bit there was a dimple as a sedge came to the surface with its wings cocked together over its back. It hesitated there for several seconds for its wings to dry, and then took to flight. At first it would fly only a foot or two, then dip down to touch the water before taking off again. Gradually the intervals lengthened and the sedge was in full flight.

These were large insects and at times they popped out of the water with the sound of a rising trout. The hatch increased and soon there were sedges coming up all around us. Then suddenly, not 20 feet away, there was a gulp where a sedge had risen and disappeared into the jaws of a Kamloops. It was time to fish.

I set my fly gently out into an open spot where it floated nicely, helped by the well-greased line. Sedges were coming up steadily and for a while nothing else happened. Then suddenly a trout rose at my fly, and in my excitement, I jerked it away before the fish could take it into its mouth. On my next floating cast, I managed to hook a fat two pounder that danced and ran for 10 minutes before it would come to net.

By this time sedges and trout were rising all around us, not in the least disturbed by our casting or by a fighting fish. Malcolm had tied into a nice one that, finally landed, weighed more than three pounds. I broke off a fly on a trout that took with a downward strike and felt very solid and heavy. It was fast and furious fishing. The Kamloops took our artificial often enough to keep us keyed up to the bursting point. All of the fish were bright and active as tigers on the run.

We fished until it was pitch dark and, although we had caught but eight trout, every minute of the two hours was stuffed with concentrated action. As we slowly rowed into the dock we could hear trout still rising and sucking in the sedges. For sport like that who wouldn't drive the 389 miles from Seattle several times a season?

Lowland Lake Trout Fishing. The State of Washington, or the Pacific Northwest for that matter, can hardly hope to equal the marvelous fishing that British Columbia offers in its Kamloops lakes. For one thing, the fishing intensity is immeasurably greater in Washington, and, for another, most of the Northwest lowland lakes are readily accessible by road, many of them, furthermore, located very near centers of population.

However Washington has made a valiant attempt within the past six years to keep up with the demands of half a million eager anglers. With the aid of a large hatchery program, millions of trout are planted every season. With the increase in rearing-pond capacity, a majority of these fish will be of legal size when planted.

Because of this program, every angler may expect to take several limits of rainbows, silver trout or cutthroats during the first month of each trout season. They probably will not be large fish—in fact, most of them will range between six and ten inches. But this size of trout satisfies the picnic fisherman who drives his family into a parking lot at a resort lake. Lakes close to the larger cities cannot stand this sort of pressure long and within three to four weeks the cream of the planted trout have already been skimmed off.

In east central and northeast Washington there are a number of lakes distant from population centers that produce large trout throughout the season. These lakes apparently carry a good supply of food and, when given a chance, trout grow rapidly. In some, the rainbows will average nearly a pound with a fair number running up to two and three pounds. In a few, the odd trout of four to five pounds—nearly always rainbows—can be taken still fishing with bait.

There is always some holdover of trout each year in lakes along the coast which will grow to fair size. In some lakes one may expect to pick up a sprinkling of twelve inchers and the occasional 14- to 18-inch lunker. In most cases these will be rainbows as the cutthroat program has not advanced far enough to build up much of a surplus stock as yet.

There are lakes not more than 60 miles from Seattle, such as Kapowsin, McMurray or nearby Ballinger, that turn out a few 15 to 18 inchers each week-end during the spring and fall. Most of these trout are taken still fishing or on a troll as they are bottom feeders and will hit a fly only under unusually propitious conditions. As a consequence, the bulk of the trout catch each year from the lowland lakes will be the smaller trout—the 6- to 10-inch planted youngsters.

The Lake Poisoning Program. The Game Department hopes to be able to improve the trout population both as to size and quantity through the aid of its poisoning program. Many lowland lakes hold such a horrible mixture of trout and miscellaneous rough fish, consisting of perch, shiners, squawfish, bull heads or carp, that the game fish hardly survive. By poisoning these waters to kill off the undesirables the lakes are brought back quickly and cheaply into full productivity of game fish.

It was only eight years ago that Washington poisoned its first lake. This venture proved so highly successful that in 1946 the Department under its chief fish biologist C. F. Pautzke instigated its poisoning program. Rotenone or a combination of it and other chemicals became readily available after the war, and Washington began poisoning in earnest.

In 1946, twenty-six lakes comprising 726 acres were poisoned; in 1947, thirty-two lakes of 1391 acres; and, in 1948, thirteen lakes of 1200 acres were poisoned. In both 1946 and 1947 this was by far the most ambitious schedule undertaken in the nation, as 41% of all the waters were situated in Washington. The cost of the program for the past two years has been $43,000.

After a lake has been poisoned, and allowed to lie fallow for a period of three months to a year, it becomes an enormous banquet table of rich nourishing trout food. Trout fry planted therein grow in a single season into legal size fish at no further cost to the Department.

The story of the fall and rise of Pass Lake is one of the most exciting and unique chapters in the poisoning program on the Pacific Coast. This 95-acre lake, nestled up against the main highway to Deception Pass Bridge, in the past decade rose from nothing to become one of the great rainbow lakes in the Puget Sound country only to drop down to nothing again. About ten years ago nobody fished it. Then it received a planting of rainbows which grew phenomenally. It was discovered by a few anglers and the rush was on. Then in 1942 it was opened to fly fishing only, and for a few years it provided superlative angling for prime two- to five-pound rainbow trout. Then it started to go down, and soon you were lucky to take a couple of 14 inchers. Its fishing grew so bad that in spite of some objections it was decided to poison the lake in the spring of 1946. Although 1,500 trout, mostly small ones, were killed, close to 500,000 undersized perch were destroyed. These perch, present in such great numbers, explained the poor fishing.

In May of 1947, a first planting of cutthroat fry and later a second one was placed in the lake. In the fall of that year biologists took net samples in the lake and found that the "cuts" from the first plant had in 5½ months grown to 11-inch, one-half-pound trout. No fishing was permitted that year and the lake was not thrown open to fly fishing until the trout season of 1948.

It received a phenomenally heavy play on opening day and the fish proved to be prime bright 10- to 14-inch cutthroats, and, although it did not produce any really fast fly fishing during the wet, windy summer of 1948, it put out a steady return of about two fish per trip per angler for that year. It is planted with fry each spring and these 6- to 8-inch trout are taken in large numbers each fall.

A glance at these figures will show what a poisoned lake can do in its first year of fishing after the treatment. A count of 2,348 anglers at Pass during the season of 1948 caught 3,080 cutthroats averaging 13.9 inches or 1.32 pounds, plus 5,370 "cuts" averaging 7.5 inches or 0.36 pounds. This was an average of two fish per trip in the spring and 1½ large fish and four small trout during the fall. (The lake gets badly in bloom during July and August and is fished very little.)

Chapter Two

MOUNTAIN LAKE FISHING

When the God of the Outdoors created Washington's Cascade Range and the wilderness of the Olympics, he scattered hundreds of mountain lakes amid their towering peaks. These crystal clear basins of water set like sapphires and emeralds amid the snow fields and tree-clad rocks were known only to the mountain goats for hundreds of years. But as the fisherman crept ever northward up through the river valleys of the coast, he cast longing eyes at the lofty mountain ranges and wondered what lakes could be hidden in the valleys and the upper benches. And

27

as time went on, this curious human species, emulating the mountain goat, built trails into the hills and later with back-pack and pack train carried trout into virtually every one of the barren upper lakes. The trout flourished in the cold clear waters, and today are there awaiting the hardy hiker who desires virgin angling combined with unsurpassed scenery.

Mountain trails that reach like twisting lengths of rope from the lowlands up into the hills are to be found thickly threaded all through the mountain ranges of Washington. You find them starting off from modern four lane highways, from government camp sites, from railroad crossings, and from swinging bridges over rushing rivers. They meander across the flats and then carefully weaving along contour lines and around cliffs gradually work right into the hills. The most famous are those belonging to the Pacific Crest Trail System, triangular white and green signs of which can take a hiker all along the entire summit of the Cascades from Canada to California.

Fishing in Lake Isobel. The mountain angler is most interested in his own particular trail, the one that takes him up to his chosen lake. On a June morning you and your hiking partner may have decided to climb into Lake Isobel, which lies a short 54 miles northeast of Seattle. You not only hope to pick up a few large fat brookies, rainbows and maybe even some mackinaws, but you are also anxious to see if the lake is as entrancingly beautiful as you remembered it from the year before. You park your car at the end of the old tote road, shoulder your Trapper Nelson packs, one of which holds the rubber boat, and with metal rod case in hand to use as a cane, turn your steps into the narrow path that leads up to the lake.

The pink fingers of dawn are reaching into the eastern sky. The air is cool and moist, and the thick ferns lining the trail drip heavy dew onto your clothes. You switch back around a jutting cliff, and the trail heads steeply up through spindly alder brush.

Thimbleberry bushes studded with pale white blossoms grow in thick clumps and in the open the salal brush is all in bloom. You find an occasional salmonberry bush and you pop one of the tart reddish yellow berries into your mouth. The remembered flavor is still there. The brush gives way to second growth as you switch to the left, and now you can look out over the valley below, where the Skykomish River twists its way into the distance, unfolding a scene of breath taking beauty before your eyes.

Small firs and hemlocks, perfectly formed, crowd close along the trail, their branches all candle-tipped with new growths of brilliant green. You are really climbing now, bracing your feet against each protruding rock to prevent back-slipping. Then you plunge into a shadowed tunnel of taller trees where the mountain walls are closing in on both sides.

In places such as this, mountain trails are apt to show signs of age. In the shade of tall conifers the path is spongy soft with moss and the turf is thickly blanketed with old needles that swallow up silently the scraping sound of your hobnailed boots.

You are now going up steeply again. On every side tree trunks, ramrod straight, reach up a hundred feet toward the sun. There are firs and hemlocks and now and then a growth of cedar—gnarled giants, many of them four to eight feet through at the base, with striated trunks and occasionally with tops wind-twisted or broken off in a jagged gash.

You glimpse a thread of white water weaving down the steep hill on your right and you stop to have an ice-cold drink from a noisy brook. The trail gets steeper and more deeply rock pitted—evidence that torrents from the melting snows of spring, using it as a watercourse, had plunged recklessly down its center. The slopes on each side of the trail turn into sheer cliffs, and the walls close in ahead of you in a blind draw. Then the trail turns into an old puncheon pathway made of rudely split cedar boards that, in a series of twelve switchbacks, scales the cliff. To your left, a veil of water is washing down the same wall of rock, spilling out of the lake above. You push through thick, seemingly impenetrable huckleberry brush, take another step, and—without warning—there's your lake!

Barely twenty feet away, its clear waters are lapping against a huge cedar log. You realize with a start that the cliff you have just scaled is a natural dam that holds Lake Isobel in its vast hollow in the hills. You look up to see the mountain sides, tree-clad and rock-girt, rimming the lake, and reaching up to snow-capped summits.

You dump the rubber boat out of the pack, and start pumping it up. Your partner lines up the rods, threads on line and ties on a tiny bucktail coachman fly. Part of the lake is still in shadow and you paddle the small boat to that side. Partner flips his fly toward the shore. It floats a second or two, sinks, and has twitched along hardly a foot when there is a swift flash through the crystal-clear water. He has hooked into a fat 14-inch rainbow that shoots out of the water in a silvery arc and drops back with a swirl of foam.

You work slowly up the lake, taking turns to cover the shoreline or the few submerged rocks or logs. Isobel is an extremely deep lake with only a narrow shelf along the shore where a fly will work at all effectively.

After several hours you have traveled half way up the lake and have taken rainbows, brook trout, silvers and a couple of 20-inch mackinaws that struggle deep and are only brought to net after a great deal of head shaking.

You come at noon to a camp site and brew a pot of tea with a party of four who have hiked in the night before. Then you stretch out in the bright hot sun and soak in the clean wine-like air. As you watch a fleecy cloud drift past one of the mountain tops, you wonder why all of us spend so much time down in the valleys. Life is so intense and hurried down there in the smoky man-made cities. But everything is so quiet, so clean, so fresh, so peaceful up here in the mountains. You forget your daily frustrations and troubles and come down that evening refreshed and ready to tackle with new vigor the problems of the coming week.

A Virgin Lake Country. There are literally hundreds of lakes in the high country of Washington that call the hiker and the angler. Through the efforts of the Game Department, pack strings have distributed trout in the more accessible altitude lakes and, since the war, the Department has acquired an airplane which is utilized to drop trout fry into lakes "way back in."

In addition, that unselfish hard-working tribe of fishermen, the Trailblazers, have been planting lakes for the past decade. This band of sportsmen, though small in number, explore the Cascades for new barren lakes, and when they have found them, stock them with trout they have backpacked in. With fry furnished by the Game Department, they successfully put the lakes into production. It is due to them that many of these remote lakes are now good fishing spots.

Unless one has made a study of contour maps of this region, one will be utterly astounded at the vast number of altitude lakes open to a week-end angler out of the metropolitan district of Seattle. The mountains are full of them. Many of the valleys and watersheds are as thickly studded with sparkling lakes as if they had been dropped from a Paul Bunyan sprinkler. Although the majority of these "high-up" lakes remain untouched by civilization, they are at the same time easily accessible from the Seattle district in a week-end trip. Many of them can be fished in a single day, while others, a few miles further back, are better suited to an overnight hike. The fisherman can drive forty miles out of Seattle's city limits, park alongside a trunk highway, and by the time he has hiked over the first ridge, he is in back country that has remained unchanged since the days of Lewis and Clark.

These hike-in lakes of the Cascades and the Olympics have not yet been commercialized. There may be a few Forest Service shelters or cleared camp sites at some of the better known spots. There is usually a raft or two hidden away along the shore line, and in a few isolated cases rowboats or dugouts are available. However, at some of the more popular lakes that can be reached in a two or three hours' walk, it is likely, during the summer, that a party of anglers will have come in Friday night or Saturday morning. In these circumstances the rafts will be in use. For this reason, a portable rubber boat is almost a necessity for the Sunday angler.

But the lakes are never crowded. You do not find empty tin cans or paper bags scattered about, the usual signs of the auto tourist. A short walk along the shore line, and you can always find a secluded camp site. It may have a nearly vertical slant and have to be cleared of rocks or brush, but you will find yourself as aloof from other humans as if you were in the middle of the Klond'ke.

Fishing After the Spring Break-up. The unofficial opening for the "high-up" lake addict has traditionally been the Fourth of July. All of the lower altitude lakes should be open at this time, but some of the higher lakes, mainly those above 5,000 feet that are situated deep in steep valleys, may still be frozen over. Between the two extremes, you may find some that may be only half free of ice or be ice-rimmed along one shore. Fishing can be excellent under such conditions.

If the angler can hit a lake just after the ice has gone off he is apt to find the trout furiously hungry after their long imprisonment beneath the blanket of ice. At these times, the fishing can be so fast it takes your breath away, as the trout are inclined to hit any lure offered them.

I remember one spring when Jack Litsey and I hiked into Cottonwood Lake around June 20th. It is about a six-mile hike. The trail winds up around Lost Lake and then follows the contour line through the open park-like pine slopes of Eastern Washington. As we got up to the 3,000-foot elevation snow patches appeared under the trees and soon the trail was hidden by several feet of hard-packed winter snow. We managed to stick with the almost obliterated path and topping the 4,200-foot contour we dropped into the narrow valley that holds the very small lake. The south shore, where grows the single huge cottonwood tree, was free of snow but the north side was rimmed with ice and two feet of snow lay beneath the trees. By the time we had blown up the rubber boat, it was after ten o'clock. In slightly over an hour we were through fishing as there were two limits of brook trout resting in the creels. They had hit with abandon, taking any fly that was flipped out to them: bucktail coachman, gray hackles with yellow bodies, queen of the waters or carot nymphs. None of the fish were large—they ran uniformly between 10 and 12 inches—but they were fast as lightning. Their flesh was deep pink, firm as marble and, fried crisp and brown for the next day's breakfast, they were as delicious a morsel as any mortal could ever desire.

Brook trout do very well in mountain lakes and, although they do not attain great size, they are always firm-meated and excellent eating. They will usually hit readily for two to four weeks after the lakes open up, but seem to taper off during the bright hot days of August due, probably to sluggishness induced by warmer water.

In the old days, a great many cutthroats, of both the native and the black-spotted Montana varieties were planted in the mountain lakes. In some of the lakes they were able to reproduce naturally in the inlet creeks and have provided steady fishing. In others, they have not propagated but have grown to good size—twenty to twenty-six inches.

Along with the state-wide emphasis on planting of rainbow trout, a program for the hatching of 22,000,000 rainbow eggs in 1950 has been announced. The mountain lakes are receiving, at present, more rainbows than any other variety of trout. These fish evidently do well in the clear lakes, and while, like the brook trout, they do not often grow to the enormous size that they attain in the lowland waters, they are fast-jumping, furious fighters.

A few golden trout were planted by the Department and the Trailblazers several years ago and they may still be taken in a few lakes. During the past two summers, grayling trout from Montana have been planted as fry in mountain lakes in Skagit and King Counties. There is no information up to this time how they have taken hold.

The altitude lakes of Washington and Oregon carry virtually the same varieties of trout and will respond to the same fishing technique. British Columbian waters differ because of the presence of Kamloops in lakes around the four to five thousand foot levels. California has a few cutthroats, some introduced brook trout and brown trout, and many resident rainbow. In addition, California is famed for its golden trout which are eagerly sought for each year by the hardy anglers who make summer climbs into the high Sierras.

Fishing Mountain Lakes with Bait or Spoon. Although the mountain lakes may be regarded as well-nigh virgin waters their trout are, at times, as hard to catch as their more sophisticated relatives in the lowlands. The high-up lakes are invariably "gin clear" and under a bright sun objects can be picked out clearly on the bottom at thirty feet. Many of them are rock-lined and offer very sparse plant growth, and few hiding spots except in the deeper water. A cruising trout in the shallows near shore can be easily put down or frightened away by a clumsy angler making sudden motions or undue noise.

In such lakes, under the bright sun of July and August, fishing during midday is an almost fruitless undertaking. But if the sky is overcast or if there is a breeze to riffle the surface, you can fish successfully throughout the day. Otherwise the most productive periods are apt to be in early morning or late afternoon when the sun has dipped behind a ridge and part of the lake is in shadow.

Many of the "high-up" fishermen use bait or spoon in taking trout. When still-fishing they will anchor just at the edge of a drop-off or near deep water and use single eggs or worms, as they do in the lowland waters. As feed or fresh eggs are not legal in most of the upper lakes, the angler must depend on deception. Most of them use a whippy trout rod and very light tippets for their leaders. A weight test for the tippets of one or two pounds is usual, and it takes a light touch to land heavy trout on such tackle.

Trolling from a raft is hardly practical, so that the spoon anglers seldom use this type of fishing. However, a small spoon in sizes one or two, with a split shot for weight, may be cast a good distance off a raft with a fly rod. If it is then allowed to sink and retrieved with slow, easy jerks, it will often take good trout when they are not rising or not feeding near the surface.

High-up Trout on the Fly. The main problem in mountain lakes for the fly fisherman is—how to cover the water? Most altitude lakes of the Cascades do not permit offshore casting because of the nature of the terrain. However, in a few lakes set near or above timber line, the angler can fish from shore without interference for his backcast. There may be a rock slide or section of shore line where you can walk along and whip out a fly. At other lakes there may be a flat surrounding the inlet and, if the lake is not too shallow at this point, it should be an excellent spot to try a fly. Or if the creek does not enter the lake by a waterfall or steep cascade the inlet itself may show good results.

In some lakes there may be a stream that rushes down the steep mountain side to enter the lake in a small bay. Often a fly cast out into the riffle where the creek enters the lake and allowed to float out with the current until it gradually sinks will take fish. Trout like to lie along this riffle waiting for food to float down and will strike at a fly drifted without drag.

But in many of the mountain lakes the steep hillsides slip right into the water, and are usually so covered with buck brush, salal, huckleberry and trees that fly casting from the shore is impossible. Occasionally a tree which has fallen into the lake will afford a precarious footing for casting but, even so, it is a long climb through brush between trees. Therefore the fly flitter should be able to get out onto the lake. A raft will do very well unless the lake happens to be so large or so windswept that propelling the usual waterlogged raft is too hard a task. In the smaller bodies of water one can paddle up against the wind and then allow the raft to drift back again down the lake. The angler can stand and cast either to shore or out into the lake without having continually to resort to the paddle.

As an angler usually wears hobnailed shoes when climbing up to high altitude lakes he must be careful not to step onto his fly line when stripping in a wet fly. As many rafts are not too secure, and he must jockey around to keep his footing, it is not too easy to keep the line from underfoot. One sure safeguard against cutting a fly line is to use a stripping basket. A canvas basket such as that described in the chapter on steelheading is light and can easily be tied onto the top of the pack.

At best, a raft is cumbersome and unwieldy and often a Sunday hike-in angler will find all the rafts taken by earlier arrivals. At many lakes, trees suitable for raft building cannot be found, and in the case of lakes situated above timber line, there will be no timber at all. However, at the lower altitude spots a stout hand axe may often save the day in that it will enable the angler to construct a one-man raft. Many old time hikers carry, besides the axe, a securely wrapped parcel of 10- and 20-penny nails and bailing wire in the back pocket of their cruising jacket for such use.

A rubber boat of the two-man type will solve all water transportation problems. It carries easily on a pack board and two men can easily backpack the boat, bedrolls and food necessary for an overnight hike.

An effective method of fly fishing with a rubber boat in an unknown lake is to let the man who rows "nymph" his fly slowly about 75 feet behind the boat. His partner may then cast a fly into the likeliest-appearing spots. Wherever or whenever trout are located by either method both anglers can take to casting.

If the boat is too crowded for two creels the fishermen can use a dampened cloth sack in which to protect the catch from the heat of the sun. As the midday summer sun at the higher altitudes beats down relentlessly, he must be very careful that his trout do not turn soft or that the flesh does not separate from the bones. The fish should be cleaned soon after catching and taken ashore at intervals. They should then be wrapped in damp ferns and placed in a creel that is kept in a shady spot.

On such a day an angler must also watch the air pressure in his rubber craft. Mornings in the mountains are usually cold and the fisherman is apt to pump in all the pressure that his boat will take. But this air will expand in the heat of the day and air should be released at intervals to prevent the boat from "blowing up." For the same reason, hike-in anglers in Washington seldom use the charged cylinders that come with the surplus navy boats. It only takes ten or twelve minutes to pump up one side of a boat and the partners can take turns doing so.

Hiking Clothes and Equipment. Clothing suitable for high-up lakes fishing should be found in the wardrobe of most western anglers. To start at the bottom, most hikers will recognize that proper footwear is one of the most important items. The shoe must be well fitted so that it does not chafe the heel or cramp the toe. A boot eight to ten inches high equipped with a row of hobnails with a few calks in the instep is preferred by many. "Hobs" are good on slick hillsides or loose rocks and the calks will help you to stick on a log when jumping between windfalls. Soft wool socks worn over an inner light pair of nylon or lisle help to keep the feet happy. Shoes should be well greased before every trip. The hiker will have to do some wading through creeks and when standing on a raft he is often ankle-deep in water. Even the best grade of leather will stiffen under such conditions unless it is cared for and softened with a good application of boot grease.

A pair of "tin" or khaki pants is customary depending on the preference of the angler. The tin pants are excellent protection when hiking through brush or devil-clubs and take a long time to wet through if one should happen to hit a rainy day. However, they are much warmer than light khaki and for this reason many prefer the latter type. A few hikers still wear the western blue jeans or "levis" but with surplus suntan pants available everywhere they have been largely supplanted.

A woolen shirt is good for early morning and the wearer does not require any other upper clothing except perhaps a fishing jacket in which to carry his tackle when he is out on the raft. A light slicker that can be rolled up and tied to the pack is good protection against sudden summer showers.

The preferred type of pack in the northwest is the "Trapper Nelson." This is a pack board which rests easily on the shoulders. A rubber boat can be strapped to the board and a sleeping bag can be tied on top and carried without discomfort. For an overnight hike, your partner can carry the food and small articles in the carrying bag that comes with the pack board.

An aluminum case is the safest means for carrying the fly rod. You can tape a protecting pad on the bottom of the case and then use it as a staff. A folding net should either be tied onto the rod case or strapped onto the pack board.

One of the fascinations of mountain lake fishing in the Northwest lies in the fact that the angler can be his own explorer and plan a trip into a lake without the aid of guide or pack horse. All that he needs is a geological survey contour map and the urge to climb over the next ridge and find a "lost lake." At the better known lakes he will find a path that a blind man could follow. But before getting into other spots he may have to consult his map and a compass most of the way. He may have to fight brush at the start and then clamber up rock slides and steep cliffs with no trail to guide him. But when he does find the lake, he has the satisfaction of having pioneered the way in all by himself.

Washington's "High-up" Lake Country. Although it takes a bit of studying to locate these seldom-visited spots there are many mountain valleys that can be fished on a week-day where other anglers will infrequently be found. The following list, which attempts to enumerate only a few of the better known mountain lake districts, can be used as a basis on which to plan either a Sunday trip or a whole summer vacation.

Western Washington: the Snoqualmie Pass District. In the Snoqualmie Pass area, after starting up the highway out of North Bend, you can branch off up the Middle Fork of the Snoqualmie and head either for Pratt Lake which contains rainbows and eastern brooks, for Thompson for rainbows and Montana black-spots, or for Myrtle for rainbows. Going further up the Pass you can strike into Tuscohatchee for brookies and rainbows. The Mountain Cabin Memorial Association has, with the co-operation of the U. S. Forest Service, just erected a shelter cabin there for the use of the public. From there you can go into Blue for brookies, Mason for rainbows, Melakwa for brooks and rainbows, Snow for rainbows and black-spots, or Derrick for cutthroats.

Over the hump on the open pine slopes of eastern Washington the angler will find good country back of Keechelus Lake. Lakes in this section include Lost for brooks and rainbows, Cottonwood and Twin for brooks, and Stirrup for rainbows and brooks. Then up the Salmon Lasac country north of Cle Elum there lie a number of scenic lakes, including Pete for rainbows and brooks, Spectacle for brooks, Hyas for rainbows and brooks, and Waptus for brooks and rainbows.

The Skykomish District. Perhaps the most prolifically lake-studded section near Seattle, if not in the Northwest, is that found up the South Fork of the Skykomish River. Here the lakes are clustered as thick as raisins in a fruit cake, ranging in size from bodies of water two miles long to small pot-holes in an alpine meadow. A few of the more easily accessible spots will be sure to have several parties of fishermen every Sunday while the more remote will be visited on only a couple of week-ends each summer.

This is a region of breath-taking grandeur. The peaks run up to eight thousand feet, many of them snow-capped. There are slopes of virgin timber never touched by man extending in every direction as far as the eye can see, there are whole hillsides covered with heather and alpine flowers, and of course there are the lakes. Many of these lie in chains with the lower lake sending its outlet cascading down over a thousand-foot-high ridge. From these vantage points the fisherman can feast his eyes on scenery that if it were in Switzerland, would have a funicular railway

Top: Deep Lake nestles in its deep valley below Cathedral Peaks in the High Cascades. This lake is reached in a half-day horse-pack trip out of Salmon La Sac country.

Right: Art Coffin, Yakima, a member of the State Game Commission, helps to cook breakfast on a horse-pack trip into the High Cascades. He is cooking over a sheepherder's stove brought in by horseback.

Washington's high country and its mountain lakes are powerful lures for the exploring angler. The spine of the High Cascades is dotted from the Canadian border to the southern border of Oregon with jewel-like lakes. The high-lake fishing season runs from early July into September, and during this period the mountain ridges and valleys are crisscrossed by alpine trails. While a weekend jaunt into the hills is feasible by back-pack, anglers who like to spend a week or more in the high country usually make it by a horseback safari. Such trips may be arranged through packers located in most of the mountain areas of the Northwest. The Forest Service or State Game Departments will furnish lists of reliable men who operate guide and pack services.

A Typical Seep Lake—Big Windmill below O'Sullivan Dam

The seep lakes of the Columbia Basin, created by mighty Coulee Dam, are an angler's dream come true. Not in existence prior to 1951, the new waters, after plantings by the State Game Department, immediately developed into a fisherman's bonanza. They have since produced some of the finest trout and spiny-ray fishing to be found in the Northwest. When Coulee was built it had two purposes—to provide electric power and to store water to irrigate the tremendous basin below it. That it also happened to form a series of new lakes was an unexpected dividend.

When the waters came, huge lakes including Banks, Potholes, and Evergreen reservoirs were formed. The Potholes Reservoir, a 29,400-acre, man-made lake, was filled with perch, crappie, bass, and carp, and was later planted with rainbow. A huge canal led out of the reservoir to provide water for irrigation for the lands lying between O'Sullivan Dam and the Columbia River.

This main canal was simply a large ditch dug through the volcanic waste lands. Soon water seeped through the porous rock that formed the sides of the ditch. Early in 1951 game men riding through the district found to their surprise small potholes and lakes that had formed in the coulees and draws. These lakes range from 20 to 100 acres in extent. This type of run-off continued until the whole district below O'Sullivan was dotted with seep lakes. The same type of lakes were being formed in the Quincy district.

These new waters, which were barren of fish life, were fabulously rich. Their fecundity was almost unbelievable. Token plantings of rainbows in a few of the waters grew so rapidly that fish biologists could hardly believe their eyes. Hampton Lakes, which received one of the first plants, grew a 10-pound, 2-ounce rainbow in 28 months. Half Moon Lake produced an 8-pounder in 2½ years. In the majority of the lakes anglers grew accustomed to creeling 2 to 4-pound rainbows that had grown to that size in two years' time. Some of the trout grew so fast that they turned into "pancake" trout, as broad as they were long.

A trio of fast-growing seep lake rainbows. The one at the top is just two years old. The smaller ones have been in the lake only one year. The bottom trout is one of the pancake type.

A pair of Burke Lake rainbows up to 3 pounds caught on Carey Special flies.

After Atlantic Salmon at Hosmer

Hosmer Lake in Oregon is planted with Atlantic salmon—the only body of water in which these fish may be taken along the Pacific Coast. It is also the first "fishing for fun" lake to be established in the Pacific Northwest. This type of lake is a modern concept in angling in which all fish caught in a designated body of water must be released and none killed. In April, 1966, Lake Terrell in Whatcom County, Washington, was opened under the same type of management. It holds cutthroats.

Located about 50 miles west of Bend, Oregon, along the Century Drive, Hosmer was rehabilitated in 1960 and has since been planted annually with Atlantic salmon from brood stock held at the Wizard Falls Hatchery on the Metolius River.

Hosmer consists of two shallow lakes connected by a winding channel. The upper lake is four to eight feet deep with a whitish pumice bottom over which fish may easily be seen. The photo here shows three fishermen motoring through the channel between the two lakes, with the South Sister in the background.

Almost everyone fishes Hosmer with a dry fly, usually in sizes from 10 to 16. Caddis flies with orange or yellow bodies are effective as well as the standard gray or black dries . . . but only barbless hooks are permitted. The best time to fish Hosmer is from the latter part of May through June.

heading into it and a high-priced hotel placed in the center. But the only charge to fish these "sky" lakes is that expended by a good pair of lungs and legs used to hiking.

I remember once hiking into Copper Lake and in the dark of a warm August night spreading the bed roll on the ground next to the open shelter. It was the first time we had been in this spot and it was too late to see anything of the mountain scenery. But when I awoke at early dawn the next morning, the sight was such that I lay in the bed roll for half an hour just soaking in the beauty of the rugged surroundings. Here lay the blue waters of Copper Lake unruffled and darkly mysterious in the early half light. Across the lake, the sun was turning pink the summit of the six-thousand-foot ridge that rose steeply from the further edge of the lake. Snow was still hanging in the upper gullies. All the trees and rocks were fresh and new in the dew of morning. A camp robber was teetering on a branch overhead waiting for us to start breakfast. The stiff hike in had already been repaid by a satisfaction we could never buy in the city and the fish we caught afterwards were just the extra dividend for a trip already made worth while.

This section along the South Fork of the Skykomish River includes the watershed of the Miller River. Lakes in this district include Dorothy Lake for brooks and rainbows; and Snoqualmie for cutthroats and black-spots. Then over to the Foss River chain which we have just described, where you find Malachite Lake for black-spots and rainbows; Copper Lake for the same; Hart Lake for rainbows; Angeline and Chetwood for rainbows and golden trout; and Delta for rainbows. Another trip leads into entrancing Necklace Valley that holds a series of beautiful small lakes stocked with rainbows by the Trailblazers. Going east over the ridge, you come to Marmot for rainbows and goldens; Square for cutthroats; Surprise for rainbows and brooks; and Josephine for rainbows and black-spots. The area north of the Skykomish contains fewer lakes but most of them show extra good fishing. Two of them, Eagle for cutthroats and rainbows and Sims for cutthroats, are unusually good.

Other districts in western Washington that will appeal to the hiker-angler include the Skagit Valley that reaches up into Canada, and the wild, seldom-explored district around Glacier Peak. One of the noted lakes of this section is Byrne Lake north of Kennedy Hot Springs, a long hike in but a grand lake for large rainbows, brooks and cutthroats.

Eastern Washington: Chelan—Bumping River—Mount Adams. South and east of this district lies the Lake Chelan country. Its main interest is Lake Chelan itself, which is 52 miles long. It is situated in a precipitous gash in the mountains 6,000 feet deep and possesses unparalleled beauty. It is virtually untouched by the tourist. It holds cutthroats, rain-

bows, silver trout, and Dolly Varden and there are many fine fishing lakes
in the surrounding hills. The starting point for these spots and best place
to secure information is at the town of Chelan.

Over towering Chinook Pass into eastern Washington, south of Chelan, one may digress up Bumping River to tap a plateau dotted with
mountain lakes, each teeming with trout. To list a few there are Twin
Sister for rainbows and brooks; Pear for rainbows; Apple for brooks;
Dumbell, Frying Pan, and Jug for brooks; and Cramer and Dog for
rainbows.

In the southern part of the state, north of the Columbia in the Mount
Adams district, you will find a very beautiful alpine country, open for
easy hiking. Mount Adams and Mount St. Helens loom up in sight much
of the way along the Forest Service road from Carson to Randle. From
this road that winds along at 4,000-foot elevation you sight lakes and
odd lava formations from now-extinct volcanoes. From here you can
reach Mosquito Lake for brooks, black-spots and rainbows; Council for
brooks and black-spots; Goose for brooks; and Steamboat, Placid and
Blue for brooks and rainbows.

The Virgin Lakes of the Olympics. Another paradise for the
"high-up" angler is the Olympic Peninsula with its little-known Olympic
National Park. This territory—the last untouched virgin wilderness in
the United States—is crisscrossed thickly with trails but contains no highways to attract the tin-can tourist. With a timberline at about 5,000 feet
one can easily tap many isolated mountain lakes, the majority of them
now within the boundaries of Olympic Park.

The best known of all the lakes in this region is the unbelievably beautiful Lake Crescent, which is nine miles long and circled, along one shore,
by the highway. This lake of a deep blue color is set down amid surrounding peaks that rise directly from the lake's shores. It has the distinction of holding two species of trout—the Beardsley and the Crescenti—
not found anywhere else in the world.

You can spend a week or a month hiking through the park either from
north to south, up the Elwha River and then down the Quinault, which
takes you from the Strait of Juan de Fuca to the Pacific, or from east to
west going up any of the numerous river valleys. Although firearms cannot be carried in the Park, the hiker will sight bands of Roosevelt elk,
many deer and occasionally a cougar.

Here are several suggested pack trips.

First, one can start up from the Hamma Hamma River and then take
the short stiff climb to Lower Lena, which contains rainbows, some of
large size. Proceed to Scout Lake, at an altitude of 4,300 feet, with rainbows, some of them lunkers. Then around Mount Stone to Hagen Lake

at 5,400 feet with rainbows weighing up to five pounds, and from there to the top of the ridge and along it to the Stoneway Trail and the First Divide. From here you can make several choices as to how you will get back to a highway. One route would be over to the Duckabush River, visiting Heart Lake which holds rainbows and Marmot also holding rainbows. Then you can circle back to Hood Canal, from where you started, either by way of the Duckabush or Dosewallips watersheds. Alternatively you can turn south west down the East Fork of the Quinault and through Enchanted Valley to the highway at Lake Quinault.

Another way to get to a highway would be to go back to Hood Canal by way of the North Fork of the Skykomish River by the Hammer Way Trail. You could, on this route, go to Smith lake, 3,700 feet high, containing brooks, rainbows, and black-spots; Flapjack Lakes, 3,500 feet with rainbows; and then out to Lake Cushman via the Staircase Trail.

A second trip would involve going in from the ocean side and. heading up the Quinault, striking Margaret and Mary Lakes at the Low Divide. These two lakes, situated at an altitude of 3,606 feet, are 17½ miles in by trail or 27 miles from the end of the road up the Elwha. They hold brooks, rainbows, and black-spots. Two miles away behind Mount Christie are the Martins Lakes, the larger of which holds some lunker black-spots. The Seven Lakes Basin lakes which hold brooks and black-spots lie in a beautiful scenic setting and may be reached from Sol Duc Hot Springs.

The Lakes of Rainier National Park. Although Washington's other National Park owes its fame to towering Mount Rainier, it holds as well some interesting alpine lakes. Most of these lakes are tapped either from Chinook Pass or from the Mowich or Yakima Park entrances. The Crystal Lakes are a short stiff hike from Chinook Pass, but they contain some lunker black-spots. Mowich Lake, one of the most beautiful lakes in the Park, may be reached by an easy grade from the Mowich entrance. It holds brooks, rainbows, and black-spots. Through the Carbon River Gate one can take the long hike into Lakes Ethel, James and Marjorie, which formerly put out wonderful catches of black-spots but which now hold mostly rainbows.

Through the Nisqually entrance one can make an easy hike into George Lake—4,232 feet elevation—where on July the Fourth you can see masses of avalanche lilies in a park-like meadow at one end. It produces fine brook and rainbow fishing. Following up the contour from Lake George one goes about three miles up over a ridge to drop down into Goat Lake. During the first week in July the hiker will tramp through hillside after hillside carpeted with bright alpine flowers. Goat Late at one time provided excellent brook-trout fishing.

The Yakima Park entrance gives access to several small lakes and potholes many of which contain trout, mostly brooks. This district is a fine one in which to do some exploring against the backdrop of Mount Rainier, fondly called "the Mountain" by Washington alpine hikers.

For the fisherman who does not wish to make back-pack trips into the "high-up lakes," pack horses may be rented that will take him into virtually any one of the districts of the Cascades or Olympics. For information write to the U. S. Forest Service.

Chapter Three

THE CONTEMPLATIVE FLY-TIER

Coming as it does near the end of winter, March has always been the finest period of the year for the trout anglers of the Northwest to relax. It is the month when they do their best fireside fishing.

In the Eastern trout belt outdoor sportsmen have lain dormant for most of the winter and have had several months to catch up on their fly-dressing home work.

But not so in Washington. Anglers have been on the go since the close of duck hunting, chasing steelhead or scouring the salt-chuck for young king salmon. But by the time March rolls around, the steelhead season is on its last legs and the overworked "Ike Walton" can spend a week-end at home without feeling that he will miss out on a "hot" steelhead trip.

As the trout season will open sometime in April, there is by this time a whole mess of gear to be got ready, and it is kinda' fun to start planning about the lake to fish opening day. So, while sitting snug at home at a basement work bench, winding and varnishing a fly rod, or talking at lunch time with a buddy over last year's opening day, one's mind keeps busy with trout lore. If the angler happens to be a fly fisherman who dresses his own flies, he has a wealth of wonderfully alluring work projects to be accomplished during this leisure month.

For the active angler there is something to this fly tying that is much more than turning out well-dressed patterns. It complements and broadens his angling life; it adds new glamour to every fishing jaunt; it removes the necessity of his making a limit catch to get the full enjoyment out of a week-end excursion. For no matter how long he has been "rolling his own" flies, his interest is renewed and he sprouts different ideas every time a new fishing season approaches.

Fly making is not a limited hobby. The practitioner takes out of it just as much as he puts into it. It is an art that can grow with the years; a craft which is never perfected but which can be made as fully scientific as desired. The fly dresser can be purely utilitarian in his approach and tie up the common patterns, to make up a liberal supply in the various sizes to have ready for the start of every trout season. In the Northwest he can specialize—become an expert on devising flies for certain species of trout, or make extensive studies of trout food. Then each season he can attempt to make a more perfect imitation of the natural bait, whether it be insect or nymph or minnow.

But no matter how deeply he goes into his hobby he cannot help, if he is a true disciple of Izaak Walton, but put some of his own personality into his flies. They will be as recognizable as if they were branded. After the season has started, he can pick up a discarded fly with a broken hook point and immediately identify it as his own, or make a shrewd guess if it has been dressed by one of his fellow anglers.

A First Lesson in Dressing a Fly. Various circumstances start a sportsman on the alluring pastime of making his own artificial flies. He may have learned it from his father in his youth, and taken to fly dressing as a matter of course; he may take lessons from a professional; or he may be a fisherman who just likes to work with his hands and turns to fly tying because it fits in so well with his fishing.

Or, like myself, he may be forced into it because he can never find the kind of flies that he wants on the market. The hackles of commercial flies are always too heavy; their wings are not cocked at just the right angle; or they just don't conform to the type of insects that breed in his part of the country. The last was my trouble. Somehow or other, I had rather definite ideas about the kind of flies that I wished to fish with, but I couldn't find them anywhere. Or if I had them dressed to order, there was considerable difficulty in getting them tied just so; and then the first time I cast them, I would get another idea and there was no way to put it into effect. So I had to learn fly tying in self-defense.

Being one of those mortals whose fingers are mostly thumbs, I had a frightful time at first. I bought the only book I could find at the time, George Holden's *Streamcraft*, sent away for a vise and materials, and started in. Nothing went right and though I succeeded in tying a hackle, it was more of a feather duster than a fly.

But at this period there lived in Seattle a one-handed fly-tier, Dan Conway, who has since gone to that Happy Fishing Country from which there is no return. Dan learned to dress a fly when he was a boy in Ireland. Although he had his left hand amputated in his mature years he lost not a whit of his skill and could dress a truly beautiful fly with the one good hand and an iron hook for the other.

Dan's brogue was as thick as a Dublin fog especially when loosened with a drop or so of "reel-oil," and the flies he made were the most perfect that I had ever seen. One of his favorite patterns was a teal and red, dressed wet, and the wings were cupped as evenly and perfectly as if they had been placed there by nature. He took an uncommonly long time to select feathers, it seemed to me, but when they went onto the hook they matched exactly. Each black stripe of teal feather fitted the stripes of the other in spacing and width just as if they had been drawn by a draftsman.

"Never make a poor fly," said Dan. "You're trying to please yourself and you don't want anything second rate. If it ain't right tear it apart and start over again."

Charley King and I learned to tie together and we never forgot some of Dan's firm-rooted principles.

"Always make true patterns," he would keep saying. "Find out the exact dressing and stick to it."

He had an odd wine-red shade of wood that he shredded out and tied "dubbin" style for the bodies of one type of teal and red. We secured a piece of this yarn and haunted department store counters until we had matched it. This was a lesson that has stuck with me ever since and I have always tried to keep patterns true, although scarcity of good materials during the war years made this a difficult task.

Dan Conway's "Special." Dan's pet fly was a variation of the Yellow

Hammer which most of the anglers who knew Dan called the Conway Special. Dan sold a few of them to fishermen who he thought would use them properly, and as I never could get enough of them, that was one pattern that I had to learn. It was rated the best fly on sea-run cutthroats for our local rivers, and had such a fishy look that just holding one of them in your fingers sent anticipatory thrills chasing up and down your spine.

The Conway Special was tied wet on number six thin wire hooks in two types, which differed only in shades of wool used for the body. One was dressed with a rather light-yellow yarn and the other with a yarn of an orange-yellow cast. The hackle, which was tied palmer, matched the wool color as closely as possible, and was dressed sparse so as to sink readily. We absorbed another lesson on this fly, for we had to learn to match body and hackle even if we had to dye them together to do it.

Dan tied the wings of his Special of white goose quills, cut rather thin and cupped over the hook in a manner that was so fishy I used this method in every wet fly of that type that I dressed thereafter. By matching quills that tapered out, the wings of the fly were curved to a point that gave them a peculiarly enticing action. Dan would use only one kind of feather—the primaries from the wings of an adult snow goose. The fibers of these feathers hung so closely together that the fly could be used day after day, and the wings would remain intact and not shred out as they would if made from the domestic quill. This teaches another lesson: that the very best feathers and animal hair can usually not be purchased but have to be collected.

My First "Pet Pattern." Although I started tying flies in late fall, I did not have to wait until the next spring to try them out, but would test the patterns on one of the year-round lakes near Seattle. In this way I learned the different riding, sinking and floating qualities of hackle dressed in all the methods that I could devise. It was on one of these lakes, Sammamish, that I first discovered that an original pattern could take fish.

I happened to have the tail of a gray squirrel that was given me, and dressed up a fly with a yellow silk body, palmered gray hackle and the squirrel hair for wings that turned out to be so good looking that I had to use it at once. So the next morning—a cold drizzly one—I drove out to Sammamish to try for cutthroats from the shore. I cast with the fly for a long time and nothing happened. So I put on a Conway and a trout rose that didn't take. When it was about time to start back I tied on the squirrel tail once more.

I cast it near a bunch of tules and was stripping it in rather carelessly when I felt a solid jolt. I set the hook and my line ran out so fast I almost fell over backwards. Then my fish rose and swirled on the surface, and although it looked large enough for a salmon I knew by its color that it was a cutthroat. No, I didn't catch the trout. It played around in the open for a bit and then suddenly ran into the tules and broke me off. Needless to say, I got a big thrill out of hooking that fish, but, as it turned out, the pattern didn't mean much for I never set it into another fish and soon quit tying it.

Collecting Feathers for Flies. When I started collecting feathers, I discovered that this was a part of fly making that stretched the hobby around the year and mixed up my fishing with my hunting to the point that I hardly knew where one stopped and the other began. How fortunate I was to live in a state where nearly every type of game bird was to be found!

Duck shooting immediately took on an added importance. It always had been a thrill, of course, to bring down a mallard on a long cross shot. But if that mallard happened to be a full-plumaged drake, my pleasure was increased four-fold. I would stretch out the broad strong wings and visualize all the dry flies that they contained. I would stroke the barred flank feathers, lifting them up, the small ones and the large heavily striped ones, and imagine the Grizzly Kings, the Professors, the Queen of the Waters, the Mallard Spiders or the May Flies they would make. If my hunting partner wasn't an angler I would usually have the barred flank feathers of all his greenheads stuck away in an inner pocket before we separated that night.

Fully feathered teal drake have never been too common here around Puget Sound, and the barred flank feathers from each drake we brought down were carefully stored in moth-proof boxes. Widgeon were easier to get, and soon there were plenty of boxes of gray and brown barred feathers on the storeroom shelf, as well as matched wings.

Since I did not manage to go goose shooting for several years after I had started the fly tying, the highly prized goose wings had to be begged from old-time goose hunters. At times the wings were bloody and bedraggled, but almost every season, at least one pair of nearly perfect wings would come to hand. Then they were spread out and carefully the matching quills were cut from each wing and fastened together with a rubber band. Now I always had the makings of a set of white wings by simply picking out the matched quills of the right size. Of recent years, however, although juvenile snow geese are the type most commonly shot on the Skagit Flats, I manage to bring down each season at least one of the showy great-winged adults, and I now have a fine reserve of "snow quills."

The Brad's Brat. So in this month of stay-at-home angling, I find time to check over the fly materials I have been collecting for many busy years, adding moth crystals, and making sure that the feathers have been correctly labeled. George Tephey has again sent me a box of Michigan deer tails—those fluffy white-tails that make the most superior buck-tail flies. They have been washed in warm water and soap so that they are pure white and brown, all ready to use. One tail has been dyed a rich hot orange as I tied up some "Brats" to use on the winter steelhead fly fishing trips that I made last month. That orange and white bucktail combination, when wet, produces an illusive shade that sea-going trout find very desirable. It is one of my year-round patterns. I tie it up on heavy hooks, in 1 to 2/0, for those high water turbulent rivers that hold winter "steelfish."

Then there are always a few number 12's in a "lake" fly box, to use as an exploratory fly on rainbows in lowland lakes. Dressed sparse on number 6 hooks it is a close second to the Conway Special for sea-run cutthroats. It is of course my stand-by for summer-run steelheads. In fact, it was devised originally for these fish. The steelhead fly box always holds "Brats" in sizes 6 to 2 dressed bushy for early season, and very sparse for low-water-late-summer-hard-to-interest steelhead. We always include some of the same sizes on trips to British Columbia to mix in with the Black O'Lindsays and the dry sedges.

Dragon Fly Nymph Patterns. No matter how many of them I tie each spring I need a new supply of those opening day specials—the Carey Special and the Carot Nymph before the next season rolls around. So out come the boxes holding the "chink" feathers, some filled with the brown rump feathers and some with the green feathers of the cock chinese pheasant. The sight of the gaudy feathers always brings back memories of those trips over the Hump to eastern Washington for the opening of the "chink" hunting season. Usually we have gone to the Okanogan where the bare brown hills and sage brush slopes are interspersed with apple orchards heavy with bright red winesaps. But at other times we have been southeast to the Palouse country whose rolling hills and vast wheat fields are a welcome change for eyes accustomed to the narrow canyon-like streets of the city.

This Carey Special is a versatile pattern. It probably resembles the dragonfly or the damselfly nymph to the trout and is a "taker" in our lowland lakes. It is best fished either as a nymphed fly or as a wet fly that is cast out, allowed to sink and then slowly stripped in. This fly seems to achieve a very "live" action of the hackles that simulates a living creature. It seems to take trout under all conditions, whether the air is near freezing in April and thin sheets of ice cover the shallows, or whether the days are hot and sunny as they are apt to be in October.

The body of the fly may be tied of many different materials, but of late years I have found that dressing the complete fly with rump feathers makes the most effective pattern. This dressing calls for a body made with a rump feather, preferably a different color from the wings, and with uniformly long fibers. The feather is tied in at the tip after the tail is fastened, and then wound down the body, as if it were yarn catching the fibers under with each revolution. If a few fibers happen to escape they can be snipped short and the ragged effect thus secured adds to the killing qualities of the pattern.

A Pass Lake Pattern. There is another dressing of the damsel nymph that has also proved to be a good early season fly. It originated as follows. The year that Pass Lake was legally restricted to fly fishing only, the Washington Fly Fishing Club held a picnic there in May, which the majority of the club anglers attended. I had fished the lake the fall before and early that spring, and noticed damsel nymphs were present both in the stomachs of the fat rainbows as well as in the water.

Bringing several nymphs home in a formalin solution, I sat them on the work table with an assortment of hair of various types and started experimenting. A dubbin body of wolverine fur mixed with red fox, combined with guard hairs and hun feathers, seemed to produce a close replica and I dressed several like this in sizes 6 and 8. Doc. Brown, Reuben Helm and myself had used them on several trips and found that they were effective in taking rainbows, Loch Levens and even small bass during our April trips.

To return to the picnic, fishing at Pass Lake was very slow that day—in fact the trout virtually stopped rising to any sort of fly. Of the forty anglers who were furiously covering the water from dawn until the noon dead line, only two men took fish. Reuben Helm netted three fat rainbows and I caught one. All four of these fish were caught on the new damsel nymph. Needless to say, from then on the pattern was firmly established.

The Carot Nymph or The Cutthroat's Delight. The Carot Nymph, an adaptation of Hardy's partridge and orange, has been another all-season fly for lowland lakes. It will take rainbows and brook trout, but it is especially effective on native cutthroats when used in small lakes or beaver ponds on overcast or rainy days. Often the angler will raise a lunker cutthroat on a Carey Special but the trout will refuse to seize the lure. In such cases a stunt that often works is, instead of casting back, change to a number 12 Carot Nymph. Then cast into the same spot and be ready to set the hook immediately, because the trout will usually hit as soon as the fly touches the water.

The Hungarian partridge has not been too plentiful in Washington and supplies of these skins are limited. As the season on "huns" was closed from 1946 to 1949, most hunter-fly tiers will be zealously guarding

whatever supplies of the gray breast feathers that they have on hand. It is
certainly this hackle feather that gives the fly its taking qualities. The fly
should be tied with a short gold tag, a fat "hot" orange body without ribbing so that the wool will shred rough in use, and a hackle tied "spider" so
that it spreads out like the ribs of an umbrella. In the water, this nymph
has the real movement that gives it the appearance of a juicy morsel—a
fit meal for any trout.

From the Wood Duck to the Wet Fly. On one end of my shelf rests
a flat cedar box labeled "wood duck." I can hardly resist the temptation
at times to open the box and take out the whole wood duck skin. What
a beautiful bird! How lucky we are in Washington to have the gorgeous
wood duck as a native waterfowl. It was quite difficult during the years
when the season for these birds is closed for angler-hunters to "pass up"
a wood duck when hunting on our inland lakes. But now that "woodies"
have become legal quarry most of the local fly-tying clan own a set of
the lemon-colored flank feathers safely hidden away among their materials, so when they feel the need of making a Cahill or a Quill Gordon
they have the feathers to tie them with. Or if they feel reckless they can
dress a lemon-colored spider with a red body, unless their better nature
prevents them from committing the sacrilege of using this rare feather
to tie a wet fly.

Fly Tying While Afield. Most fly tiers at the start of their careers have
dreamed of dressing a fly right on the banks of a stream. As time goes
on the undertaking is apt to appear more and more impractical and few
of them ever get beyond the dream stage. However this project does
possess some very practical aspects. It is recommended that every practicing fly tier include a fly-tying kit in his fishing gear when making an
extended trip provided he is not limited in weight or space. Even so, he
should be able to pack nearly everythng he will need for a month in two
or three cedar cigar boxes.

The materials he selects should be suited to the country or to the type
of fishing he expects to encounter. He must have the basic tools of his
trade, of course, vise, scissors, hackle pliers, bodkin, wax, head cement,
and thread. He should also carry a good assortment of hooks to fit the
various types of fishing in the Puget Sound country; these should run in
sizes from 12 to 2/0. He should have the standard colors of hackle, of
quills, of wool and silk floss, and of peacock, as well as tinsel and chenille.
In Washington he would carry bucktail and polar bear hair, both natural
and dyed, and the special feathers necessary for Northwest patterns. With
such a kit, the angler should be able to replace any patterns he is short
of or dream up new ones if those on hand prove ineffective.

Many of us in the Northwest carry such a kit whenever we go into

British Columbia for Kamloops trout or when we take a vacation trip here in our own state. But the only time that I remember actually tying flies along a river was on a steelhead trip that I made to the Wind River back in the early nineteen-thirties.

I had never fished this stream before, but I had been told that a double gray hackle was the taking fly that summer, and four flies of this pattern were mixed up with the bucktails in the fly box. They were dressed on a number 6 hook with stiff gray hackle tied half way down the hook, gold floss with gold ribbing for the center of the body and gray hackle for the front half of the fly. They had no tails, and their hackles were tied as in a bivisible so that each fly could be used either as a floater or a wet pattern in rough water, as occasion demanded.

Bill Booth and I made camp on the river above its confluence with Trout Creek and traveled downstream through most of the canyon the first day before we located a section of water that held fish. All of the D.G.H. were lost that afternoon as a result of mishaps and not of fish. That evening in camp I tied up six more with the vise stuck into a stump and a log for a chair.

The following morning we were back in the lower canyon shortly after dawn, and before noon I had lost all six hackles, four of them on wild steelhead which snapped off the flies without any trouble and two on bottom rocks in the white water. So back to camp, and another half dozen D.G.H. were dressed before the mosquitoes became too thick that evening. Again, all of them were lost on steelhead the next day. While it might have been lack of confidence on our part, we could not seem to interest the "steelfish" in any other patterns.

So came another day and another set of flies, and with the aid of heavier tippets (I believe that we ended up with 8/5 gut) both of us put steelhead on the beach. The fly kit on the river bank certainly paid off on that trip.

Although I have made several trips to the Wind River each summer since then for steelhead, and have carried the D.G.H. in the fly box each time, I have never since taken a summer-run on that pattern. So one never knows. Fly patterns seem to come and go in effectiveness and many an excellent imitation for no logical reason remains buried in the back corner of a fly box. Perhaps a fly needs the faith of an angler just as much as it needs its fidelity to nature. For when an angler has confidence in his fly, he will give it all he has, and fish it with every bit of skill and technique at his command. Granted that he is using the right type of fly for the water he is covering, usually any one of a dozen patterns in the hands of an expert who knows the water will take fish. And the man who knows the water best, and fishes it most patiently and carefully, will be the one to take fish, even though his pattern may not be one of those at the top of the "Best Killing" list.

Trout Flies. The trout flies illustrated facing page 42 represent only a sampling of the fly patterns that have proved successful in the lakes and rivers of the Pacific Northwest. While the majority of those shown are originals developed in the Puget Sound country, along the Columbia, or in British Columbia, a few are patterns that are used the country over. An angler who is carrying a fly box equipped with a set of these flies in various sizes should be able to take trout in this territory, no matter in what section of it he happens to be fishing.

Their dressing and a hint or two about their use are given below.

Carot Nymph: Hook; 12 to 8. Tag; Gold. Tail; None. Ribs; None. Body; Orange wool. Hackle; Hungarian partridge breast feather in either gray or brown, tied spider.

This has been a taker on cutthroats and brook trout in small lakes, beaver ponds, or sloughs. When these trout are feeding the "live" action of the hackle fibers as the fly is stripped through the water usually produces a strike.

Dandy Green Nymph: Hook; 7 to 10. Tag; None. Tail; Wisps of gray-green pheasant hackle. Ribs; Round gold tinsel. Body; A tapered body of spun mixed grass green and yellow polar bear fur (fuzz)—or any type of fur body of this color may be used.

Hackle: Gray green hackle from the back of a chinese pheasant cock, tied spider fashion. Wings; None.

A very good early season underwater nymph for lakes, good up to midsummer.

Damsel Nymph: Hook; 6 to 8. Tag; None. Tail; Section of brown mallard or widgeon divided and cut short. Ribs; Black silk thread or thin herl. Hackle; None. Body; Wolverine fur mixed with red fox dubbed for body. Wolverine guard hair tied on upper body and separated at head to form antennae. These hairs are tied down with ribbing thread to form segments in the body like the real nymph. Wing cases are of brown-tipped Hungarian partridge breast feather.

An attempted exact representation of the damsel nymph which is present in Northwest lakes in great numbers.

Yellow Spider. Hook; 6 or smaller. Tag; None. Tail; Gray mallard pearl feather. Ribs; None. Body; Yellow silk. Hackle; Mallard pearl feather tied spider fashion. Wings; None.

This is one of the all-round Northwest flies. It takes trout in lakes and is noted as a good river fly for sea-run "cuts."

There are many variations. Some types are dressed with red or green bodies and others have silver tinsel ribbing. Or a brown or a lemon-yellow dyed mallard feather may be used for the hackle. Frank Headrick has had luck using this fly in a size 6 on summer-run steelhead.

Carey's Special. Hook; 6 or 8. Tag; None. Tail; Fifteen strands badger hair or wisps of rump feather. Body; Peacock quill (optional badger, moose mane, peacock herl or rump pheasant feather). Hackle; Chinese cock rump feather tied spider fashion. Wings; None.

This represents the nymph of the large dragon fly which is one of the very common lake foods available to trout along the West Coast. It is almost exclusively used in lakes. Either the brown or the greenish rump feather may be used.

Black O'Lindsay. Hook; 6 or 4. Tag; None. Tail; 8 to 10 wisps ginger and bluejay mixed. Ribs; Round gold tinsel. Body; Bright yellow wool. Hackle; Under hackle is chestnut; over hackle is bluejay. Wings; Under wings are fibers of peacock swords, over wings are barred mallard or teal. Shoulder; Eyed jungle cock feather.

A very popular pattern for British Columbia. It makes a fine exploratory fly in lakes and will take sea-run cutthroats.

Silver and Mallard (Nation's Fancy). Hook; 4 or 6. Tag; None. Tail; Golden pheasant tippet wisps. Ribs; Round silver tinsel. Body; Rear, ⅝ silver tinsel; front, ⅜ black wool or floss ribbed with silver tinsel. Hackle; Badger tied ahead of wings. Wings; Barred mallard.

A Bill Nation pattern designed for the Kamloops of Paul Lake but a good lake fly all over British Columbia.

Silver Brown. Hook; 8 to 6. Tag; None. Tail; Wisps red breast feather from golden pheasant. Ribs; None. Body; Flat silver tinsel. Hackle; Dark red game cock or brown grouse feather. Wings; Slender strips golden pheasant from center of tail feather.

An effective pattern for early or late fishing for cutthroats or rainbows, mainly in lakes.

Teal and Red. Hook; 8 to 6. Tag; silver (optional). Tail; Golden pheasant tippets. Ribs; Silver tinsel. Body; Red Wool. Hackle; Brown. Wings; Teal breast feathers.

A good pattern in lakes or streams, mainly for cutthroat, or, in British Columbia, for Kamloops. It may be varied with a yellow body.

Queen of The Waters. Hook; 8 to 12. Tail; None. Tag; None. Ribs; Gold tinsel. Body; Orange wool. Hackle; Brown, palmered entire length of body. Wings; Gray pearl mallard.

This fly, on the West Coast, is usually dressed wet with the wings cupped so as to give plenty of action. It is very effective on brook trout under normal circumstances.

Alaska Mary Ann. Hook; 6 to 10. Tag; None. Tail; Scarlet hackle wisps. Ribs; Silver tinsel. Body; White chenille. Wings; White polar bear. Shoulder; Eyed jungle cock.

Developed in Alaska, it is reported to be an imitation of the fin of a Dolly Varden. A good fly to use as an attractor in swift-flowing coastal rivers for trout.

Double Gray Hackle. Hook; 4 to 8. Tail; None. Body; Rear third, gray grizzly hackle dressed as in a bivisible; middle third, gold floss ribbed with gold tinsel; front third, gray hackle dressed as in rear.

This is the oversize version of the gray hackle—yellow body. It is designed for fast rivers where it will float readily in white water. It is a taker of steelhead wet or dry. It has also proved effective as a dry floater for big rainbows in mountain lakes.

(This, and the next three dry flies, were dressed by Letcher Lambuth to imitate western insects.)

Orange Sedge. Hook; 8. Tag; None. Tail; None. Ribs; Brown hackle stem. Body; Bright chestnut hackle feather stripped one side, twisted on orange waxed silk and wrapped on, then projecting fibers trimmed off. Not much taper. Hackle; Dark brown. Wings; Dark grizzled brown western red deer hair divided and upright.

The orange sedge is a good all-season fly for coastal rivers in the West, as the sedge will hatch out most of the summer.

Red Upright Dun. Hook; 10. Tag; None. Tail; Six or eight ginger hackle fibers. Ribs; Ginger hackle stem. Body; A ginger hackle stripped on one side and twisted on waxed yellow silk. After this is wound on, the projecting fibers are trimmed off.

Hackle; Ginger. Wings; Barred wood-duck, rolled and divided.

This is the western version of the well-known fly.

Blue Upright. Hook; 8. Tag; None. Tail; Six or eight blue dun hackle fibers. Ribs; None. Body; Stripped stem of peacock herl very thin; no taper. Hackle; English blue dun. Wings; Barred mallard, rolled and divided and tied upright.

This western manner of dressing the popular fly is good during the early season.

Western Yellow Stone. Hook; 8. Tag; None. Tail; Two short ginger hackle stem tips scraped with thumb nail to form a "U." Ribs; Ginger hackle stem. Body; Bright yellow mohair twisted on waxed yellow silk—not much taper. Hackle; Ginger. Wings; Medium grizzled mule deer hair divided and upright.

This represents the stone fly with its wings upright as though it were just lighting or ready to take off. A good mid-season fly.

Fifth Row. California Coachman. Hook; 10 or 12. Tag; None. Tail; Wisps ginger hackle. Body; Peacock herl egg mass at rear; balance of body

R. Henry with his 22-pound brown trout, caught in Sullivan Lake, Pend Oreille County, on May 22, 1965. It is the largest brown ever taken on rod and reel in Washington.

Record Fish

The dream of almost every fisherman is at some time to catch a fish so large that ever after he will be the envy of other anglers. As a basis of comparison, here are some Washington State records of "big ones" caught with rod and reel:

Species and size:	Where caught and when:	By whom:
Bullfrog, 7¼ lbs.	Martha Lake, 1949	Jim Pratt
Ling cod, freshwater, 13 lbs.	Roosevelt Lake, 1955	Unknown
Cutthroat, resident, 8¾ lbs.	Coffee Pot Lake, 1956	Al Thomas
Crappie, 4½ lbs.	Lake Washington, 1956	John Smart
Rainbow, 22½ lbs.	Waitts Lake, 1957	Bill Dittner
Brook Trout, 5¼ lbs.	Bayley Lake, 1961	F. Roskelley
Cutthroat, Crescenti, 12 lbs.	Lake Crescent, 1961	W. Welsh
Dolly Varden, 22½ lbs.	Tieton River, 1961	Louis Schott
Steelhead, 33 lbs.	Snake River, 1962	Homer Scott
Steelhead, 31 lbs., 2 ozs., (dressed)	Snake River, 1963	Randy McDonald
Cutthroat, sea-run, 4 lbs.	Tahuya River, 1963	S. Thorniley
Channel Catfish, 12 lbs.	Grand Ronde River, 1964	Phillip Newbry
Smallmouth Bass, 7½ lbs.	Snake River, 1964	Bill King
Walleye, 10 lbs.	Banks Lake, 1965	Oscar Carlson
Steelhead, summer-run, 18¼ lbs.	South Fork Stillaguamish, 1965	Bob Rech
Brown Trout, 22 lbs.	Sullivan Lake, 1965	R. L. Henry
Lake Trout, Mackinaw, 30¼ lbs.	Loon Lake, 1966	Ken Janke
Largemouth Bass, 11½ lbs.	Newman Lake, 1966	Don Milleten

Dry Falls, a "Quality Lake"

Dry Falls lies in Sun Lakes State Park about three miles from Coulee City. As one of Washington's "quality lakes," it operates under a special set of regulations established by the State Game Department. No person may use bait of any type while fishing in the lake, and the daily limit is three trout which must be at least 12 inches in length. All types of artificial gear may be used but no outboards are permitted. The lakes are managed on a restricted season and usually only during the spring months.

This 98-acre piece of water is a highly interesting one to fish, ranging from a couple of feet in the weedy areas down to 30 feet along the sides of the hemming cliffs which eons ago were the site of a spectacular waterfall. Anglers with spinning gear can successfully troll a small spoon through the deeper water, and the shallow areas are ideal for fly fishing. Tules grow in thick clumps around some of the islands as well as through the shallow areas. In April and May the lunker rainbows cruise among the weeds and tules and may be taken on flies, either wet or dry. A small nymph fly or any of the Carey Special flies are "taking" patterns. On calm mornings or in late evening a dry fly will take the big rainbows.

The lake is planted with fingerlings each year, which normally grow to 12 inches by the next spring. In addition, the lake has many hold-over trout fish running from 14 to 20 inches.

The author and his labrador, Jet of Bikin, who is leaping from the boat to retrieve a trout that has just been hooked on a fly.

NORTHWEST TROUT FLIES

a: Carot Nymph. **b**: Dandy Green Nymph. **c**: Damsel Nymph. **d**: Yellow Spider. **e**: Colonel Carey Special. **f**: Black O'Lindsay. **g**: Silver and Mallard (Nation's Fancy). **h**: Silver Brown. **i**: Teal and Red. **j**: Queen of the Waters. **k**: Alaska Mary Ann. **l**: Double Gray Hackle. **m**: Orange Sedge. **n**: Red Upright Dun. **o**: Blue Upright. **p**: Western Yellow Stone **q**: California Coachman. **r**: Bucktail Royal Coachman, (dry). **s**: Montana Buck. **t**: Flying Ant.

bright yellow rayon. Hackle; Ginger. Wings; White bucktail tied upright.

This is a representation of one of the many forms of the May Fly, and imitates a female found on a western river.

Bucktail Royal Coachman (dry). Hook; 4 to 12. Tag; None or gold optional. Tail; Red hackle fibers or golden pheasant tippets (optional). Ribs; None. Body; Peacock herl with scarlet red band of silk or wool in center. Hackle; Brown. Wings; White bucktail tied upright.

The bucktail royal is one of the most widely used flies on the West Coast. It is dressed dry in all sizes to take trout or steelhead. Then it is dressed wet, like any other bucktail, and used in small sizes for trout or larger sizes for rainbow or steelhead.

Montana Buck. Hook; 4 to 8. Tag; None. Tail; Golden pheasant tippets. Ribs; None. Body; Golden color silk or wool. Hackle; Gray grizzled hackle palmered. Wings; Deer body hair-gray-tied upright.

Very good fished either wet or dry for cutthroats or rainbows. It will also take steelhead.

Flying Ant. Hook; 8 to 10. Tag; None. Tail; None. Ribs; None. Body; Rear half, peacock herl; front half, red silk (orange silk optional). Tapered. Wings; Gray hackle tips tied semi-spent fashion (brown hackle optional).

This is a land-bred insect and should be fished dry, or slightly submerged as a drowning fly. A killer when the flying ant emerges.

Migratory Trout and Salmon Flies

The type of sea-run cutthroat, steelhead and cohoe fly shown facing page 156 is being developed on the Pacific Coast. Although a few of them have been illustrated before, most of these are original patterns that were devised in the Puget Sound country.

Conway Special. Hook 4 to 8. Tag; Gold (optional). Tail; Red and white hackle fibers. Ribs; Gold. Body; Yellow wool palmered with yellow hackle. Hackle; Red and yellow. Wings; White goose or swan feathers with a thin strip of red on each side.

One of the most effective sea-run cutthroat flies on the coast. It is also good as a summer-run steelhead fly. It may be dressed with bucktail instead of feather wings.

Shammy Royal. Hook; 6 or 8. Tag; Silver. Tail; Strip of chamois. Ribs; Silver. Body; Black chenille butt; balance of body red silk. Hackle; Furnace. Wings; White bucktail.

These "shammy" flies with their enticing action are very effective on sea-run cutthroats.

Nation's Silver Tip. Hook; 4 to 8. Tag; None. Tail; Six strands of golden pheasant tippet. Ribs; None. Body; Rear half, flat silver tinsel; front half, black floss. Hackle; Speckled gallina. Wings; Light mottled turkey with a few strands of tippet inclosed. A side striping of red swan may be used if fly is dressed for coastal rivers.

This is another one of the Bill Nation flies that was dressed for British Columbia lakes. However, as it is intended to represent a small minnow, it may be classed also as a migratory fish fly. With the red striping it will be good for cutthroats and probably for steelhead.

Shammy Bee. Hook; 6 or 8. Tag; Silver. Tail; Strip of Chamois. Ribs; None. Body; Alternate bands of red and yellow chenille. Hackle; Red and yellow. Wings; White bucktail.

Steelhead Flies

Orange Shrimp. Hook; Summer-runs 4 to 6; winter runs 4 to 2/0. Tag; Gold. Tail; Red Hackle fiber. Ribs; None. Body; Orange wool. Hackle; Orange. Wings; White bucktail and, when procurable, jungle cock feather extending at least halfway up the length of the wings.

A very good early season fly, or for winter runs.

Purple Peril. Hook; 4 to 8. Tag; Silver. Tail; Wisps dyed purple hackle. Ribs; Silver. Body; Purple dyed floss. Hackle; Purple. Wings; Gray or red deer body hair.

This has proved an effective dry fly here for steelhead, and it will also take when wet. It is especially good on dark days.

Brad's Brat. Hook; Summer runs 4 to 6; winter runs 4 to 2/0. Tag; Gold. Tail; Orange and white bucktail. Ribs; Gold. Body; Rear half orange wool; front half red wool. Hackle; Brown. Wings; Orange and white bucktail. Shoulder; Eyed jungle cock (optional).

The orange bucktail used should be about 1/3 the amount of white.

Killer. Hook; 4 to 6. Tag; Silver tinsel. Tail; Red hackle fibers. Ribs; Silver. Body; Red wool. Hackle; Red. Wings; Black deer tail (bear hair optional). Shoulder; Eyed jungle cock—an essential part of this fly.

Very effective in some rivers—one of these is the Wind River.

Skykomish Sunrise. Hook; Summer-runs 4 to 6; winter runs 4 to 2/0. Tag; Silver. Tail; Red and yellow hackle fibers. Ribs; Silver. Body; Red chenille. Hackle; Red and yellow. Wings; White bucktail.

Kalama Special. Hook; 4 to 6. Tag; None. Tail; Red hackle fibers. Ribs; None. Body; Yellow wool. Hackle; Grizzly palmered. Wings; White bucktail.

A very effective pattern on the summer-runs in Washington's Kalama River.

Lord Iris. Hook; 8 to 1. Tag; None. Tail; Golden pheasant tippet. Ribs; None. Body; Silver tinsel. Hackle; Orange. Underwing; Two orange hackle; peacock herl; two badger hackle; golden pheasant crests. Overwing; Red, orange, green, and blue goose or swan wing flight feathers married together. Topping; Golden pheasant. Shoulder; Eyed jungle cock.

One of Preston Jennings patented flies, it has proved a very effective all-season fly for large rainbows. An imitation of the common minnow, it is taken with determination. A good early season cutthroat fly in small size. It has taken steelhead when used in the same manner as the bucktail flies.

Golden Demon. Hook; 4 to 8. Tag; None. Tail; Golden pheasant crest. Ribs; None. Body; Flat gold tinsel. Hackle; Orange. Wings; Brown bucktail. Shoulder; Eyed jungle cock.

This Oregon and California steelhead pattern has been effective in Washington. It has proved very good when rivers are tinged in early season with snow water.

Steelhead and Cutthroat Flies

Black Gnat Bucktail. Hook; 4 to 6. Tag; None. Tail; Scarlet hackle wisps. Ribs; None. Body; Black chenille. Hackle; Black. Wings; Brown bucktail.

This is another southern pattern that is used in Puget Sound waters. A variation used in the Stilliguamish—the Hoyt Special—is dressed without the bucktail and with bushy grizzly hackle only. These dark flies are takers in silt or snow colored water.

Lady Godiva. Hook; 1/o to 3/o. Tag; Silver tinsel—usually embossed. Tail; Red and yellow swan married. Ribs; Silver tinsel flat. Butt; Red chenille. Hackle; None. Body; Yellow seal's fur. Wings; Underwing sparse white polar bear; overwing red bucktail.

This is Judge Ralph Olson's pattern that has been a killer for him on winter steelhead in the Skagit River and has taken several *Field and Stream* prizes. Judge Olson states that he does not like hackle on a steelhead fly. He prefers the larger sizes 1/o to 3/o for winter fishing, and this pattern is especially good on the overcast days that come so often in winter. For bright days, he varies it with a similar pattern—the Orange Wing. This has orange tail; orange butt; silver tinsel ribs; yellow wool body; and wings made of white and orange polar bear fur.

Minnow. Hook; 6 to 8. Tag; Silver. Tail; Peacock herl. Ribs; None. Body; Silver tinsel for belly; overbody, peacock herl tied down at bend of hook with the tinsel. Hackle; None. Wings; None. Head; Peacock herl.

This is a taker when used on sea-run cutthroats in rivers when the humpback salmon fry or similar types of minnows are on their downstream migration.

Wind River Optic. Hook; 4 to 6. Tag; None. Tail; None. Body; Silver tinsel—usually flat, but may be heavy round. Hackle; None. Wings; Burnt orange bucktail. Head; Hollow brass bead clamped onto shank; enameled black with red "eye" with a white dot.

This is one of the variations of Jim Pray's noted Optic fly. It is an effective pattern used as a sunken fly in deep pools.

Cohoe Flies

Candlefish Fly. Hook; 2/o to 3/o—long shank. Tag; None. Tail; None. Ribs; None. Body; Thin heavy silver tinsel. Hackle; None. Wings; Polar bear streamers. Body; Underbody, three layers consisting of natural white, pale green, and pale blue; leave part of white at bottom and then mix. Median line is bright carmine. Back; Yellowish blue-green and a French blue (of a gray tone) blended together.

When colors are mixed, the hair itself is blended when dressing the fly.

Double Hook Cohoe Fly. Hooks; 1/o. Tag; None. Tail; None. Body; Flat silver tinsel. Hackle; None. Wings; Underbody natural white; upper-body bright blue—both polar bear.

An example of a double-hook cohoe attractor pattern. The eye of the extra hook is turned upward and is attached with 8- to 12-pound test nylon fastened down under the body.

Ghost. Hook; 2/o to 3/o long shank. Tag; None. Tail; None. Ribs; None. Body; Heavy silver tinsel. Hackle; None. Wings; Polar bear. Mixed pale blue and medium pale green.

This is an "attractor" type of fly that will be good either for feeding or spawning silvers.

Herring Fly. Hook; 2/o to 3/o long shank. Tag; None. Tail; None. Ribs; None. Body; Thin, made with heavy silver tinsel. Hackle; None. Wings; Polar bear. Underbody is natural white with a touch of green; median line gunmetal gray; back is a full rich green with a few strands of olive for topping.

When the above flies are dressed for casting, they should have their wings no longer than the bend of the hook. For trolling, however, they may be much longer.

PART TWO

PART TWO

Chapter One

A SHORT HISTORY OF THE PACIFIC COAST STEELHEAD

The migratory trout of the Pacific Coast—the steelhead and the sea-run cutthroat—are two unique species, for they are found nowhere else in the world as native fish.

These two grand sport fish, which provide some of the most exhilarating trout fishing in America, make periodic runs up the coastal rivers from California to Alaska. They have developed their peculiar characteristics in an environment of fast-rushing rivers, and conifer-clad watersheds supplied with pure snow water from the mountain reservoirs of the coastal ranges. It appears that these fish do not adapt themselves to any other environment.

Because of the climate and the types of river on the Pacific slope, various methods of angling for these fish have been developed which differ greatly from the methods used for Atlantic salmon and sea-trout. The

Pacific Coast Steelhead

Northwest is so far away from the population centers that anglers from the East or Middle West are usually completely unfamiliar with these Western angling methods. The Easterner must be prepared to drop many of his firmly rooted convictions on fly and bait fishing and be ready to try out the western manner if he hopes to become an adept taker of the Pacific migrants.

Most American anglers know the steelhead by reputation only. They know little about his habits and life cycle. And before they can hope to become well-rounded western anglers they must first learn something of the life history of these trout.

Steelhead trout have been fighting their way up the turbulent rapids and waterfalls of the western rivers for centuries but the complete details of their life cycle are still not fully known.

However, the facts of the steelhead's life cycle that are of most interest to the sportsman are now generally known and accepted by fishery men. In the first place, from the physiological viewpoint, the steelhead is not a distinct species but a western rainbow trout that has spent a portion of its life cycle in salt water. There is no real structural difference between a steelhead and a rainbow. Ichthyologists state that a young wild steelhead eight inches long that is ready to migrate to salt water will have the same scale count, the same number of anal rays and gill rakers, as a rainbow resident in the same river. The count of rays in the anal fin of the steelhead is 9 to 13, commonly 10 to 12. The count of scales along the median line is 45. The flesh is usually a deep red in color.

In fact, in water systems such as Lake Washington a five pound "rainbow" would have to have its scales read in order to determine whether it had ever made a salt water migration and was, therefore, a steelhead or had been resident in fresh water all of its life cycle. A fresh-run steelhead would naturally look different than a lake rainbow, but a steelhead that had spent a year or so in a lake would not.

Types of Migrant Rivers. Although steelhead trout are found in most of the ocean rivers of California, Oregon, Washington, British Columbia and Alaska, the streams that produce the really exceptional runs all possess certain characteristics in common. They are all rivers the upper branches of which reach up into mountain foothills. They are fast-flowing streams, many of them glacial, that run over rocky bottoms to the sea. They usually have wide beds toward their mouths with many gravel bars. Most of them have tributaries that flow through box canyons, alternating pools and white-water rapids with portions that are rather inaccessible to the angler. There are usually long stretches in the upper rivers containing gravel reaches that provide ideal spawning beds for salmon and steelhead. There are resting pools and deep-flowing runs where the migrating fish may lie until they are ripe enough to move onto a bar of gravel where they can make their nesting bed.

The greater percentage of the steelhead in these tributaries are winter-run fish; that is, trout that have come into their parent streams during the winter months. A smaller number enter many of the same rivers during the summer and are known as summer runs.

The details of that portion of a steelhead's life that is spent in fresh water are now well-known to ichthyologists. But when the fish enters the sea, it goes on a pilgrimage that until now has remained a closed secret. Whether during this phase it remains close to its home estuary or whether it ventures far out into the ocean depths like a chinook salmon has never been determined. It is to be noted that few steelhead are taken by commercial anglers from the ocean.

It is known that the bulk of the runs approach the rivers in which they were spawned in late fall. Here they lie off the estuary for a certain time until their spawning urge coincides with the right water level in their parent stream. They then leave the salt chuck and swim into the river. Depending on water conditions, they may rush far up the stream during a flood period; or if only a slight rise has taken place in the level of the water, they may rest for a while just above the tidal section of the stream, and later on make a leisurely journey to their spawning grounds. Other conditions too govern the time of each run's journey. Some winter steelhead come into a stream with tight strings of eggs or firm lengths of milt and these usually rest in a lie pool for their spawning time to come. Others may remain out in the salt chuck and not come into a river until they are almost ready to spawn.

This recurring surge of different groups up a stream is what adds variety and uncertainty to sportsmen's catch of these trout. With every rise in water the angler may expect a new run into a river. On the other hand, given a long cold spell of several weeks when water levels become stabilized, the steelhead will be inclined to remain out in the salt water. During this time, no new fish will come into the mouth of the stream. When the thaw comes, there will be a sudden rise in water which may bring the fish into the river in a tremendous run that may travel far upstream. Under such conditions most of this run will be untouched by anglers, for floods and muddy waters make fishing well-nigh impossible.

An ideal season from the viewpoint of the steelhead fisherman is a series of high waters—not floods—interspersed with short stabilizing periods when waters are fishable and the steelhead are to be found in those portions of the streams open to fishing. A successful winter season may depend almost entirely on water conditions. If the runs are apportioned throughout the season, then fishing can be good. But if the bulk of the fish go up on a couple of flood periods, then fishing can be poor.

Spawning Habits. The bulk of the steelhead customarily spawn from March into May and their eggs hatch out in forty to fifty days from the time they are laid, depending on water temperatures. Although the upper reaches of many rivers are utilized by spawning fish, most of the eggs hatch out in the smaller tributaries. The fry will remain in its home creek for a period, and when it approaches fingerling size it will move down into the main river. These young trout will then spend twelve to eighteen months in fresh water and then move downstream toward the sea to begin their salt water existence.

The steelhead is sought by sportsmen during every phase of its existence in fresh water from the time it has reached the legal length of six inches and has come into the main river. In the State of Washington, the Game Department has given these downstream migrants some measure of protection by not opening river fishing until late May.

The small number of steelhead which manage to recover from their spawning labors and head down river for a second trip to salt water were once caught quite extensively during April and May. But since streams in Washington have been closed at this time, very few of these "racehorses" have been caught.

The greater part of the sportsman's catch of steelhead are the prime newly run fish on their spawning migration upstream. Although at first glance it would seem poor conservation policy to take fish just before they have spawned, like most salmon, steelhead are not available to the angler before this time. Much protection is given these spawning fish by closing the upper reaches of rivers and most of their tributaries during the season. In this way, once the steelhead have reached their spawning beds, they are safe.

Artificial Propagation. The State Game Departments of the Northwest states have attempted in the past to maintain steelhead runs by restricting the fishing season and by protecting the fish on their spawning beds. But with the greatly increased fishing intensity during the past decade for these migratory trout, in addition to these measures, some means had to be found to increase the runs or to build up the steelhead population in rivers where they have steadily declined.

Although artificial propagation sounds like the solution, it is not quite that simple. In the first place, steelhead eggs, unlike rainbow eggs, cannot be purchased in the open market. And although there is no real difference between a rainbow and a steelhead, one cannot expect that rainbows will turn into steelheads simply by planting them in a coastal river. Up to the present, in any case, such plantings have not worked out. Steelhead eggs must therefore be obtained from the wild fish. In order to do this, traps are located in the headwaters of a good steelhead river, and the trout are held until they are ready to be stripped. This is work that not only requires long experience but a good physique as well. It is only necessary to watch a good hatchery man strip the eggs from a struggling 16-pound female to get some idea of the labor involved.

The big trout is first bailed out of the holding trap in a net. The stripper then holds the thrashing form across the middle of his body and starts pushing the orange-red eggs into a shallow pan. After the steelhead has been cleaned of most of its two to five thousand eggs, it is returned to the stream to recover and perhaps make a second spawning migration. (All salmon are killed before being stripped of eggs at a hatchery since they would die in any case. Their carcasses are then frozen to be used as food in the same hatcheries.)

After several females have been stripped of eggs, a male fish is selected and its milt milked onto the eggs. Under natural spawning conditions, the milt must meet the eggs within seconds after being released or the latter will not be properly fertilized. But when stripped dry, fertilization does not take place until water has been added to the pan.

The buck steelhead usually ripen later than the does, and they are usually returned to the trap to be used again and again as their milt ripens.

The eggs are hatched and the young fish whenever possible are planted as fingerlings. It has been found that if these fingerlings are planted in the lower section of a river, they will move into the sea immediately and thus escape being caught by a trout fisherman. It is customary to plant a trapped river with the maximum number of required fingerlings before allotting any of the hatchery fish to some other depleted stream.

Chapter Two

CATCHING STEELHEAD ON BAIT OR ARTIFICIAL LURES

The steelhead trout even in its home country of the Pacific Northwest is fast becoming the most highly prized trout trophy available to American Izaak Waltons. As the king of trout, the steelhead rules supreme along the Pacific coast. Although the boundaries of his kingdom extend from Alaska to northern California, its center and capital is to be found in the Puget Sound country.

Virtually all rivers, some of them nationally famous, that flow into Puget Sound or the ocean, from Vancouver Island on the north to the

Rogue in Oregon, are thoroughfares at some season of the year for the sea-going rainbows. Nowhere else in the world except along this northern strip of the Pacific are these migratory streaks of dynamite, these aristocrats of fresh water sport fish, available to the angler as a native species.

Difficulties of Winter Fishing. That every angler in the Northwest has not long ago been inoculated with the deadly virus of steelhead fever is probably due only to one circumstance, namely, that the greater percentage of steelhead ascend the rivers in this section during the months of December to March when all but the fever-ridden anglers have put their tackle away until the next trout season.

There exists however a small group of these hardy, enthusiastic, unreasoning anglers who live normal lives for nine months of the year only to become fishing fools for the remaining three. For "once a steelheader, always a steelheader."

To the ordinary citizen, the very thought of wading a stream in midwinter, or even standing on its frozen banks, brings on a bad case of chills. What must he think of steelheaders who, their reddened hands stiff with cold, bait hooks with clammy hunks of cluster salmon eggs, and then proceed to wash their numb digits in the raging torrent; who fish when at times lines swell to double their size with mush-ice coverings and guides fill up so with ice that casting becomes almost impossible? Should this ordinary citizen be told, in addition, that steelheaders often cast from frozen dawn to dismal dark without getting even a "bump," much less a fish, his astonishment would turn to scorn.

But, never fear, the steelheader knows what he is doing; if he thinks about it at all, he in his turn feels very sorry for the stay-at-home angler who has never experienced a steelhead's run. He knows that he has to take a few frozen-up days (they don't come too often considering the season as a whole) when ice covers the sloughs and early morning fishing is mighty tough. But he knows too that such a morning usually turns into a crystalline day. He knows that the river will be clear, the air bracing, and, if his luck holds good, he should run into fish.

Maybe just around that bend off the gravel bar, where a swift run against the far bank swirls over hidden rocks, he will feel that soft nudge at his bait. Just a touch that barely stops the regular bobbing of his rod tip. So he sets back with a heavy "sock"—and wait—is it?—yes, there it is—the throbbing surge of life out at the end of the hundred-foot cast.

He keeps his rod tip up as with a savage rush the steelhead streaks downstream, melting line off the reel. There is no stopping the trout as it bores into the current and the angler runs along the bar desperately trying to retrieve some line. The "steelfish" stops only to shoot up into the air, its glistening silvery body slicing back into the water as it heads back upstream. So angler and trout battle it out. If the leader holds and the fish doesn't come "unpinned," it is finally landed—a trim streamlined dozen pounds of energy and dynamite. That's what gets a steelheader out on a stream, and that's what keeps him plugging away through good days and bad ones.

Appearance and Size of the Steelhead. The steelhead trout when freshly run out of the salt chuck gleams silver in color like a salmon, but, as we have learned, it is really only a rainbow that has acquired an ocean education. Almost without exception, all rainbow or steelhead spawned in any of the streams of the coast that run freely to salt water will swim out to sea when they have reached migratory age.

The steelhead may remain in salt water for from one to four years, as it does not come back into its river until it is ready to spawn. Biologists C. F. Pautzke and R. C. Meigs of the Washington State Game Department in their study of the Puget Sound steelhead of the Green River state that the most rapid growth of these trout is during their first year in fresh and the first year in salt water. After a year at sea if the steelhead has reached maturity and is ready to make its spawning migration, it may weigh around four pounds and measure 24 inches in length.

While the weight of steelhead ranges from jacks of a couple of pounds up to grandpas reaching 28 pounds, the majority of these fish caught in the winter in the Puget Sound country weigh from six to 10 pounds. A 6-pound fish is considered just fair; an 8-pounder—medium; but those fat 10- to 14-pounders are highly prized. Anything between 16 and 19 pounds causes its captor's chest to swell with pride. But the ironheads between 20 and 25 pounds are rare indeed. Those in this class exhibited in Seattle each winter could be counted on the fingers of both hands. These huge trout are usually once-in-a-lifetime prizes, and many an angler will fish for 20 years without tying into one of these lunkers.

A convenient rule for computing the weight of steelhead is to add one pound of weight to the basic scale of four pounds for every inch over 24 inches. Thus a 28-inch fish should go eight pounds in weight. However when fish get over 30 inches in length they tend to weigh over the scale. After their first year in the salt chuck these trout grow slowly and the majority of them over 12 pounds in size have spent three to four years at sea. Like the Atlantic salmon these steelhead may make several trips to sea and back again to spawn. However, the percentage of fish that Pautzke and Meigs found to have returned for a second spawning went as small as 5 to 6.9% of the marked fish on which they had a check.

When a steelhead first pokes its nose up the home river it is steel-gray on its head and over its back, while the rest of its body is bright silver, well spotted on the back and over the tail. At times a steelhead will be caught 15 to 20 miles up from a river's mouth with sea lice still adhering to its body near the anal fin and showing the purplish iridescent gleam to its sides that comes only from the ocean.

After these trout have been lying in a river for several weeks, they lose their silvery freshness and begin to take on the appearance of a rainbow trout. Their gill covers become tinged with dull scarlet and a reddish streak extends along the median line. By the time the steelhead have reached their spawning beds they have become very dark—some almost purplish or black—and have little appeal for the sportsman.

In the rare cases when steelhead survive their spawning period along with its dangers, they "brighten up" for their second downriver journey. They lose their dark color, some taking on a rusty cast, and a few retain their rainbow stripe. These spent fish tend to be long lanky specimens with all of their fat used up. They will be found descending streams usually in early spring from April to June and formerly many were caught during this period.

These downriver fish are feeders and tend to hit lures readily. However sportsmen discourage the killing of such spent fish as they happen to catch during the latter part of a season. They argue that if the fish has lived through one spawning time it should be afforded every opportunity to fatten up and reach the sea for a second run.

Some of the old-time steelheaders refuse to beach a fish that has started to darken or that shows a rusty cast, and usually release the dark ones they hook. It is generally thought that a prime fresh-run steelhead, perhaps with sea lice still clinging to it, will be a more rugged fighter. Moreover its flesh should be firmer and less dry than when it has lain in a stream for a month and is almost ready to spawn.

Experts state that the dark coloration of a steelhead is mainly a spawning dress and not wholly due to the influence of fresh water. They claim that during long periods of low water, steelhead are apt to lie off the river's mouth and commence to darken up before they leave the ocean. But whatever the cause of this change of color, anglers prize a new ocean-run steelhead above one in any other condition.

By far the most commonly used technique in winter steelheading along the Pacific coast is bait casting with clusters of salmon roe. In fact a conservative guess would place the number of steelhead caught in the Puget Sound country with this lure as 95% of the total.

A very few anglers use spoons. In some of the Columbia River drainage, crawfish tails are utilized and occasionally a hook with red yarn is used. But the angler who casts a fly consistently during the winter for steelhead is a rarity.

A small band of conservationists, alarmed over the greatly increased intensity of winter steelheading and the consequent gradual decrease in the number of the trout themselves, feel that the use of salmon eggs as bait should be banned. Looking a decade ahead, they claim that this fine sport cannot possibly be maintained if egg fishing is permitted. When steelhead are lying in an accessible drift the entire group can be cleaned out by a steady procession of experienced anglers using salmon roe. With new roads opening up and the use of boats even in the rapid coastal streams becoming more prevalent, it is felt that not a sufficient number of fish will escape to their spawning beds to maintain the population. While they feel that the sportsmen are entitled to a fair share of the yearly crop, this harvest should not be so large as to deplete the species.

These conservationists contend that strict regulation will be necessary in the not too distant future to uphold the runs. Shortening of the fishing seasons and artificial propagation cannot accomplish it alone. They feel that various types of spoons or devon minnows, yarn lures, or bait such as shrimp or worms, should be substituted for the salmon roe. All of these lures would afford as much, if not greater, sport, and at the same time allow for more steelhead to escape.

On the other hand, many of the best-known steelhead rivers on the Olympic Peninsula flow through Indian reservations in their lower reaches. Indians customarily net these rivers heavily during the winter season. Although the sale of steelhead is illegal in Washington under the original Indian treaties, the tribes can ship fish outside of the state without coming under the state laws. Many sportsmen feel that as long as the Indians are permitted freely to net and sell steelhead, the number taken by anglers fishing with salmon roe is not the main factor contributing to the decline of the runs.

Steelhead Tackle and Rods. Although the modern winter steelheaders of the coast may differ somewhat among themselves in their choice of bait, their choice of tackle will be rather uniform. Most anglers now use a rather springy rod, eight to nine feet long, with a two-handed cork or wooden grip. This rod usually comes in two sections with the length of the butt varying from 36 to 52 inches, while the tip may be four to six feet in length. It is usually of split bamboo, although the new glass tips, tubular metal, or beryllium copper rods are now being manufactured for the Northwest steelhead fisherman.

The tip of the rod should be light, with enough suppleness to indicate the lightest strike of a fish and at the same time with enough backbone to carry the heavy lead necessary to drift some of the fast, large coastal streams.

The long rods have come into favor over the casting rod mainly because they enable the angler to "feel the fish" when drifting a fast run.

In addition, they permit him to play a fish with the tip as he would with a fly rod and help to keep the big trout out of snags or brush along the banks of a stream.

Reels and Casting Technique. Any good bait casting reel that will hold at least 100 yards of line is preferred. However, these reels must be sturdy to stand up to the incessant casting which must be done in all sorts of weather—rain, sleet or frost. Moreover, when playing a heavy fish in fast water the reel takes much punishment and it must be a strong one to last for more than a season or two.

Although the steelheader's cast may appear a bit awkward to the bass angler, he does place his bait out long distances, often under adverse conditions. Due to the fact that there are always two to three feet of terminal tackle extending beyond the tip, a vigorous side cast is necessary. This swing may come from either the right or left depending on the direction of the current or overhanging brush, and at times may be executed underhand or with an overhead swipe coming past one shoulder. The best form is secured with a firm sweep combined with an extra application of power just before the thumb is released from the reel.

Lines. Twenty-five years ago, when steelheading on the coast was in its infancy, the customary tackle was a stick of bamboo about 10 feet long on which guides were taped. Any reel that could hold the raw silk line then in vogue was utilized, and this line was cast out of a basket or directly off the water onto which it had been stripped after the previous cast. Later, when multiplying level-wind reels became popular, the silk casting line was universally adopted. Now with nylon line available, the first choice seems to be clear monofilament nylon, second, braided nylon line and the formerly popular silk casting line falling to third place.

The use of continuous lengths of monofilament nylon line has become general on the West Coast only since 1945. Used in weights of 8 to 12 pound test, sufficient length for most purposes may be placed onto the reel without backing. It casts easily, and due to its small diameter, it sinks more quickly than silk when drifting through a fast run. Moreover it does not soak up water, and therefore will not freeze up or become fuzzy with ice crystals as a silk line will. It therefore can be cast in freezing weather when a silk line would be almost impossible to operate.

Its main shortcoming is that, when using a level wind reel, if too much pressure is placed directly on the line coming off the spool, the taut line is likely to bury itself into the core of line left on the reel. If not watched carefully this may cause a backlash or fancy tangle on the reel itself. To overcome this the line should always be grasped above the reel when an attempt is made to loosen it or to break it free when snagged on a rocky bottom or other obstruction.

Braided nylon will freeze up quicker than the single filament and it is generally believed that it does not stand up as well for this rugged winter fishing. However it does have more stretch, which helps to loosen up a line when snagged on bottom.

Good pre-war silk lines are excellent but they are very scarce, and as mentioned before they do ice up badly under extreme winter conditions.

Leaders. The tendency since the war has been away from heavy lines and now lines testing from 8 to 15 pounds are quite generally used. This in turn allows the use of lighter leaders. Today, the eight-pound-test leader is almost standard although fishermen occasionally go up to 10- and 12-pound test when a stream is badly off color or snag infested.

When rivers are low and clear, a 6-pound, or in extreme cases, a 4-pound-test leader may be necessary. This is light terminal tackle when you consider the turbulence of the rocky coastal rivers and the fact that you can hang onto a 14- to 18-pound steelhead most any time with this equipment.

There is no standard length for the leader as it may vary according to the particular fancy of the angler. However, most leaders used in the Puget Sound country vary from 18 to 26 inches in length. When the water is high and off color, length and size will not matter. When rivers are way down, the longer leaders may improve your chances of getting strikes.

Hooks. Hooks of the Seely Octopus or the Mustad Italian Point types are used in sizes from 4 to 5/0. However, hooks going from 1/0 to 3/0 will meet most of the usual conditions found in winter fishing. These hooks are of round silver wire, offset, with a round bend and a very sharp point. They are the same variety of hook used by anglers who spin for salmon in the Northwest.

Hook-up for Leaders and Sinkers. Various methods of tying the leader to the hook are used but a modified whip finish, as illustrated on page 69 holds well and permits the leader to be pushed back through the eye of the hook so that it may be looped over the eggs.

When tying, the hook is held between the right thumb and forefinger point upward, and a wide loop of the leader with its end extending along the hook to its bend is also held by the thumb and finger. With the two first fingers of the left hand, the loop is brought over the point of the hook. Then by turning the fingers over in the loop it is crossed over below the hook and the same arc of the loop is again brought over the hook point. When about 5 or 6 turns are made over the shank of the hook the surplus leader is pulled back through the eye until the turns are held tight.

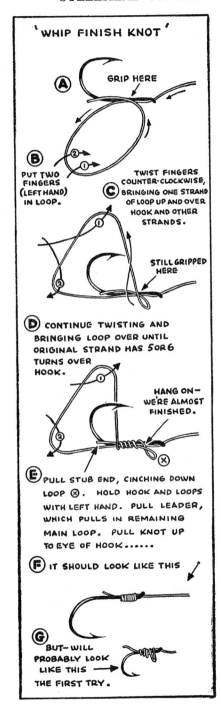

'WHIP FINISH KNOT'

(A) GRIP HERE

(B) PUT TWO FINGERS (LEFT HAND) IN LOOP.

(C) TWIST FINGERS COUNTER-CLOCKWISE, BRINGING ONE STRAND OF LOOP UP AND OVER HOOK AND OTHER STRANDS.

STILL GRIPPED HERE

(D) CONTINUE TWISTING AND BRINGING LOOP OVER UNTIL ORIGINAL STRAND HAS 5 OR 6 TURNS OVER HOOK.

HANG ON— WE'RE ALMOST FINISHED.

(E) PULL STUB END, CINCHING DOWN LOOP ⊗. HOLD HOOK AND LOOPS WITH LEFT HAND. PULL LEADER, WHICH PULLS IN REMAINING MAIN LOOP. PULL KNOT UP TO EYE OF HOOK......

(F) IT SHOULD LOOK LIKE THIS

(G) BUT— WILL PROBABLY LOOK LIKE THIS → THE FIRST TRY.

The sinker should be attached to the loop of the casting line by a short section of drop cord 3 to 5 inches long. See illustration on page 70. This drop cord should be weaker than the casting line so that it will break first if the sinker should become snagged on a rock. As a consequence only the lead will be lost and the leader will be freed. Carpet thread makes a fine lead fastener, and a spool of it should always be carried in the angler's pocket.

The most popular type of lead in use today is the pencil type which may be purchased by the pound at most sporting goods stores. This comes in pliable lengths of lead ranging from 3/16 to 5/16 of an inch in diameter. The angler cuts the lead into lengths varying from two to six inches, and either pierces one end or notches it with a pair of cutting pliers. Some steelheaders carry a coil of this lead in their pockets and cut off the length required for the water that they happen to be drifting.

Use of Salmon Roe. With the type of hook-up described in the foregoing section, salmon eggs, worms or crawfish tails may be used as bait, or a spoon or devon minnow be substituted. But salmon cluster eggs, as stated before, lead all other steelhead baits in use on the West Coast.

Salmon eggs may be purchased in any tackle store in glass jars usually in the pint or half pound sizes. Originally, these eggs were all wet packed; then a brand of dry eggs became popular. Within recent years, an oil pack has caught the fancy of steelhead enthusiasts. This egg is less messy to use and holds together well on the hook.

The strings of salmon eggs are cut into lengths that will fit readily into the jar. The angler, usually on the river bank, cuts these strings into

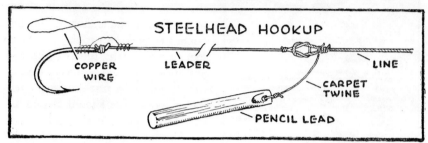

"gobs" about the size of a pecan or walnut. It is well to snip along the membrane holding the eggs in sections within the string as this will help to keep the cluster intact longer when cast.

A rather large bait can should be strapped to the waist to hold the gobs of eggs. In addition, a cloth is usually looped through the belt for use in wiping off the hands after baiting up.

As salmon eggs, at best, are difficult to keep in a cluster due to their tendency to string out in the water, various methods are used to help keep them on the hook. One is to push the leader back through the eye of the hook and then pull this loop over the cluster. Another is to tie the eggs on with red cotton thread. A third method that has proved very practical is to use a six-inch length of light copper wire similar to that used in electric cords. One end of the wire may be fastened in the eye of the hook and then wound around the eggs. This wire may be unwound when the eggs are gone and used on a new gob and it will usually last as long as the leader.

Preparing Fresh Salmon Eggs. Steelheaders fuss a great deal about salmon roe bait. Some prefer light-colored eggs, while others like those of a deep red tint. But without exception all of them feel that "fresh eggs" or eggs just taken from a female steelhead are much to be preferred. Fresh eggs milk readily in the water and many anglers believe that fresh-run steelhead will hit a gob of such eggs when they will not look at a "store" egg. For this reason a female or hen ironhead is prized and most fishermen hope to take at least one such fish on every trip.

Eggs freshly cut from a fish are hard to use as they string out rapidly and will last for only a cast or two. Most anglers harden them up at home. A popular method of doing this is to lay a string out on a length of paper toweling and then sprinkle both sides with salt (a mild cure type is excellent) or borax. The string is then wrapped in several rolls of toweling and is allowed to harden overnight. If it is to be used soon, the string is wrapped in newspaper and placed in the ice box. If it is to be kept for a week or two, it may be cut up and packed in a jar and then placed in a refrigerator. Eggs should be hardened up just enough to hold them together. If too much salt or borax is used, or if the eggs are left out to dry too long, they become so hard that they are of little use as bait.

"*Strawberries.*" In many of the large very fast rivers, "strawberries" are commonly used, as they will hold up well in the tough fast rapids and stand a lot of casting. A strawberry is merely a gob of eggs tied up in a red or white square of net, veiling or cheesecloth. The material may be procured in a department store. A rather bright red is the preferred color and it should not have too small a mesh. This material should be heavy enough to hold the eggs but, at the same time, it should be frail enough so that it can be pulled off the hook by hand without having to be cut off with scissors.

Cut the material into 3½-inch squares, lay eggs in the center of a section, gather in the edges, and wind red cotton thread tightly around the top so that the eggs are held in a firm ball. Finish up with a couple of half-hitches. Snip off the extra material and you have a gob of eggs closely resembling a real strawberry.

When baiting up a strawberry, the hook should be impaled immediately below the knot on the netting and the gob of eggs pulled well onto the bend of the hook. The point of the hook should always be left free so that the barb may be set into the striking fish without any interference.

If all this "egg talk" appears to be excessive, remember that salmon roe is a very messy part of steelheading. If it is handled correctly much of the difficulties may be overcome. And when fish are few and far between, the angler who presents his egg cluster in the best possible manner is the one who will pick up the strikes. A fresh gob firmly wired on, covering the hook and milking as it works through the drift, will take steelhead when a strung-out piece of white will not attract even a Dolly Varden.

Steelhead Slang. Most steelheaders in the Northwest speak a vernacular that may need some clarification to make it understandable to the visitor. Salmon or steelhead eggs are called "goof," and a cluster of eggs a "gob." A "splatter cast" is a poor cast which results when a steelheader makes a powerful flip, the reel backlashes, and the bait, in mid-air, suddenly scatters loose eggs about the immediate vicinity.

A "drift fisherman" is one who casts and drifts his bait down through the runs and riffles. A "plunker" is one who casts out into a deep hole, allows his bait to sink to bottom, places his rod in a forked stick stuck in the bank, and then patiently awaits results. A "cracker" is the tyro, amateur or beginning angler, and is a term sometimes applied to one who never seems to learn how.

A "spawner" is a fish all ready to go through its spawning functions. A "preacher" is a spawner that is very dark in color. A "racehorse" is a spawned-out fish headed back downstream for the ocean.

The term "cleaned" refers to the occasion when a fish hits so hard and furiously that it takes hook and bait by breaking the leader. A "bump" is the gentle strike of a fish betrayed by the gentle bobbing of your rod tip. The word "unbuttoned" or "unpinned" is used when a fish, usually a salmon or steelhead, that is apparently well hooked, suddenly gets loose, generally during a run, without breaking any tackle.

A female steelhead may be called a "lady," a "hen" or a "doe." The male is termed "buck," or "rooster." A "jack" is a male steelhead that has returned ahead of its run and is therefore always smaller in size.

Migratory Streams and Drift Fishing. The actual act of fishing for winter steelhead may appear simple but to do it efficiently and successfully takes a liberal mixture of fish sense and knowledge of migratory streams. Most of the Pacific Coast rivers are fast. Rushing out of the foothills, they wind down rather narrow valleys through canyons and over rock-strewn courses in their upper reaches. Where the stream runs a straight course there will usually be a long fast drift. Then when it swings into a bend up against a cliff or clay bank it will deepen into a pool flanked by rapids above and below.

As the watercourses approach the ocean, the larger rivers usually swing back and forth across a wide channel caused by floods and spring freshets. Such streams show long gravel bars which are ideal spots from which to cast or from which to play a fighting steelhead. The smaller rivers tend to be well brushed along the banks with snags rather prevalent and, as like as not, a small log jam at each abrupt bend.

No matter how many times I fish our coastal rivers, I am always astonished at the violent contrast between winter and summer fish populations. For instance, during August, the Green River will flow at summer low and the best one can hope for will be a few downriver migrants six to eight inches long. But in January, from the same innocent-appearing run that slants over against that high clay bank, will come a 15-pound streamlined streak of silver—a slashing fighting package of power and beauty—a fresh run steelhead. One can hardly believe one's eyes unless one has become accustomed to the great harvest of the sea during spawning runs.

These sea-going rainbows do not lie in these drifts very long—they are just passing through. So the angler must learn to know the routes that a steelhead takes in heading for its spawning grounds. He must recognize the swift runs that hold fish for a while and learn to spot the lie holes. He must judge the type of water suitable for drift fishing and the spot where the plunker has the advantage. In other words, he must learn his rivers and learn them well.

Drifting is by far the most popular and productive method of fishing for steelhead as it enables the angler to search out every bit of available water. The principle of drifting is to cast out into the current, allow the sinker to touch bottom and then bump along over the rocks through the run until the line has straightened out below. The gob of eggs is supposed to drift down ahead of the sinker just off the bottom of the stream in the zone where the steelhead are lying.

The angler should start at the head of a riffle and attempt to cover all of the run. If he is unfamiliar with water he should start off with short casts and gradually lengthen them until he has reached over against the opposite bank. He should cover all of the drift by gradually stepping down the bar. If he is familiar with the river he may try with his first cast to put his bait into the spot where he has taken fish before. In this manner he does not scare the steelhead out of a shallow lie either by dropping lead too close to him or by drifting line over him.

The weight of the lead should be adjusted to the speed of the water. An ideal drift is one where the sinker drifts evenly and not too rapidly through the run. With too light a lead, the bait will not reach bottom and will hurry through too quickly. With too heavy a lead, the bait will tend either to hang up or if the water is slow, will not drift at all.

Most steelheaders cast a bit upstream to get their lead down quickly and then wind the surplus line onto the reel when the drifting starts. A large bow in the line is not good as it often prevents feeling a strike or may even prevent the setting of the hook. Toward the end of a drift, with a tight line, one may slowly feed line by the reel to cover more water. When there is sufficient depth below, one may allow the bait to rest for a short period at the end of a drift. This often attracts a strike.

The reel should be adjusted so that the lead will pull the line freely through the guides when thumb pressure is released from the reel. One should learn to cast with an arched throw from either side. Get the bait straight into the air so that it will drop straight into the current. Both the wrist and arm should get into the swing as the long rod requires a bit of power to make a long cast with a light lead. The fact that the line can be reeled in only up to the lead, leaving more than two feet still extending beyond the tip, makes such casting more difficult than casting a bass plug. A two-handed cast is best executed either underarm or over the shoulder. Let the reel run freely until just before the bait hits the water, when it can be thumbed to a stop.

Sensing the Strike. The one really difficult phase of bait fishing for steelhead is to "feel the strike." The hefty sea-going rainbows in most cases take bait with the gentlest of nudges. It is hard for a beginner to realize that such a powerful fighting trout can hit a lure with so little force. The explanation undoubtedly arises from the fact that these trout are not too active and do not like to move from their lie spot to hit a bait. The gob of eggs will be drifting down a riffle and if it happens to go past a steelhead the trout may slide over a few inches and open its mouth to suck in the bait. As soon as it feels the pressure of the line it will let the eggs go. Therefore, unless the angler sets immediately and does so with a heavy strike, he will probably fail to hook the fish. When making a long cast with some bow in the line (a tight straight line is difficult to maintain at all times) one has to set with a force that would be sure to pop the leader if the line were out only a short distance.

Sometimes in fast runs a steelhead will hook itself. The angler will feel the halting of his bait, and almost immediately there will come that throbbing jerk at the end of his line that tells him he has socked into an ironhead. But in most cases he must learn to distinguish through hard-won experience, the differences between a "rock bump" and a strike. The angler casts out into the run and, as his bait bumps along the rocky bottom, he feels this movement as it is telegraphed up through the rod and at the same time he sees the bobbing of the tip.

Suddenly the bait stops. Is this a fish or just a rock? That's the big question and only the old-timer, after many winters of drifting, can tell for sure. If the bait should stop and there should follow several little twitches of the rod tip as if a 6-inch trout were nibbling on the eggs, that's a steelhead for sure, and you had better set hard and fast. But if the bait stops for a short second and then goes bumping on it may, or may not, have been a fish. Of course, one can set on every suspicious bump or hesitation during the drift. But the angler runs the risk of many hook-ups on the bottom with a large percentage of lost hooks and sinkers.

Steelheaders who have been drifting for years have learned to sense that indefinable velvet nudge that means a steelhead and not a rock. When this "sensing a strike" becomes second nature, then the fisherman has conquered the difficult hurdles and is well down the homestretch to becoming a good steelheader.

When a steelhead hits the bait but is not hooked it usually strings out the eggs, which becomes evident as soon as the bait is reeled in. This shows that a fish has been located and one should try to put a new bait back into exactly the same spot, as the fish will usually hit again. However the eggs may also have been stripped off by hooking onto the bottom temporarily or onto a snag, so that this is not an infallible sign.

When the steelhead are finicky and taking bait with an upstream run or heading in toward the angler it is difficult to "catch up" to the fish and get the hook really home. At such times many anglers run back up the bank attempting to hold a tight line and at the same time socking back on the rod until they are sure that their fish is well hooked.

Anglers are apt to argue more about the feel of a steelhead's strike than any other phase of this sport, but they seldom agree on a definite description of what it is like. In the final analysis, the strike of a steelhead on bait is really not a strike at all but a nudging or a mouthing of the eggs. There is none of the sudden jerking down of the rod tip and the screaming of the reel that occurs when a trout, a salmon or a muskie strikes.

Remember that a fresh gob of eggs will usually be more appealing than a strung-out bait. Therefore it is well to change the eggs often even though it may slow up the casting. After all the main idea is to hook a fish and not to demonstrate one's casting ability.

Steelhead Water. How does one recognize good steelhead water? This again comes with experience. Of course some anglers are so blessed with a liberal gift of "fish sense" that they can, after a few trips, recognize what constitutes the lie spots or resting drifts in a strange river.

A good drift is usually one that runs along fairly fast, is four to eight feet deep, with places in the current where a fish may rest with little effort. Perhaps a good measure of the proper current speed is one that travels at about the same rate that a man would normally walk.

Those swirls or small slicks on the surface usually denote spots beneath which a steelhead can rest off the bottom just lazily fanning its fins. Where a drift comes over a white-water rapids and then swerves into the opposite bank a good casting spot is usually just along side the swift current, or anywhere down through the center of the run. Where there is a long, shallow, fast rapids in a river, steelhead are apt to lie just above the run in the fan of the next drift if the water there is deep enough to hold them.

In the smaller rivers where drifts are shallow and very fast, steelhead will usually lie only in the deeper portions. They may also be found close up to sunken logs, behind a clump of snags or along a tree that has fallen down into the edge of the river. These objects break the current flow enabling the fish to obtain food with a minimum of work.

Plunking. The really deep pools or eddies are not good drift spots. These are fished mainly by "plunkers," who cast well out into the pool with a heavy lead and allow the bait to sink to the bottom. They then set the rod up on a forked stick and await developments. Older anglers often utilize this method and a quartette of old cronies can, with the aid of a good warming fire, spend the day happily reminiscing over past fishing trips. They often catch fish and many of the lunker steelhead are taken in this manner.

When rivers are too high and rather too much off color for good drifting, the plunkers come into their own. The steelhead are likely to be on the move under such conditions and may come nosing along the bottom to bump into the eggs gently bobbing in the current. Then the angler's rod tip will start jerking, his reel singing, and he must jump fast to take up slack and start playing his fish.

The Olympic Peninsula Streams—the Bogachiel. Every angler has his favorite steelhead rivers—streams that have been good to him in the past—places that he yearns to return to season after season. Some of them may be nearby rivers, places he can reach in a short drive. They may be heavily fished, but he usually knows the drifts so well that competition, unless it is too pronounced, will not keep him away. Or he may like to hit the rivers further afield, away from the big cities, where conditions more closely resemble those of pioneer days.

The Olympic Peninsula rivers have always had a great appeal to me. They are short streams running out of the Olympics directly into the Pacific. Most of them are still untouched and unspoiled. There are no hamburger stands, gas stations or cabin camps strung out along their banks. One has to learn how to reach their upper reaches by traveling over difficult roads or over brushy trails. But they usually hold fine runs of steelhead during the winter season.

The Quillayute chain is one of great promise to the steelhead angler. The Quillayute itself is just four miles long and pours into the Pacific between the Indian villages of La Push and Mora. It is formed by the Bogachiel, Soleduck and Calawah, all of them premier steelhead rivers. Steelhead start heading up the broad Quillayute in December and are still going upstream in April. Except for periods of freezing weather when the waters are low and clear and the fish are likely to remain out in the ocean awaiting a taste of rainwater, limit catches can be made as soon as a run is located in the river.

A famous spot is the long riffle at the head of the Quillayute just below where the Bogachiel and Soleduck join. Steelhead may come into this stretch between tides and if an angler hits a run of fish fresh out of the Pacific he will have a red-letter fishing day that he will never forget. Then as these ocean-raised rainbows head up either the "Bogy" or the Soleduck there are long sections of beautiful drifts that produce superlative fishing. Some are only a few feet off a highway and others are half-mile hikes through the brush. Some drifts are never touched unless one can drift the stream with a portable boat.

I remember one early March when Charley King and I enjoyed the superlative sort of steelheading you dream about the rest of the year. There had been a rise in the water level the week before but rivers for that long week-end were clear and at normal level.

Our best fishing was in the Bogachiel, one of Washington's most lovely rivers. It is a fairly large stream with fast deep drifts and long pools. Much of the bottom is small gravel that permits clean drifting. Although it flows through a section that was cut over years ago the river banks are still tree-covered. Except for an occasional small farm or homestead cut out of the timber, the stream has the virgin untouched appearance it must have had when Indians were the only people to tap the tremendous runs of salmon and steelhead.

We had found a few fish upstream, particularly in a long fast drift too wide to cover completely that flowed up against a gravel bank. Our side of the river was alder-grown to the water's edge and one had to wade out in order to have room for the side cast. The upper end of the run did not show any signs of fish. But toward the center, Charley had a bump and reeled in to find his eggs stripped clean.

We were casting only a few feet apart with myself downstream. After several drifts I got in a long cast that put the bait way over towards the gravel bank. It bobbed down with the current hitting nicely along the bottom, passed through an inviting circle of slick water and just before the bait straightened out downstream the bait stopped.

There was that indefinable feel of a strike. I socked back hard, and the line started to pull off the reel in heavy surges. There was that old tingling of the spine that always comes when a steelhead goes into action. The line melted off the reel and a silvery form came out of the water far downstream. The heavy water and the brush just at my back made the playing of the fish rather difficult but I managed to keep the trout from running down into the next riffle.

Charley, with a wide grin splitting his face, had continued casting and suddenly he startled me with a wild whoop. I looked back and could see his rod tip jerking viciously. Two fish on at once in a fast riffle and no gravel beach to land them on. This promised to be good.

After several jumps and a lot of horsing around out in the current my fish finally tired and I was able to work it in toward the bank. Charley's however was still boring away out in the center of the riffle.

Just then a sudden rain squall blew in from the Pacific, and as I had not worn a hat my glasses became so rain-spattered that I could hardly see. As a consequence, when attempting to get the big trout above me so as to let it drift into shore where I could scoop it up, our two lines became tangled. Everything looked rather hopeless for a bit but Charley passed his rod underneath and released the tangle, and I managed to see enough to beach the bright ironhead. Then in a few minutes more Charley slid his fish up into the alders.

The next day we located a run of steelhead in one of the lower riffles of the Bogachiel that had just come in out of the ocean. This riffle, which is some distance above the junction of the Soleduck and the Bogachiel, runs along a gravel bar and is shallow but fast well out to the center of the stream where it drops off into a narrow ledge chute on the opposite bank. This channel is filled with large rocks and snags and, although it often holds fish, it is extremely rare that one can drift through it without hanging up and losing an outfit.

However this morning we had put on a light lead and cast only half-way across the stream, in this way preventing a hook-up. Fish had been taken in the Quillayute the day before and we figured that these new fish would rest in our riffle after fighting up through the turbulent rapids below.

Just as Charley's bait swung about three quarters of the way through the arc of its drift he had a soft stop, heaved back on the rod, and was fast to a nice fish. He worked it up into the head of the run, fighting it in the fast current at his feet. I moved down below him and just as he was beaching his I hung onto another ironhead. This was a stubborn fish with lots of power that kept well out in the current and wouldn't be budged. But it finally tired and I slid a beautiful 14-pound buck out onto the gravel bar.

Both of our fish were so silvery bright that they gleamed like new molten aluminum, and both had a slight purplish iridescent cast down their sides. As we handled them a few of the scales came off onto our fingers, a sure sign that they had been out of the salt chuck only a short time. Both had sea lice glued onto the slight depression near the anal fin.

I stepped back to the edge of the bar and on the first cast set on another steelhead. This was a much faster fish, inclined to short, fast rushes and swirls on the surface. When it was beached it proved to be a female of about ten pounds. In the meantime Charley had cast out from our "pitcher's box" and after several attempts felt that velvet stop, and with his powerful sock, hooked another fighting ocean-trained rainbow.

We were using 6-pound-test leaders with about a two-inch length of lead. We had fresh eggs from the day before, salt-treated the previous night, that were wound onto the hook with light copper wire. We changed bait almost with every cast. The big trout in the fast water hit with a very light nudge and it required some experience to know where to place the cast and when that momentary stop in the drift meant a strike.

Finding a run of active fish in a riffle of this type, where the casting is easy and the current is strong, and the steelhead dash about with the abandon of winged rockets, is the fulfillment of an angler's wildest expectations. You are not hurried, you know that you can hang onto a steelhead most any cast, and you can take time to savor the magic of this winter morning.

There is a film of the famous Peninsula mist in the air (rain to the uninitiated) and the day is mild. All of nature has been washed as fresh and clean as a tall fir on a mountain ridge. The white rocks on the bar beneath your feet run into the limpid clear river that sings its song of heady triumph over its almost completed journey to the sea. The cottonwoods stand dark and stark against the sky; the smaller alders gleam wanly white against the deep green of the fir and cedar ranked behind them. A pair of "golden eyes" appear around the upper curve and swing downstream overhead with their whistling wings.

Boat Fishing. In the section of the ocean highway south of Forks leading down to Aberdeen are several rivers that would be shrines in the hearts of anglers everywhere if their possibilities were nationally known. There is the Hoh, an Indian river, which at times holds runs of ironheads behind every rock. There is the Queets, which, although netted intensively by the Indians, every year turns out several lunker steelhead going over 20 pounds. Then further south lies the legendary Quinault, famous for big steelhead in January and December as well as summer runs in its upper reaches in August and September. And finally there is the Humptulips, not too heavily fished because of its inaccessibility but worth a lot of exploring.

The short, small rivers running northward into the Straits of Juan de Fuca, although seldom fished except by Peninsula anglers, are prolific producers. They bear romantic names such as Pysht, Lyre, Hoko and Sekiu. The Elwha, the largest one, because of a high dam, holds steelhead only in its lower reaches.

Many of the Puget Sound rivers are so filled with rapids, snags and white water that they are ill-suited for boats. However the rubber raft, which can easily be transported, has opened up many stretches of streams seldom touched by anglers previously.

Some conservation-minded sportsmen deplore the popularity of boat drifting, for they feel that the steelhead should be allowed resting spots in each stream where they will not be disturbed by the fishermen. In fact the Washington Game Department has already banned the use of boats for fishing in some of the heavily worked streams near Seattle. These include the Green and sections of the Stillaguamish and the Skykomish. These regulations pertain only to fishing from a boat as it would take an act of the legislature to prevent the use of a boat for transportation purposes only.

However there are a number of coastal streams which are either so large or their banks so obstructed that they can be fished efficiently only from a boat. Typical of these are the Cowlitz, a wide navigable river entering the Columbia, and the North River, a brushy stream flowing into Willapa Bay. On the Olympics in the Quinault and the Queets the Indians use large dugout canoes and outboard motors to navigate upstream and then float back downstream, fishing both ways.

Boat Drifting the Skagit. The one river in Washington in which boat drifting is the accepted manner of steelheading is the mighty Skagit. One of the largest streams in the Northwest, and one which produces large runs of king salmon and steelhead, the Skagit flows from the Canadian border south and then west to join the waters of Puget Sound in Skagit Bay. Its upper reaches from Concrete to Newhalem, and its tributaries such as the Sauk and Suiattle, contain miles of excellent gravel spawning beds. There is no pollution in these waters and although much of the watersheds have been denuded of timber the water levels are fairly constant. The upper reaches of the river from Diablo Dam into Canada are, of course, closed to migratory fish but hold good populations of large rainbows and Dolly Varden trout. The portion of the main river in Washington above the dam was opened to sports fishing in May, 1950.

The Skagit is much too large a river to be waded at any season of the year, and a boat is necessary if one wishes to cover the various drifts which swing from one side of the river to the other. Boats are usually placed in the stream below Concrete and taken up between Hamilton and Sedro Wooley. This is one of the few streams in which competent and experienced guides own boats and regularly pilot fishing parties during the season.

The Skagit has a long season—December through March. The better-known guides are usually booked a year ahead for the months of February and March, which are the better-producing periods. Their boats are 16 to 20 feet long, wide of beam, and so stable that they can accommodate up to four anglers, who can stand and cast at the same time. As these guides make daily trips they keep track of the runs and should be able to locate the drifts in which the steelhead are resting. Charges run from $21 to $30 per boat per day regardless of whether the party consists of one or four fishermen.

Many anglers who "know" the Skagit drift it in their own boats and although it is a rugged stream with very swift current and some fast rapids, a good boatman should have no difficulty. There are a few boats that can be rented from guides, but anglers usually transport their own boats by trailer. There are many accessible bars from which to launch a boat. These include a spot downstream from Marblemont, and others at

Rockport, at a point just below Concrete, at Pressentine Ferry, Birdsview Ferry, the Hamilton Bar, Lyman Ferry, Utopia, and Mount Vernon.

One needs a good anchor and at least 75 feet of manila rope to hold the boat in the swift water. The rope should be run over a pulley wheel in the bow and the boat should be allowed to swing into the current when anchored. When drifting it is well to go downstream stern first. A man should be kept on the oars when going through one of the rapids. When a good drift is located the boat should be anchored to one side so that the cast and drift will be in the "fishy" water. At times when a big fish is hooked the angler must be put ashore in order to beach the steelhead away from the fast current.

Cluster eggs made into strawberries are almost universally used as bait in boat fishing. Anglers cast out into the current and allow their bait to bump the bottom until it straightens out below the boat. When anchored in the current many anglers permit the bait to rest for a period downstream at the end of the drift and often in this way catch a fish. As a heavy lead is necessary in much of the water a rod with a stiffer tip than normally used in bank fishing is preferred by many. A net or gaff is always carried in the boat to land the fish while out in the stream.

The Skagit is noted for large steelhead in the 15- to 20-pound class, but the average will run closer to 8 or 12 pounds.

The lower river just above and below Mount Vernon is customarily fished from anchored boats. Lines equipped with heavy leads will be cast out and the bait hung up on bottom in the manner employed by plunkers. The anglers then sit back at their leisure waiting for a cruising steelhead to take the eggs.

But there are many drifts, particularly upstream from Lyman to Rockport, where steelhead can be caught from the bank. These casting bars are rather far apart and one must learn how to get into each one and the best spots to fish at various stages of water. In addition, the Skagit provides some of the best fly fishing for winter steelhead in the state. The "fly runs" and proper tackle will be discussed in the next chapter.

Light Steelhead Gear. There is an ever-growing group of light-tackle enthusiasts who use a fly rod for their winter steelhead angling. These fly rods are usually 9½ feet long with stiff action and may have an extra length attached to the butt joint so that they can be cast in the regulation two-handed manner.

Clear single monofilament line is used, 8 to 12 pound test, which may be carried on a regular casting reel, or on a large diameter casting reel such as the Winona. When using very light lead, such as one to three buckshot, the line may be stripped into a basket strapped to the waist and then shot across stream with a flip of the wrist. The light line has little water resistance, sinks readily, and can drift over brush, behind logs, or under overhanging trees, thus getting into the seldom-fished spots. In the smaller streams this light lead, especially in low clear waters, will not frighten the fish. However when you tie into a large trout in the brushy creeks it will be difficult, although sporty, to land on the light gear.

This same type of rod and gear is utilized by a small band of anglers when fishing for the summer-run fish and late winter runs with bait. However instead of cluster eggs they use a small hook on which they impale one or two single salmon eggs. Their leaders are light, testing perhaps 2 to 4 pounds. They must be highly skilled at playing heavy fish on light tackle ever to beach a steelhead in fast water.

As they are fishing rivers usually low and clear they seldom use more than one or two buckshot for weight and drift their bait through the fast riffles without touching bottom. They attempt to drop it down into pockets behind rocks where the steelhead may be resting. In the deeper holes they usually cast upstream so as to sink the egg, and then allow it to drift slowly and deep through the pool.

A stripping basket will help to make the distant casts, as even a long flip can be achieved out of the basket without tearing off the egg. Steelhead tend to take these single eggs lightly, and the angler must exercise great care both in setting the hook and playing the fish. It is a ticklish though sporty type of fishing and perhaps as many fish are lost as ever are landed.

Some of these fly rod addicts use "yarn" lures instead of bait. Using a 2/o or 3/o hook, pieces of peach-colored yarn extending over the point will be fastened at the eye in sufficient amount to cover the point and to fluff out in the water somewhat like a gob of eggs. This yarn is cast out with a sinker and is bumped along the bottom like cluster eggs. At times it is very effective in streams the size of the Puyallup, Stuck or Satsop, and appears to take best when drifted through a fast riffle. It has also been used with success in the Skagit when the river is down and the water has lost its snow cast.

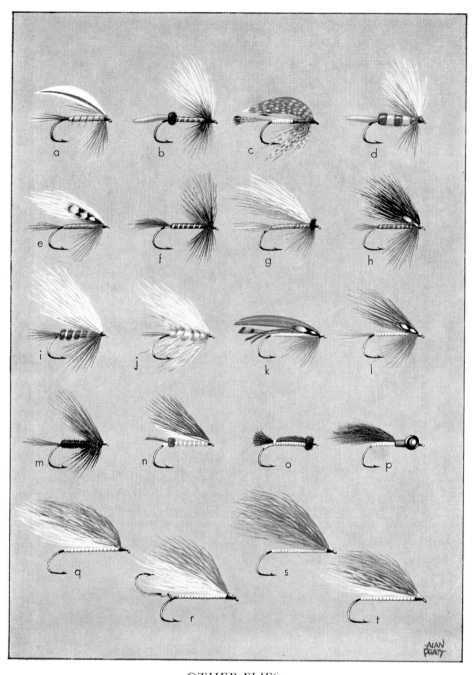

OTHER FLIES

a: Conway Special. b: Shammy Royal. c: Nation's Silvertip. d: Sammy Bee. e: Orange Shrimp. f: Purple Peril. g: Brad's Brat. h: Killer. i: Skykomish Sunrise. j: Kalama Special. k: Lord Iris. l: Golden Demon. m: Black Gnat Bucktail. n: Lady Godiva. o: Minnow. p: Wind River Optic. q: Candlefish. r: Double Hook Cohoe. s: Ghost. t: Herring.

Happy anglers land rainbow trout at Diamond Lake in the southern Cascade Mountains.

A fine catch of bass from the Owyhee Reservoir in Southeast Oregon —which also contains crappies and rainbow.

Rearing Pond on the Skagit

Late each spring, steelhead fry are released into 27-acre Barnaby Slough on the upper Skagit River. They are fed with dry pellets and are permitted to grow in the wild under natural conditions. Then the young migrants are released in April each year into the Skagit and its tributaries. The largest number of migrants from Barnaby was the 250,000 sent out in the spring of 1968.

In the 1967-68 winter season, biologists reported that 75 per cent of the sports catch in the Skagit were adult steelhead heading back to Barnaby. During December and January, these Barnaby fish crowd into the Rockport section of the Skagit in such tremendous numbers that boat fishermen cause traffic jams in that section of the river.

The success of Barnaby has triggered the establishment of other rearing ponds. The Whitehorse Ponds on the North Fork of the Stillaguamish is another highly successful operation. In 1968, 278,000 young migrants—winter steelhead, summer steelhead, and sea-run cutthroats —were released from Whitehorse into a number of Snohomish County streams. Ringold Ponds on the upper Columbia, Whistler's Bend on the North Umpqua (Oregon), and Medco Bend on the Rogue River (Oregon), have also proved successful rearing ponds.

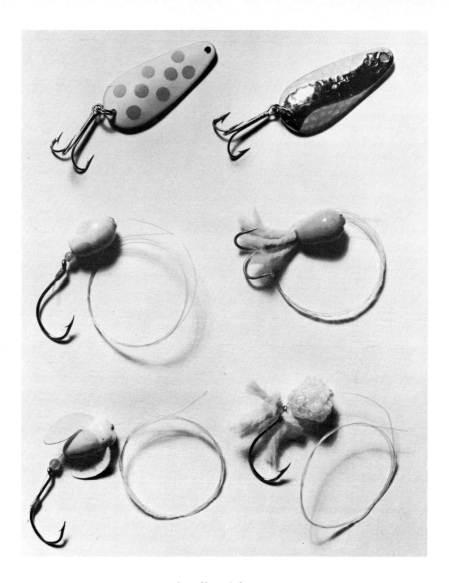

Steelhead Lures

Shown here are steelhead spoons and bobbers available in most sporting goods stores in the steelhead states: *top left*, a clown spoon, yellow with red spots; *top right*, a hammered brass spoon with a line of bright red lacquer at either edge; *middle left*, homemade clown bobber, white with red dots; *middle right*, a Sammy Special, a small red bobber developed by Willis Korff; *bottom left:* a winged bobber, a spin-n-glo; *bottom right*, an oakie drifter dressed with strands of red and green yarn.

Chapter Three

TAKING STEELHEAD ON A FLY

Although the Northwest anglers who take steelhead on bait or spoon outnumber fly fishermen at least ten to one, the latter are the most rabid, fanatical group of anglers on the Pacific coast.

They have to be. The very nature of their sport—its unpredictability, the long hours of casting often necessary to produce a few strikes—calls for a singleness of purpose possessed only by the zealot. But once an angler has become inoculated with the fever he becomes a rabid disciple of this type of fishing for life.

Not everyone makes a good steelheader. If you are the sort of angler who gives up easily, who must have action every hour, you won't like "fly flitting" for the huge migratory rainbows. If you must catch fish the first few times out on a stream you won't like it either, for some anglers put in several seasons before they beach their first fish.

Steelhead are more like big game than like ordinary trout. They are hard to find, hard to take, and the limit is low. While most western states allow 15 to 20 trout per day, the usual limit on steelhead is two or three, and it is a red-letter occasion when you take a limit. So it requires a lot of stick-to-itiveness and dogged persistence to take these fish consistently. But once you have tasted the excitement of the sport you are forevermore a member of the clan. You will continue to be a trout fisherman part of the year but when the steelhead are running, then you forget everything else and start stalking these huge migrants day after day.

Although all steelhead will hit a fly, the ones usually taken by this method are the fish called "summer-runs" or the fish that come into rivers from May until October. At this season of the year coastal streams are usually clear and low, and the weather is warm enough to make casting a pleasure. The fish are prime—a long way off from their spawning time. They are fat and crammed to the gills with pep, energy and dynamite. To the angler from the East who is fishing the coastal streams for the first time all steelhead look alike. They are whopping big trout and he would give almost anything to get any one of them out on the end of his line. But to the veteran steelheader there is a big difference between the two races of sea-going rainbows.

The winter fish is always, like a Pacific salmon, near its spawning time when it enters a river. Some may be "riper" than others but all of them are making their run for the express purpose of seeking a spawning bed. But not so with the summer-runs. These trout are all of them at the very absolute summit of their life cycle. They have stored up enough energy and oil to withstand their long sojourn in a river riffle before they spawn. Their eggs or milt are just developing and the fish are more active in every way. Although they feed sparingly anglers do find food in their gullets occasionally. They will therefore rise readily to the fly.

Most anglers agree that these summer-runs are much the sportiest of all the steelhead on a fly rod. They appear to possess more energy, reserve power and fight. When hooked, they will show longer and faster runs. Many of them are jumpers—fish that will come out of the water in leap after leap of clean beautiful symmetry. Occasionally one hooks a steelhead that puts up a very poor fight but there are fewer of these "duds" among the fish that come in during the summer months.

One of the main differences from a sportsman's viewpoint between taking steelhead on bait or on a fly lies in the way the lure is struck. As we stated in the previous chapter, steelhead do not strike a bait at all. Rather they nudge or mouth it so gently that it is extremely difficult to know when they are taking the hook into their mouths. But when a steelhead takes a fly it invariably takes it with all the force and dash inherent in its perfect streamlined body. It is perhaps the most powerful strike that ever falls to the lot of a trout fisherman. It comes out of the blue with such devastating vigor that the angler, at first experience, is utterly dumfounded. If he doesn't lose the trout, he afterwards sits and wonders that his leader and rod did not break under such a furious onslaught.

In appearance, the winter fish are inclined to be rounder and not as streamlined as their summer counterparts. Most of the winter runs are shining silver in color when they first come out of the ocean into the river, but they darken quickly—especially the bucks—as they ripen up. The summer fish are also silvery when fresh run but they soon take on a rainbow stripe along the lateral line and a touch of red on the gill covers. They are likely to remain in this color phase all through the summer and fall. Later they will darken, their gills become dull red, their stripe more crimson, and their white bellies will turn a dirty off-white.

What causes summer run fish to enter a stream when they do has never been determined by ichthyologists. It is one of the many mysteries connected with the steelhead's life cycle. Most major migratory rivers have a few steelhead coming in the year round. But in a few of the streams the migration of summer fish may be as large or larger than the winter arrivals.

In the Columbia River drainage, one stream where some exact figures are available, the bulk of the steelhead that remain in the lower river come in during the winter months. These fish ascend the streams that join the Columbia below Bonneville Dam and provide the fine sport fishing for steelhead that is available in this area from January to April.

But the steelhead headed for the upper reaches of the Columbia and its tributaries even as far east as Idaho are summer migrants. The steelhead that have been counted over Bonneville Dam will illustrate the difference between the winter and summer migrations in the same river:

TABLE OF STEELHEAD ESCAPEMENT OVER BONNEVILLE
DAM FROM 1938 TO 1949

Month	Year					
	1938	1939	1940	1941	1942	1943
January		23	5	37	4	14
February		19	96	76	37	18
March		560	1,688	1,641	256	654

	1938	1939	1940	1941	1942	1943
April		8,110	4,125	6,392	3,642	3,374
May	6,622	1,587	988	1,518	4,159	4,698
June	2,382	1,490	4,489	994	1,588	1,564
July	19,455	36,581	61,175	21,940	19,905	7,755
August	29,231	38,062	46,071	29,600	41,973	29,894
September	46,618	33,891	64,377	50,542	76,622	41,051
October	2,264	1,264	1,786	3,980	2,411	2,444
November	339	216	292	1,063	566	573
December	92	119	59	304	182	92
Total	107,003	121,922	185,161	118,087	151,345	92,131

Month	Year					
	1944	1945	1946	1947	1948	1949
January	50	1,003	63	197	154	1
February	157	1,078	551	321	119	—
March	1,019	3,066	3,040	1,968	1,631	1,689
April	6,142	4,685	9,839	6,889	4,473	3,293
May	2,227	1,557	5,481	2,025	1,170	1,712
June	1,169	1,109	3,265	1,595	1,895	1,264
July	21,868	24,600	20,559	28,134	33,191	34,314
August	24,508	40,483	58,356	40,819	53,621	54,281
September	35,907	40,194	38,296	50,025	40,609	20,786
October	6,129	1,925	2,067	2,905	1,742	1,161
November	1,119	302	262	443	381	686
December	226	142	769	113	76	98
Total	100,521	120,144	142,548	135,434	139,061	119,285

Steelhead experiment in the North Fork of the Stillaguamish River.
The Game Department of Washington is attempting to pry open the
lid that hides the secret of the two runs of steelhead. The North Fork of
the Stillaguamish River, which was closed to fly fishing way back in 1939,
has always carried a fine run of summer fish. The bulk of these steelhead
after their journey up the main river turn up the North Fork and ascend
that stream for about 15 miles to where Deer Creek, a large tributary,
enters the river at the small hamlet of Oso. Few summer-run steelhead
ever ascend the North Fork above this point.

Both winter- and summer-run steelhead go into the North Fork of the
"Stilly" and up into Deer Creek to spawn. They both use the gravel bars
of the Creek for spawning during the months of March and April. It
would be extremely difficult to distinguish beyond the question of a doubt

between the two races when they are using the same spawning redds. Moreover, while the waters of Deer Creek are high and discolored in the spring, it has proved impractical to try to catch the big spawners in the riffles of the upper canyon. So the Game Department, at the request of the Washington Fly Fishing Club, built a trap in lower Deer Creek to take summer fish on their way up when they were the only steelhead present in the stream. This trap was completed in 1945 and, after the first heavy rain of August, seventy-five mature fish were taken and transferred to a circular pond at the nearby Arlington Hatchery.

Now it is a very hazardous undertaking to hold a wild steelhead trout in a hatchery pond from August until March. These big rainbows refused to eat. As far as the hatchery men could determine, they never touched any of the food given them. Once fifty-one pieces of food were counted and placed in the pool, and the same number of pieces were removed a day or so later. In addition, the big trout scuffed up badly after being in the trap and confined in the small round pond. Fungus growth appeared on most of them by the end of February. However about 30 of the fish lived through the winter and between March 2nd and 30th of 1946, 35,000 eggs were stripped from eleven females. Out of these eleven fish, seven died during the egg stripping but the balance were placed back alive in the Stillaguamish River.

There was a remarkably good hatch from the 35,000 eggs, with only a 3% loss. Even up to the spring of 1948 there were still 24,000 fingerlings surviving that ranged in size from 3 to 10 inches.

Although rainbow and steelhead fingerlings are virtually exactly similar in appearance, there is one characteristic in which they differ radically. At Arlington there are always many circular ponds holding rainbow fingerlings during the spring. You can approach one of these ponds, dabble your fingers in the water, and the rainbows will swim up eagerly to be fed. But when you approach the pond of steelhead fingerling they flash away from you and school up as far away as they can get from the intruder. This primitive instinct, fear of man or a moving object, may be one of the traits that differentiates a steelhead from a brood-stock rainbow.

Finally in the spring of 1948, five thousand of the larger fingerling summer-run steelhead were marked with an internal red tag and fin-clipped as well. Then on April 11 they were planted in upper Deer Creek. The balance of the young steelhead were fin-clipped and planted in Squire Creek, a tributary of the North Fork about ten miles above Deer Creek. At the present time virtually no summer runs ascend the North Fork to this point.

Some of these marked fish may come back in 1949, after a year in salt water, weighing three to five pounds. But the majority will probably remain in the salt chuck for two years. If they return as summer fish the experiment will be an outstanding success. For it will prove, for the first time anywhere, that summer-run steelhead will run true to race and that they can be propagated artificially. If this is the case, they can be established in coastal rivers that at present do not carry runs of steelhead during the summer season.

Fishing the Wind River Riffles. For many years past, except during the war, I have gone to the Wind for the 4th of July. The Stilly may be only 56 miles away and the Wind River 250 miles, but the lure of the canyon of the Wind lures me each season. Much of this river between Trout Creek and the suspension bridge lies in a deep narrow canyon that is not only difficult to wade but especially hard to fly fish. There are, nevertheless, spots where one can get down to the river and follow it for several bends before having to climb out again.

Here and there are long pools that always hold fish in their clear depths. Or there will be short flats in the fast water where there are small holding pockets under rocks where steelhead like to rest. One has to fish a river for some time in order to find these spots, but unless the river changes course during a spring freshet, steelhead will usually be found in the old familiar places.

There are three flat spots in a long fast run in the Wind where a trail hesitates on the river bank near the center flat. The river splutters and ripples over rocks, tumbling along at a fast rate, but there is a very evident narrow channel where the currents from both sides merge into that inviting fast slick. I like to hit the spot when the sun is barely topping the canyon wall.

You must wade out on slippery rocks so as to make sure that the fly will swing directly into the slick and float down through it instead of whipping rapidly across it. I make my first casts short and with intense anticipation watch the fly as it is sucked under to drift into the head of the pocket. It doesn't always produce, of course. Steelheading isn't that easy.

But once in a blue moon, there will come that terrific sock, like the jolt of a pile driver, that even when half expected always comes as a shocking surprise. Without an instant's pause the rocket-like dash down through the rapids begins.

I scramble madly to the brushy bank trying to follow the fish downstream. Too much line out in this welter of rapids means a lost fish. While I hold rod up with the reel screaming, the steelhead comes out into the air sixty feet downstream and falls back with a splash, scattering a spray of water rainbow-tinted by the slanting sun. All of this slam bang action has happened in a dozen ticks of my "pocket Ben."

Now I am up on a huge rock with line out of water and have the fish safely past that limb that juts out into the current. My heart is back where it belongs and I know that I have won the first round. Then my fish does a savage double roll and jerk, but I have an easy touch on the line and nothing gives. There is a short run upstream, the fish stops, and then streaks down to the end of the flat. So far so good. Then without an instant warning the trout heads for the opposite bank. It runs up between two rocks, turns and comes back downstream by another route. There is an instant of pulsing life at the end of the line—a short heavy stop—and then nothing. I know that my fish is free, I exhale my pent up breath, relax, and reel in the line and find that only two feet of leader is gone. Lucky it didn't take it all!

I wade back to shore, squat on a partly rotted log near a tall fir until all the turmoil boiling inside me has calmed down. A big old bumble bee buzzes over my shoulder to light on the flower of a columbine, bending it over as it sticks its head down into the bell of the flower. I have a whole day before me, with a wide choice of boiling runs to choose from and no reason to start in before I am ready to go. This sure beats city life all hollow!

This trying to land a "steelfish" in the swift riffles in the Wind canyon is a battle rarely won, but even when lost, somehow completely satisfying. You know that all the cards are stacked against you, the odds on the steelhead are 50 to 1, but what of it? You get paid with excitement, and who wants to eat fish every day anyway?

Wind River Pool Fishing. But the Wind does present water that isn't all dashing rapids and slippery rocks hemmed in by steep canyon walls. There are also deep holes and long pools where the water quiets down and one has a chance to play a fish. There is one spot where the canyon widens out and the river slows down a bit to spread out into a long, deep, slow-moving ellipse of water we call the Rock Pool. Here for more than the past fifteen years I have taken steelhead every summer. After a long stretch of fast shallow runs the river makes a gentle bend to widen and slow up against a huge rock. Then it shallows out again into another series of riffles.

In order to reach the Rock Pool you drop down from the canyon rim on a steep trail through a thick growth of alder, hazel and fir with a tangle of ferns carpeting the ground. If this is a pre-dawn trip, it will still be murky as you hit the river and take the meandering trail downstream. Above the pool the river tumbles noisily through a fast run and looks darkly mysterious as you feel your way across.

You set up your rod on the small sand bar at the fan of the pool and that old familiar tension starts mounting within you. You haven't visited the pool for a year and you are wondering if it will be holding fish today. The surface in the half-light looks like dark molasses—slick with little evidence of drift. You thread line through the guides, bend on a 9/5 leader and open up the fly box. Just then there is an explosion out in the center of the pool as a huge trout broaches the surface in a roll that sends a series of rings across the pool to your feet. You glance at your partner, gulp, and say:

"They're here waiting for us!"

Your hands tremble as you pick out a Polar Shrimp fly feeling that white bucktail wings will show well in the dim light. You are now completely engulfed in a surging tide of excitement. Every nerve is tingling. You feel fully alive and there is an urgency to living that you never capture in the ordinary routine of a business day. Your partner takes a coin and asks:

"What do you want?"

You answer, "Heads."

He flips it into the air and it lands between your feet with tails uppermost. He walks downstream about ten feet, wades out into the quiet pool and steps out onto a flat rock which comes up to within six inches of the surface.

This is the hub of the pool, the spot from which he can cover the water best during this morning period. Through trial and error over the years we have worked out the procedure. He starts to cast, letting his fly carry out over the pool, allowing his line to sink and then at the proper moment stripping it in. He covers the water clockwise in a fan-shaped segment that takes in all of the lie spots he can reach. You walk upstream and start drifting through the riffle at the head of the pool.

Partner has 30 minutes to spend on the Rock and during that time he has not had a touch. You take his place for the second shift from the vantage point. You first cast upstream at an angle where your fly will be grasped by the current and carried down into the pool. You then strip the line slowly with even jerks into your stripping basket. You then repeat with a cast a bit downstream.

There are certain pockets that you remember where the fish are apt to gang up. You watch the line before you and as it pulls over a flat rock six feet away you start stripping it in. Experience has shown that at this point the fly will be retrieved through a space between two rocks far out in the pool that is another resting spot. You work down to the fan of the pool where the water shallows and hurries on to break into the rapids below.

It is intensely engrossing casting. Big steelhead, 8- to 15-pounders, are rising at intervals, mostly just rolling, but a minute ago a bright lunker—

a living piece of silver sculpture—knifed out of the dark surface. Your fly drifts into the boil of the rise and you wait tensely for it to stop. But it doesn't. Any second you expect a hit. You know that it will come without warning—come with the dead jolt of running into a stone wall—and usually it will be on the retrieve.

You change flies and put on a Brad's Brat. Still nothing happens. Your 30 minutes are up and your partner takes your place. You take time out to sit on a rock and watch him cast. You aren't as keyed up now and you can relax to drink in the details of the picture that Nature has painted for you.

The steep bank across at the head of the pool is thickly grouped near the top with tall fir trees old and darkly green. There is one clinging to the edge of the cliff that you know will tumble down one of these years. Across from you the hillside is a lighter green of cutover brush with that whitened stub that you aim your casts at to hit one of the pockets in the pool. You glance downstream to see the canyon walls reach up— up—so high that the trees appear as pointed shrubs along its rim. You two are all alone—no other anglers—no sign of civilization—no other noises but the eternal chatter of Wind River.

The sun's rays are creeping down the walls of the canyon behind you as Partner steps off the Rock with nary a hit and you take his place. You are hoping that the fish will hit this time, as they seldom take a fly after the sun hits the surface of the pool.

You have changed to an Optic, dressed on a number 6 hook with a slim silver-tinsel body, a black head, and orange and black bucktail wings. For some reason we have never been able to figure out a dark fly is a taker in the Wind. The Killer pattern, too, which has a red body and coal-black wings, has always been good. When stripped in slowly, there will often be several flippers or young steelhead following along after it. They rarely do this with the lighter-colored, more gaudy patterns.

You made a series of casts that covered the whole fan of the pool. Then a fish boiled near the far bank. Your cast was a long one, the fly drifted nicely, and you commenced stripping in the line as it pointed down current. You had about 35 feet of line in your basket when with startling suddenness the line stopped as if hooked solid to the bottom. This was it.

You tense and wait a second, glancing into the basket to see that the line is coiled evenly without any kinks. Then come two savage jerks like the pull of a horse, and the line begins whipping out through your fingers. The coils come out of the basket in such vicious haste that if one of them fouls, the tip of the rod might break before the leader could snap. Then the line tightens like wire in the guides, the reel starts singing, and at that moment the steelhead shoots up into the air in an awkward leap, falling back on its side.

You yell, step off the rock with rod held high and reel screeching and stumble ashore. Your fish is still headed up the pool on the same run. Then it stops—rubber-banded on the surface—goes down—and then swims right at you. You reel madly, backing up at the same time. Then the fish shoots back into the center of the pool and leaps twice—high clean jumps. Then it goes down again and starts that angry series of bulldog jerks from side to side so characteristic of the fighting steelhead.

You try to appear nonchalant before Partner but it isn't any use. He knows that you are excited; you know that you are excited; and the fish is not only excited but going crazy all over the place.

"Whoopee, this is what we came for," you yell and keep right on dancing up and down the sand bar. The trout dogs for a bit and then goes into another series of electrifying stunts. You know that it is a large trout and only put on enough pressure to keep the fish working. Finally after 45 sizzling minutes the steelhead wears itself out and you slide onto the tiny beach a beautiful fat rainbow-tinted thirteen pound buck.

After placing the fish in a thick clump of ferns still damp from the morning dew you sit down to compose yourself. Soon the thousand volts of ferment that have been traveling through your spine ease off. Your feeling of excitement merges into one of satisfaction and contentment.

Steelhead are the most peculiar citizens of the game fish tribe. They are unpredictable, erratic, inconsistent and completely fascinating. Why they strike at certain times and then lie dormant at others is an enigma that we have never been able to unravel. Just consider this Rock Pool.

Here we have been casting it steadily for nearly four hours, combing every inch of the water in which, from past experience, we know that fish lie. And not until just about an hour ago did we get a strike. At times we have cast the pool for two days in succession, morning and evening, and never had a touch. Then on the next trip down we would have fast, furious action almost as soon as we started fishing.

Why should they allow a fly to be dragged past their noses for hours and then suddenly slam into one coming down exactly the same pathway? And why, almost invariably, if one of them hits, do they suddenly become active and take flies freely until several are hooked? And why again do they afterwards go dead again and completely disregard all offerings?

This Rock Pool is a fine proving ground, as one can always tell when the fish are present and one can cover them efficiently at all times. It may not offer the same difficulties as casting to steelhead in a riffle. But it does present enough facts to indicate that generalizations about these rainbows are as unreliable as tips on the stock market.

Steelhead Tackle and Rods

The steelhead fly angler on the Pacific Coast, like the big waters he casts over, is a rugged type of fisherman. Everything about his fishing is on a big scale, his casts are long, his flies are far from dainty, and his quarry, as trout go, is tremendous. His rivers are fast and furious, tough to wade, hard to fish, and present problems that the light gear of a lake or eastern trout angler could hardly cope with. However, although these anglers have developed a technique well-suited to the brawling rivers where the huge migratory rainbows live, their fly rods are not as heavy as one might anticipate.

The two rods most generally found in the hands of Northwest anglers are 9 or 9½ feet long. These are usually rods with a rather stiff, powerful action, ones capable of handling a long line. The action generally lies toward the center of the rod and the tips are never soft or whippy. This type of rod is preferred because it will carry a long cast without pushing the rod. While a great many of the riffles may be covered with 55- to 65-foot casts, it is often desirable to reach out 75 to 85 feet.

Most of these rods handle best with a torpedo-head type of line that carries at least a B belly. The 9-foot rod will weigh from 5¼ to 6 ounces while the 9½-foot rod will usually weigh from 5¾ to 6½ ounces.

I have a 5¾-ounce Thomas with a powerful action that has handled close to two hundred steelhead. Outside of having the misfortune of breaking several tips—not on fish—the rod is still performing well after years of use. I have never desired a longer or heavier fly rod, as this one fits me well and I can whip it over the riffles for eight hours a day without discomfort.

However there are times when a stiff wind is blowing upstream that anglers with a 9½-foot stick are able to push their flies over to the far bank which I can hardly touch. Moreover a rod of the 9½-foot length will cast easily the large flies running from two up that are sometimes used in the bigger rivers for winter fishing.

There is a growing minority of the steelhead clan who like to use 8-foot or 8½-foot rods weighing 4 to 4¾ ounces on the smaller streams. These rods are entirely capable of handling a steelhead and an experienced angler will not have difficulty with a heavy fish. But on long casts one tends to push them a bit too much and in heavy water one can rarely give the butt to a sulking fish as one is able to do with the longer rods.

Reels. Any good fly reel with an adjustable drag that will hold at least 75 yards of backing will perform well under most conditions. In order to be safe in all streams, however, one should use 100 yards of backing as a protection against the possibility of the fish going down over the fan of the riffle.

Instead of splicing the line directly to the backing, a good plan is to splice a loop about four inches long (or one that will go over the reel) in the end of the backing. Then this backing on the reel may be looped into the small circle spliced onto the end of the line. This method will avoid the need of backing for every line, but only for every reel.

Moreover one can easily remove the line from the backing for drying or for storing in the winter. Many anglers buy an extra spool for their reels and carry one spool in a waterproof bag. This is usually made to hold a greased line that can be utilized should the steelhead be taking a floating fly.

Lines. The vast majority of steelheaders use the torpedo-head type of line. Delicacy in presenting a fly is not one of the prerequisites of steelhead angling. Rather, the ability to make long casts and to keep this casting up for hour after hour are the two most important factors of steelhead technique. A torpedo-head line fulfills these requirements. Match the line to your rod and if you follow the lead of most Westerners, you are apt to resort to a bit heavier belly than the rod will ordinarily call for.

A torpedo-head line will work out easily in a couple of back casts, and then shoot the required distance. Most of the steelheading in the Puget Sound country requires a sunken line and for this reason anglers dress their lines sparingly. Graphite not only helps to protect the line, but adds to its shooting ease and allows it to sink readily. But it is so messy on the hands and clothing that it is not generally popular.

A second method of dressing a sunken line is to use paraffin. Stretch the line out between two trees or poles and then rub it well with ordinary paraffin. Then work this into the line with a soft cloth until the line appears polished. Such a waxed line may float temporarily but the wax prevents water soaking and vastly improves its shooting power.

Silk lines are much preferred over the nylon by most steelheaders as they sink much more readily and appear to stand up well through rough usage. However, when casting a dry fly or with greased-line fishing, nylon will prove to be quite satisfactory.

Leaders. A 9-foot tapered leader is quite standard among steelhead anglers and a 9/5 or one with a terminal tippet of .012 is usually considered right for most waters. Although its breaking test lies between 3½ and 5 pounds it seems to be plenty strong enough for even record fish if one dosen't bear down too heavily. The Ox leader with a tippet of .010, testing around 2¾ pounds, is also common when the waters are low and clear and is considered strong enough. A few anglers go down to a 1x leader longer than nine feet but occasions requiring this are not common.

Most of the old-time anglers used Spanish gut leaders. The Hardy Cast dyed mist color was considered the best. But today, good Spanish gut is so difficult to obtain in the West that many fishermen have turned to nylon. The silkworm gut leader will sink readily and does not slip when knotted onto a fly—both features highly desirable in steelheading. While it tends to fray, this is readily discovered and the leader may be cut and retied at this point.

Nylon on the other hand possesses the advantage of tying easily when dry but it will also stretch under stress and will slip when playing a fish unless the proper knot is used in tying the leader sections together or in attaching the fly. Nylon does not fray like gut but its surface may be nicked. If such a cut goes unnoticed, the leader may break at this spot when you are playing a fish. In very heavy water or when rivers are discolored in winter or in early spring, straight leaders 7 feet long, testing 4 to 6 pounds, are usually adequate.

Steelhead Flies. The choice of the proper fly to take steelhead is as wide open as the mountain ranges of the West. This is still too new a sport for it to have become confined to a handful of patterns. Every section of the Coast has developed flies especially well-suited for the local rivers, and new fly tiers are continually devising new artificials. In the future, a few of these may emerge as excellent takers whether they are used on the Stamp in Canada, the Stillaguamish in Washington or the Deschutes in Oregon. At present the best plan is to select your patterns according to locality, taking the advice of the experienced steelheaders of that section.

Considering the fact that steelhead are so erratic in hitting a fly, I have often wondered what advantage one pattern may have over another. Why should a Golden Demon be considered such a taker on the Rogue; a Killer on the Wind; or a Lady Caroline on the Campbell? Couldn't a Vancouver angler, for instance, do well with his favored pattern in California, or vice versa? Does experience on a particular stream count as much or more than the flies cast to the ironheads? Most coast anglers will agree that the majority of steelhead flies are either attractor (fancy) patterns or imitations, either of a minnow or of trout or salmon fry. Such being the case, shouldn't these flies work in all rivers unless peculiar conditions warrant an individual dressing?

Generally speaking, most of the good steelhead flies are dressed with wool, tinsel, hackle and deer or polar bear hair in varying combinations of white, red, yellow, orange, black or brown. Fifteen years ago there were very few patterns to choose from. Now there are dozens. In the Seattle area there are a surprisingly large number of anglers who tie their own flies. In fact most of the inveterate summer-run fishermen "roll their own," and, although there are a few basic patterns that appear in every fly box, each angler in addition is apt to have his own pet design. As many of these "pet patterns" take fish more or less consistently they can't be disregarded.

In the color plate facing page 42 I have included a good sampling of the patterns most commonly used in Washington. Many of these have not had much currency outside of this section. But I am sure that they will prove just as effective on other rivers.

Although a few hackle streamers and the regular feather wing are used for the sea-going rainbows, the hair-winged flies are by far the most popular. Eastern white-tail deer bucktail is much preferred for wings with many dressers liking the crinkly type of hair. All of this deer hair will "work" in the water with a beautiful live action. It is best to dress the fly as sparse as is consistent with the rivers to be fished. A heavy mass of buck hair will just be a gob of color in the water. But hair that has a chance to separate and spread out will impart that enticing action so desired in a migratory fly.

Deer hair is easier to work with than polar bear hair but it does not possess the sparkle or light refraction qualities of the hair from the bear of the Arctic ice floes. A good trick to remember is to use a topping of 10 or 15 strands of a bright blue polar bear hair to give your bucktail fly a dash of translucent color.

The body hair of the deer in the natural color or the white hair at the base of the tail is generally used for dry flies. It floats well and will dry quickly on the back cast.

Wool or chenille is the best-liked body material as it stands up better than silk. After a steelhead has been wrestling around with a fly for a half hour, it has to have been well and durably made to be usable again on another fish. And a fly that has taken a steelhead always seems to be a "lucky" pattern that will often produce again if cast soon over the same water.

Although hackle does add action and color to a fly it is not the important factor that it is on a dry fly. Most fly tiers dress it much sparser than is customary on the commercial fly. A few, in fact, discard it altogether. They depend on the body color and flash of the tinsel to give sufficient undercolor to the lively bucktail wings.

Speaking from personal experience, I have found that the Brad's Brat pattern has taken trout wherever I have used it. I have dressed it on hook sizes 12 to 2/0, sometimes heavy for winter and sparse for summer, mostly wet but sometimes as a floater. It of course has been one of my most consistent patterns for steelhead and about as good for sea-run cutthroats. The smaller sizes have taken trout in lowland and mountain lakes.

When the Kamloops trout in Knouff Lake in British Columbia were not rising to a hatch of sedge flies, it proved to be an effective exploring pattern in this area.

Alaska Rainbow Fishing. On the big fighting rainbows in the river connecting Brooks and Nak Nak Lakes on the Alaska Peninsula it was my best taker. In fact, in three days of fishing there in August, 1947, I completely wore out all the Brats that I had with me on the rainbows and sockeye salmon.

To digress a bit while we are on the subject of Alaska fishing, this Bristol Bay area of the far north presents the greatest virgin rainbow river fishing to be found anywhere in the world today. That is a broad statement, but the few lucky anglers who have been able to taste a small portion of the superlative angling there will back it up without reservation. There are hundreds of miles of clear rivers, carrying runs of tremendous rainbows or the sporty grayling, that have never been fished except by the huge brown bear or the bald eagle. There are scores of lakes set down in the tundra that have never floated a boat, which hold huge rainbows off every tributary creek. There are large brawling rivers where the rainbows or steelhead are so large and the current so swift that broken rod tips are a common experience.

All of this vast territory from Clark Lake on the north down the Peninsula to Ugashik and then along the north boundary of Bristol Bay to Dillingham and north is a vast wilderness, criss-crossed with rivers and dotted with lakes. Any one of them would be world-famous if it were somewhere in the United States. Here they lie, untouched by man, just waiting for a float plane to set down an angler or two.

The Nak Nak-Brooks Lake area received some publicity during the past war due to the erection of the large army air base along the Nak Nak River. A rest cabin for naval officers was erected on the River above the air base and many of them enjoyed a brand of fishing there that exceeded their wildest dreams. Today, planes may be rented from the village at the mouth of the river for the 20-minute flight to Brooks Lake.

The Fish and Wildlife Service maintains a cabin at the outlet of Brooks Lake where extensive studies on sockeye salmon are being conducted. A permanent weir guards the outlet and provides a check on the sockeye run. All of the Brooks River, about two miles long from the weir to the falls and thence down to Nak Nak Lake, provides typical Alaska rainbow fishing. While the rainbows here do not grow to the tremendous size of those found in some of the other streams they are as numerous and as hungry as trout in a hatchery trough. And you never know whether you will hook into a fat 14-inch youngster or a sprinting 8-pounder. All of them are frisky, as full of fight and vigor as a fresh-run steelhead.

Brooks River, except for its brushy banks, is a well-nigh perfect fly stream. It flows with a nice current over a bed of small rocks. It courses along in a succession of swift runs and deep pools. It is devoid of any signs of civilization. Instead of a fisherman's trail along the bank, there is the meandering pathway made in the tall grass by the huge Alaska brown bear.

I happened to fish Brooks during a period of miserable weather, when the mist curled down to the tree tops, and gusts of wind and pelting rain assaulted me intermittently all day long. But this didn't seem to mean a thing to the trout. They hit well morning, noon, or evening, savagely taking the bucktail flies that I drifted over them. Dry flies were out of the question as it was tough enough to try to cast any kind of fly—much less try to keep one afloat. The fish were all released, although I managed to weigh 11 of them that went more than 44 pounds.

At that time all of the pools in the river were filled with sockeye salmon, and those who claim that a sockeye never hits a lure should have the opportunity of dropping a fly in front of a Brooks River "red" salmon.

These were all fresh-run salmon, beginning to color up it is true, but unbruised and free of any signs of fungus and as full of pep as if they were still in salt water. In fact, I soon learned to keep my fly out of the deeper, more quiet pools. For if I stripped my fly through the slacker water I was almost sure to hang onto one of them. It would then proceed to tear all over the place in a series of leapfrog jumps, skittering along the surface in long runs or bulldogging along the bottom. As I was short of leaders (having forgotten part of my kit at Anchorage) I had to tire them out in order to save tackle. And it took a lot of playing to save a fly and leader on the four- to ten-pounders. After a number of lessons in salmon technique I learned to shun the pools.

So I kept to the riffles and fast runs where the trout were lying in preference to the salmon-infested pools. These scrappy fish could be located everywhere in the fast water. Just wading upstream through a shallow run, trailing the fly behind me on a short line over my shoulder, would produce a strike of a trout up to 18 inches. When I cast over hidden rocks or against the bank or along a snag there would usually be a lunker waiting to hit the fly and to streak off downstream. And if you couldn't follow, you had an exhilarating battle on your hands. But a lost trout meant little when there was another one ready to hit a few feet further on.

At that season of the year, all of the fish appeared to be true rainbows. They were fat trout, silvery in color when under 15 inches, but heavily spotted when mature. The spots extended from the back almost to the belly and over the tail and head. There was no distinct median line and division of steel gray and white as in a steelhead. All of them had a narrow red rainbow streak along the side and red gill covers. At other seasons there might be ocean-run rainbows here, because this stream, through Nak Nak Lake, has direct access to salt water.

The one drawback to this rainbow paradise is its inaccessibility. There are neither roads, trails, lodges, cabin camps, nor boats. As far as accommodation for the angler is concerned, there is nothing. The only possible way to get to the fishing is by float plane. And during June and July when fishing conditions are at their best, planes are difficult to charter. For at this time they are almost monopolized by the commercial fishermen and cannery men in the Bristol Bay area.

The Alaskan angler must leave all thoughts of rapid transit and airtight schedules behind him in the States. Life does not move by the clock up there and what can't be accomplished today can be put off to next week. Moreover, as you will be traveling by plane, weather will often determine when and where you will make your next move.

When we flew by Norseman plane from Anchorage to Brooks Lake the day was clear as a bell during the winding passage through the spectacular canyon of Clark Lake Pass. Then as we headed over Lake Iliamna the rain and fog settled down and soon we were flying along barely 300 feet above the tundra with fog shrouding everything. We flew over country that looked all the same, with no one having a very clear idea of where we were. But finally the pilot got his radio compass onto the Nak Nak air base tower signal and we made a landing in the river near the air field. From then on we followed the river up and around the shores of Nak Nak Lake until we reached Brooks.

Should anyone be planning a trip into this fabulous rainbow country he will probably base at Anchorage. From there he can arrange to make his plane trip into the selected fishing area. There are a number of good guides who have charter planes working out of Anchorage. The newly organized Northern Consolidated Airlines of Anchorage, have set up a rainbow tour that covers this Katmai National Monument area in which all details of air flight, camping and accommodations are fully arranged for.

The angler should bring a good bedroll north with him and wear woolen clothing but heavy underwear is not necessary. He should carry rain clothing. Take hip boots and rubber foot pacs. A small tent that can be made bug-proof should be part of the gear. Remember that you will be traveling mostly by plane and your outfit must be cut down to bare essentials. The mosquitoes, gnats, "white socks," and deer flies will be a problem but you will be able to fish with the aid of insect repellent.

In virtually all of the clear rivers and lakes the rainbow and grayling will take a fly so avidly that it is not necessary to use any other lure. However it is wise to take two complete fly outfits in case of breakage. Take along a bass-casting outfit and a supply of small daredevil spoons in case you fish one of the large rivers. Then when you become tired of cranking in the monster rainbows you can go back to the fly rod where they break off easier.

By looking at a large-scale map of the Bristol Bay region, you will realize how hopeless it is to list all the fishing possibilities, but there are a few of the lakes and rivers that are a bit more accessible which have been "tried out" by the exploring angler. These include the Tanalin River, flowing into Lake Clark, and Tularik Creek near Newhalen, both good grayling streams. The Newhalen River, flowing into Lake Iliamna, already is noted for rainbows. There is a trading post at Sieversons on Iliamna near the Newhalen where you can base. Ninety miles away at the other end of the lake there is the Iguigik Trading Post on the Kuichak River, the main outlet of Iliamna.

This Kuichak River is fast tough water holding huge rainbows in June that are rated as tackle-busters by the anglers who have watched them streak down the rapids with their lures.

Then working south down the Peninsula, Kukahlek Lake is a fine rainbow fly spot, and Nanwhyenuk, Battle and Grosvenor Lakes have shown wonderful angling. The Savonoski River, the inlet to Nak Nak Lake, is also said to be excellent. Further south the waters have seldom been fished but they hold forth alluring possibilities of world-record trout for the venturesome fisherman.

Then going west along Bristol Bay to Nushagak Bay one can head north through a region strung out with lakes and rivers like leaves on a bush. Nushagak River is rated as tops, as is the Malchatna. This is another virgin territory, little-explored and so rarely fished that very little is known about its possibilities. But the rainbows are there waiting for a modern flying Izaak Walton to find them.

Doc's Lucky Day on the "Stilly." Few anglers will probably ever cast their flies into the waters of Alaska's rainbow heaven where the trout hit at any old hunk of hair cast over them. But there is no other balm so good for a fly tier's soul as to cast his new creations over trout that are in a hitting mood. In truth many an angler has joined the steelhead-on-a-fly fraternity all because he happened to hit a lucky day on a stream. I recall such an incident that occured to Doctor Marvin Brown.

Back when the North Fork of the Stillaguamish was open to all types of fishing, I had as my fishing partner the good doctor, who was not a fly addict. We had been hunting pals for years before the trout bug somehow got tangled up with the upland bird virus coursing through Doc's veins. He was a whiz with a scatter gun and it took a lightning-fast eye to beat him out on a rising Chinese pheasant rooster. He enjoyed every minute of his days afield. He usually came back from a long drag through a sagebrush draw with long Chink tails sticking out of each side of his hunting coat and blood and dirt streaked over his face and hands.

But at fly fishing he was still a cracker. While I stuck to the feathered lures, Doc would use anything he could find. He was an expert bass plugger and was able to take an occasional summer-run on his bass rod and a spoon. Or he would even descend to using salmon eggs when the going got tough.

We had an agreement that I could go through the water first, covering it carefully and slowly with my fly. And then Doc would go into action. He would follow through with whatever he figured would take. He always carried a fly rod along but used it seldom and had never taken a fish on it.

This was all right the first summer. I was breaking him in gradually. But after several weeks had gone by the next summer, and Doc was still carrying a fly rod along but resting it up against an alder at every bar and casting with a bass rod, I rebelled.

"Shucks, Doc," I declared, driving back from the usual Thursday fishing trip, "you're never going to take a steelfish on a fly unless you leave everything else at home."

"Yes, I know," answered Doc, "but I don't cast very well. And I sure hate to see you reach the best part of the riffle while I can't even hit mid-stream."

Anyway the steelhead quit hitting about that time, Doc refused to go out, and I made several trips alone. Finally, one day, I located a fresh run of fish in the stretch we called the Upper-Rip-Rap and beached a fine bright seven-pounder. Doc perked up his ears at this but that was all. Then the next trip up the steelhead were still there and I took a couple of eight-pounders in an hour or so.

I wheeled back to town—up to Doc's office—dumped the silvery beauties on his reception floor—and rang the bell. His eyes bugged out, and he said:

"When do *we* go back?"

"Any time you want," I answered, "but you've got to use nothing but a fly."

"It's a go," said Doc, "pick you up two o'clock Sunday morning."

So up we went and I fished through the Rip-Rap run carefully showing Doc exactly where to place his fly, the angle for the best drift and all the trimmings. But though I demonstrated all the tricks, I got nary a bump.

Doc, however, blundered along behind me and halfway through the riffle, a steelhead hooked onto his fly and was off to the races. Doc yelled like an Indian, got out on the bar, with line melting off his reel. Then he groaned and cried:

"I got a backlash!"

One hundred times out of a hundred that would have meant a broken leader and a lost fly. But not that day. The steelhead rested until Doc dug out the tangle and then resumed horsing all over the place. Doc finally subdued it and dragged a shiny 6-pounder onto the gravel.

"How does it feel?" I asked.

"Wonderful," answered Doc, "now watch me catch another."

And he did—right away too. I sat on the bar—this wasn't my day—and watched. This time the click on the reel failed to work and with no drag there was line out everywhere. But Doc couldn't lose and he beached a second rooster steelhead.

"It's my turn now," I said, and started casting through the good water. But to no avail. I worked the fly as carefully and expertly as I knew how but for me there just weren't any fish in the river.

Doc with two steelhead on the bank had his limit but he was so excited he couldn't stand still and went up to the shallow fast water to try for some eating trout.

I tended to my fishing but only a few minutes had gone by when I heard a yell that echoed all over the place. There was Doc, wading down the middle of the river, splashing over his boots, his rod jerking in mad gyrations, a leaping fish ahead of him, and between yells, his begging words:

"Hey, Brad, what do I do now?"

Well, that tied up everything. I had to get out of the river, lay down my rod and go up and convince the usually sober Doc, now completely drunk with steelhead elixir, that first he must carefully play his fish—bring it into shallow water—and then gently release it.

"But, Brad, it's bigger that the first two," he expostulated.

"Don't give me that stuff," I pounded into him, "you should have thought of that sooner. You've got two fish and this one's going free if I have to bust it off."

So he released it. Then to play safe and keep him out of the stream, I made Doc take down his rod and put everything away. And he impatiently watched me cast for two more hours without ever a strike. So he had the fish and teacher had nothing. But it made a rabid fly fisherman out of Doc, and he has never used anything else on summer-runs since that time.

Fly Fishing the North Fork of the Stillaguamish. The North Fork of the Stillaguamish is the premier summer-run steelhead river in the Seattle area of Washington. Ten years ago there were perhaps a dozen anglers who fly fished it consistently for the big rainbows. Then in 1939 it was restricted by law to fly fishing during the trout season with any type of lure permissible only during the winter months. This was the first steelhead river in the United States to be made exclusively fly water for summer-runs and up to now no other steelhead rivers have been added to the "fly only" category.

But within recent years during July and August the fishing pressure on the North Fork is tremendous. A continuous parade of anglers works the riffles and deeper runs all week and there is a waiting line on the good gravel bars all during the week-ends. Considering the relentless casting that each piece of water undergoes, the take of steelhead is large. Although no exact figures are available probably two to four hundred summer-runs are harvested from a small portion of the stream during these two summer months.

Most of this ever-growing group of anglers—men, women and children—are converted trout fishermen who have taken their kindergarten course in steelheading on the gravel bars of the "dear old Stilly."

It is an ideal fly river. Every riffle that holds steelhead is flanked by a bar which permits unimpeded back casts. In addition, one can wade well out into the "flat" runs as the current is not too strong. Most of the riffles are long enough so that the big trout do not leave them. But should a large fish head back for salt water, it can usually be followed down into the next run.

Most of the riffles are deep enough to provide resting spots amid the large rocks that dot the bottom. Steelhead come up into the pools that lie between Cicero and the mouth of Deer Creek and lie there until a rain storm raises the water in the Creek. They then usually run into this Creek to await their spawning time in the deep pools in the upper canyon. Deer Creek has been closed to all fishing for the past decade.

The Use of Stripping Baskets. A casting and fishing technique has been developed in the North Fork of the "Stilly" that, while it may be peculiar to that river, could well be practiced in any other stream. This involves the use of a stripping basket which is indulged in by virtually all of the "Stilly" anglers. These baskets are either small creels, flat wire receptacles, such as are used to file letters, or canvas buckets. The creels or wire baskets are usually strapped to the waist with a belt. The canvas buckets are hung from the neck by a length of rawhide. See illustration on page 104.

The canvas bucket is usually oval in shape, about 10 inches long, seven wide and five inches deep. The bottom is sewn in and a flat steel tape ⅜ of an inch wide is sewn around the top. The heavy canvas should be varnished so that the basket will hold its shape under any sort of use. The bucket should be suspended from the neck to about the level of the waist —or at a convenient height for stripping line into it. When not in use, the bucket may be thrown over one shoulder.

The angler strips out the necessary line, makes the cast, and at the

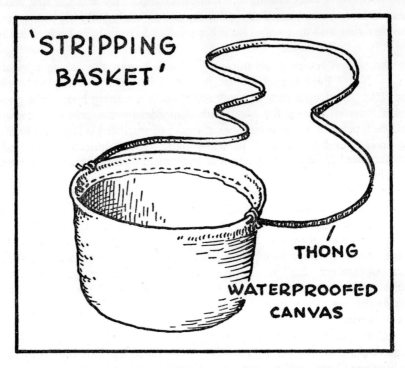

'STRIPPING BASKET'

THONG

WATERPROOFED CANVAS

end of his drift rapidly coils the line into the basket. Then simply by whipping out the torpedo head of the line, he "shoots" the balance of the line directly from the basket. In making long casts this is a great convenience as it obviates the danger of the line becoming tangled as it often does when the many coils are held in the hand. Moreover one can step downstream over logs or out onto rocks without one's line tangling and be ready to cast at once. Also should a fish take on the retrieve, the line will whip out of the basket without tangling.

Casting a Run. Most anglers like to commence at the extreme head of a run and carefully work their way completely through it to the very fan of the riffle or pool. Should the run start with a very fast riffle it is well to make short casts from a spot as well out into the current as possible. In this way try to work the fly down into the turbulent water, and allow it to hang there for an interval at the end of the drift, if it is still working out in the current.

Casting a Run in Typical Steelhead Water

Gradually lengthen your casts until the fly is flicking into the water as close to the opposite bank as possible. The angle of the cast will depend on the character of the water. If the current is very swift it may be necessary to cast upstream and then whip short loops of the line up into the current so as to allow the fly time to sink. But as one works down from the head of the run a cast quartering across will usually sink the fly into the proper water. If there is a resting spot near the far bank you should cast well above it so that when the fly drifts by it will work down through the water instead of whipping across the surface.

You should make several casts from one position, covering every possible bit of water that you can reach. Unless an angler is casting behind you, when stream etiquette requires that you do not hold him up too long, take all the time you wish to work through a riffle. A slow careful angler is the one most likely to pick up the strikes.

After efficiently covering the water from one position, step down a pace and comb the new water before you. In this manner, by the time you have reached the end of the pool your fly should have been threaded through all the water you are capable of covering. At the end of each drift allow the fly to rest an interval in case a steelhead has been following it and attempts to take it as it whips around.

One should always remember to strip in gently and slowly for several feet when commencing the retrieve. For if a fish should hit at this time a firm jerk on the line at the same instant would undoubtedly break him off. After several strips, allow the fly to swing again out into the swift water. But toward the end of the retrieve the line may be stripped into the basket as rapidly as possible.

When stripping, the rod should be held just above the horizontal, held by the right hand on the cork butt. The line should be grasped lightly between the two forefingers and thumb of the same hand. Then with the left hand the line is stripped in short jerks through the right fingers into the basket, using a light touch at all times. In this manner the line can easily be released if a fish hits during the stripping.

The reader's attention is drawn at this point to the illustration entitled "Casting a Run in Typical Steelhead Water." The drawing resembles the noted Elbow Hole in the Stillaguamish River and may be found on page 105.

The summer fish usually follow a pathway up through the main set of the current, such as is marked out with the dotted line. Crosses designate spots known as "lie water." Generally speaking, the fish will be found just to one side or the other of the fast current. The angler (the first man to the left) is fishing his side of the fast water. He will cast toward the far bank and then allow his fly to drift through the fast water until it comes to rest below him. The other anglers downstream are threading their flies through the fast water in a similar manner.

Other steelhead will take short side pathways into lie pockets or channels. One such pocket may be behind the rock in the right foreground. This will be a difficult spot to cover, but it may be done by a man with waders who gets far enough upstream and out into the current so as to allow his fly to drift down over the rock.

Other side roads will lead into the pocket below the rock in the center of the drawing, and the narrow channel above and below the snag along the far bank. To cover these lie pockets the fisherman must wade out into mid-channel so that his cast fly will drift into the pockets and settle there for a bit instead of whipping through them too rapidly.

An effective cast is attained when the angler can stand almost above the deep channel and allow his fly to drift directly into the lie pocket below the spot where he is standing.

There are various methods of fishing the fly for steelhead on the long casts but a natural undirected drift is the one most generally used in Puget Sound rivers. After the fly is cast and it is started on its way through the riffle, Washington anglers allow it to drift without giving it any action. The fly is allowed to work its way through the water as if it were a wounded minnow buffeted by the current. Usually all of the line has been cast out of the basket, and the angler watches his rod tip on the alert for that smashing jolt of forked lightning.

Veteran strippers sometimes pull about six inches of line off the reel and grasp the slack between the thumb and forefinger of the right hand so as to be able to release it and thus soften the blow against the reel of a heavy strike. But inexperienced anglers had better not touch the line at all, especially if they are confirmed trout fishermen. For their conditioned response when a trout hits is to tighten up, strike back and set the hook. In most cases this would be fatal with a steelhead. After each cast one should check the reel to take up any small portion of loose line. A small loop around the reel handle or over one finger would simply mean losing the fly and probably part of the leader.

Steelhead in fast water invariably hit like an express train, and the angler has nothing to say about hooking his fish. How these huge rainbows can put such tremendous power into their strike may be indicated by an incident that happened to me on the Wind River some years back.

One September, Reuben Helm and I were putting in the whole day down in the canyon of the river above the suspension bridge. Shortly before noon we had climbed up on to the steep cliff at the Rock Pool to look over the steelhead. The day had been a mixture of overcast and sunshine and the fish had been very active. Three of them, as we watched, moved away from their group and settled down close to our side of the river in the upper riffle.

"I'm going to try for them," I told Rube, " if you don't mind giving me directions from up here."

He consented, so I slid down the steep rock, climbed around its jutting point, and hugging the bank closely I carefully worked my way up to where the fish were resting in a small pocket. There was a large rock that I could kneel behind which would hide the movement of my rod. I stripped line into the basket and made a short cast out into the stream.

"They're still there," yelled Rube, who could see everything below the surface with the aid of Polaroid glasses. The water was gin clear, and the fish were wary and very nervous.

"Drop your fly about twenty-five feet straight out and let it drift down," directed Rube.

I did so but nothing happened.

"Your fly stays too near the surface and doesn't sink until it gets way past the fish," called out my partner, "cast further out and more upstream."

I tried this, still kneeling behind the rock where I was in such a position that I could see neither my drifting fly or the steelhead themselves.

"You're fly's coming right over them now," yelled Rube, "one of 'em is coming right at it. Yes—no—he turned away just before he touched the fly and all of the fish have headed out into the current."

Reuben had me so worked-up over the possibilities of one of the lunkers sucking in my fly that I dropped my next back cast and hung up in a bush behind me. The next several minutes were spent in loosening the line and getting the tangle out of the basket.

"I'm going to cast way out in the current and let my fly drift," I called out. The fly whipped out toward the other bank and started working downstream.

"I can see your fly," hollered Rube (it was a polar shrimp), "but no fish anywhere. But hey—wait—I see a flash—about 30 feet upstream. It's coming—a big one—right on the dead run. Whee-e! It took your fly on the run without stopping and is heading downstream like a bullet. Watch yourself!"

That I did. The smashing strike almost tore the rod out of my hand and the surplus line started whipping out of the basket and then off the screaming reel. The mad dash continued until the line was into the backing, when it slacked off as the steelhead leaped out of the water. All this happened in a few seconds. If I had neglected to straighten out the line before the cast the fish would have broken off at once. But it was securely hooked and came to the beach after a fast and furious fight.

No wonder these fish hit like a ten-ton truck when they sock a fly after a 30-foot dash at the speed of a rocket.

Covering Rises. When an angler is lucky enough to find steelhead rising in a riffle either because he sees heavy swirls or fish leaping out of the water, he is naturally greatly encouraged. These signs may simply indicate fish that are traveling through, but they may mean that these fish are active and in a position to take a fly properly presented.

One must learn to cast some distance above the rising steelhead, as a fly flipped into the spot where the rise occured will be whipped far down the current before it sinks to where the fish can see it. Try to visualize the location of the fish and endeavor to put the fly far enough upstream so that it will be well down by the time it reaches the steelhead. Do not fail to make numerous casts into the same water so as to work the fly through every bit of it. If this doesn't produce a strike keep working down through the run as the fish may have dropped downstream.

Some runs are difficult to fish because cross currents will sweep the fly over the surface, preventing it from getting down to the fish. If these riffles are not too broad or fast, you can usually cover the head of the run by wading out into the current. The old Hell Hole on the "Stilly" which was washed out during a fall freshet about a year ago was such a run. Short, and an easy cast across, it was nevertheless very difficult to fish. However, with experience I learned to mend my fly over into the pockets under the huge rocks on the further bank. But before doing so, I always drifted down through the center run of the hole, as fish often lay at the end of the fast water and would hit a fly as it whipped through. This also was a good spot to pick up jack salmon. The lower Hell Hole widened out into a deep pool which in season held resting salmon and sea-run cutthroats, but not too many steelhead.

But there was another submerged rock across and downstream—a very long cast away—that always was my target. I would attempt to lay out a long line so as to drift the fly through the swirl on the top of the rock with enough slack to let it sink down into the hole below the huge boulder. If the fly went down deep enough and a steelhead was there I usually hung onto him.

Slow-moving water is usually fished best during early dawn or after the evening shadows have started to creep out over it. But one can never tell about the fast riffles.

One sweltering day I came dawdling upstream from the Meadow Pool about noon without a strike. I walked through the cool tunnel of brush out onto the gravel bar at the Hell Hole and idly flipped a short cast upstream to the head of the riffle. The bucktail royal coachman fly was thoroughly dry and it floated high down the current. A steelhead slashed up at once but struck short and missed. Then as the fly swept downstream the fish came to the surface, made a 15-foot dash after the fly and gulped it in almost at my feet. Then in a trice it went berserk all over the run, making short quick jabs—almost too fast for the eye to follow—skittering all over the turbulent water.

It only leaped once but its underwater gyrations were superb. The sudden unexpected surge of excitement left me breathless with my heart pumping right up into my throat. Then he got down under one of the sharp rocks and in a couple of seconds had sawed off the leader.

Lie Hole Water. Although the migratory rivers of the Pacific Coast vary greatly as to size and characteristics there are certain common rules to be followed when working a stream for summer-runs. For even though these fish must go along the full length of a stream on their spawning journey, they do not hole up or rest in any section unless it is to their liking. One must learn to recognize this type of water or "lie hole" and then be able to locate it before one can hope to be a consistent steelheader.

In the first place, summer-runs like fast water and do not frequent the quiet pools or eddies. Drifts that will hold fish are usually three to eight feet deep with a riffle running through the center or along one bank. Sand bottoms are never good holding spots. Rather, the river bed should be gravel or rocks with large boulders interspersed to afford easy resting spots.

If the water is swift with a swirly broken surface, steelhead will lie in a comparatively shallow run. But if the surface is too smooth with an even gravel bottom, the steelhead tend not to rest there even if it is deep except when the sun is off the water.

When steelhead are working up a stream through shallow fast riffles they will often stop in the fan of the first good drift they reach. The water may be rather fast and slick just before it boils over into the rapids but fish will often hold here if there is sufficient depth and a resting place. Later they may move up into the deep sections of the pool above to settle down along the edge of the swift water.

Anglers should look for narrow deep channels or pockets in the swift shallow flats between pools. Such spots will often lie up against the far bank across from the casting bar and go unnoticed by the casual fisherman, but steelhead like to rest in them. It is a good plan to walk down along the bank opposite a bar when the sun is on the water to search out such pockets. Mark them in your mind so that you can cast into them when fishing later from the bar side.

The experienced angler who fishes a new river looks first for this sort of a fast run with a depth of three to ten feet. He casts it from the bar side of the stream whenever possible so that his fly will work along with the current in a natural drift and come to rest in the shallower water below his stand. He will look for slicks and boils on the surface and repeatedly work the fly through them. If there are steelhead in this section of the river he should normally expect to find them in runs of this type.

Steelhead are also found in the deeper pools but usually only in those that have a good current running through them. All of this water should be slowly worked with the fly and the extreme head of the pool should not be neglected. One good method of fishing such water is to cast the fly into the riffle above and allow it to drift into the hole on a short line so that it plunges into the deeper water as if it were any drifting bit of food. One should work this boiling bubbly water at the head of the pool thoroughly before lengthening one's line to get past the fast water. Afterwards one should start stepping down the bar so as to line the fly through all of the deep water.

Steelhead are more active in the early morning or on overcast or rainy days. Under such conditions they will often move up into the very shallow water at the head of a run where they are not apt to be found at any other time—usually just as the rays of the morning sun first glance off the riffles. If no one has disturbed this water that morning an ironhead is apt to hit a fly the first time that it drifts past his nose.

I have fished the upper Rip-Rap on the "Stilly" just before dawn when one steelhead took the fly as I was working out line, only to have Doc Brown move in behind me and hang onto another fish on his first cast while I was still playing mine. These are the sort of conditions that make steelheading appear almost too easy—but they happen only once in a blue moon. However dreams of such slam-bang action keep pulling an angler back to a river after taking many days of discouraging work.

It is surprising how a trout as large as a steelhead can remain almost invisible in shallow fast water. If they remain motionless the steel gray of their backs seems to blend into the rocks so that it takes an experienced eye to pick them out. Even under sunlight when they hang close to bottom there will not be the telltale shadow to give them away.

One September I was fishing the noted Index Hole on the North Fork of the Skykomish River with Homer Kirby. We had the hole to ourselves and although it was well past sunrise the surrounding hills kept the pool in partial shade. We had both carefully threaded our flies through the central waters of the run—the spots that usually produced at this time of day. But to no avail. Leaving Homer at his steady casting I moved up to where part of the stream narrowed to a fast run only about 15 feet wide against the opposite bank, while the main part of the river shallowed off and poured into this narrow run over a long ledge of rocks. I stood in the riffle and idly flicked a fly into the fast water in front of me. It tumbled along for about ten feet, when there was a silver flash and a steelhead rose to the fly with a swirling strike and missed.

I stood motionless and searched out every bit of the bottom below where the rise had come but could see nothing. Then I knelt down in the shallow water of the ledge, took off the Brad's Brat and bent on an Orange Shrimp. As it drifted over the same spot there was another fast rise, a swirl in the water, but again the fish did not take. I could not see the fish either before or after the strike although I was looking directly at the spot.

About this time Homer came up the bar and sat on a dry rock to watch the proceedings. I cast the Shrimp again with no response. I then put on a Killer and on the first drift got another vicious rise but neither felt nor hooked the summer-run. Again I rested the water and tried to find the fish which was rising not 15 feet away from a spot where apparently I could see every rock on the bottom. But there was not the least sign of a trout. Homer looking in from a different angle had no better luck than myself in trying to locate him.

Changing flies I tried on a bucktail coachman, dressed with hair from the base of the tail that made it a good floater. I cast upstream and the fly danced along, bobbing in the fast current, always on the surface. With every nerve tense and my heart now jumping all over my chest I watched it float over the trout's hiding place. And again there was that rise like the crack of a whip but this time I felt the heavy jolt of a connecting strike and the steelhead was on.

It turned into the current, rushing downstream with lightning speed in a single run that pulled off all the line and half of the backing. Then as I rose clumsily to my feet, the line slacked a bit as the silvery fish rose into the air in a clean leap way down the pool against the opposite bank. I followed down the bar and finally beached a prime 7-pound hen fish. As I glanced at the silvery sides and steel green back, the belly glistening like spun aluminum in the sun, it was hard to realize that such a fish could remain hidden in its shallow lie spot.

Careful Wading Pays Off. Most summer steelheaders on the coast use waders in their fishing. Hip boots will do for the smaller creeks, but in the larger rivers or for the long deep flat water, waders are almost a necessity. They enable one to cover water that could never be reached with boots and also permit one to cross a stream at the deeper riffles.

In the Pudget Sound country, felt soles are generally used as the felt insures safe footing in the type of bottoms found in the coastal rivers. Waders may be purchased in the boot-foot type equipped with felt soles. With the stocking-foot type of wader, the angler can have a cobbler cement a felt sole onto his wading shoes.

"Deep wading" anglers must avoid stepping into the shallow water of a run before they have explored the possibilities of its holding steelhead. These trout are extremely wary and will flash away from the slightest disturbance. Therefore an angler should be very careful if he happens to be the first one to approach an untouched drift in the morning. A steelhead may by lying close in to the bar, and this water should be searched carefully from the bank before starting in with the deeper wading. Also when wading alone down a run one should advance slowly and deliberately. Fish are not too frightened of an angler standing still in the water, and the cautious wader may often take a fish that the noisy fisherman will have frightened away.

I recall one Sunday afternoon when I had fished alone down the North Fork of the "Stilly" to the Meadow Pool. It was a day of sun and clouds, fine for fishing, but I had covered the fast water at the head of the pool for nearly an hour without interruption by man or trout. There were, however, occasional flips in the lower slow-moving flat of the pool that looked like rising sea-run cutthroats.

So I moved slowly downstream out from the bar, hesitating long between each downward step. It was lazy weather—hot—but a slight breeze was riffling the surface. I fished along easily with no rush or tension. Just being afield on such a day was almost sufficient award. If I took a fish, fine, but if not—there was pleasure to be gleaned from the blue sky, the deep green of the maple and cedar lining the stream, and the group of fat Jersey cows that had wandered off the meadow to cool their noses in the river.

I cast to the small rises that were breaking the surface about 60 feet across just above a sunken snag. The trout kept rising and I cast to them carefully, never moving, with the water lapping up against the waist of my waders. My stripping basket was drawn up high on my chest and I stripped almost all of my line in after each cast.

Then at the moment that I find finished stripping in from a long cast there was one of the casual flips directly out in the current not twelve feet away. Hoping for a nice sea-run, with only a few feet of my line through the tip of the rod, I dropped the fly, a Conway Special dressed with snow goose wings, over the rise.

The fly twisted along just under the surface and then—I gaped in utter surprise as I watched a silvery steelhead roll up to take the fly and then disappear as if shot out of a gun. The line whipped out of the basket like a rushing snake, the coils melting away in a few seconds. Then the reel started to sing, the fish leaped downstream under a willow—the spell was broken—and with a yell of "fire in the hole," I stumbled ashore. I was fast to a fresh-run crazy-leaping ironhead that displayed its whole gamut of tricks—now on this side of the river, now jumping near the far bank, skittering and dodging as only a steelhead can. But the hook stayed tight and I finally beached a trim 8-pound buck.

I laid the fish in the ferns under a large blackberry bush and sat down to regain my composure. I would probably never have hit in to the fish if I had floundered noisily through the drift. This was once when stealth and a deliberate approach paid off.

Fishing the Floating Fly. This fish would have taken a dry fly, as summer-runs often do when they are in a rising mood. Best conditions for the floating flies are when waters are clear, and water levels are low. Steelhead will take well in the early morning or during the ebb of an afternoon. But if there happens to be a nice riffle on the flat water of the long pools they will often rise to a dry fly when the sun is bright.

At such times one does not have to see rising fish to get strikes. If the run usually holds fish, patient casting with the floater takes fish without any trout being in evidence. This type of fly will also work well in fast swirly water when it can be cast so that it bobs down the run without too much drag.

This "fishing 'em dry" should never be indulged in by those with a weak heart. For the smashing eruption on the surface of an ironhead is startling enough to jostle the wits out of any fisherman. At times, if the fish attempts to gulp in the fly it may leave a hole in the stream as if a wash tub had been pulled out.

Most anglers who float a fly for steelhead over the Northwest rivers handle their casts very much as they do when using a wet fly. They make long casts quartering downstream and allow the fly to float until it is dragged under at the end of the drift. Very often a strike will come when the fly flips around in a small circle at the conclusion of the drift or just as it has tipped under.

The line should be greased for this fishing and a nylon fly line is ideal. The casts are generally made downstream and one works through the water in the same manner as one is accustomed to doing.

Steelhead of any size like a big fly and patterns dressed on 4 and 6 hooks are customary, although an 8 is used at times. Any of the regular patterns will do if they are dressed to float. The dry bucktail royal coachman ranks near the top of the list as it is a consistent taker. A gray hackle with a yellow body or a double gray hackle can be used as both are good floaters. A local pattern, the Purple Peril, is much used in Washington. For a brown type of fly, the Montana Buck not only rides well when dry but will take fish when it sinks.

An angler can never tell about steelhead, as we have said so many times, and they can take to a floating fly without the slightest warning. When using a dry do not forget to cover the more quiet water below the riffles, or the long flats where the water flows evenly at about a six foot depth. The small pockets out of the current or the fan of a drift are other "pay-off" spots. Allow the fly to bob along freely and retrieve it almost to your feet so as not to disturb the water by picking up line.

Steelhead are often very deliberate about coming up for an artificial. At times they will rise from the bottom of a ten-foot pool just to size up a fly on the surface. If the angler happens to be casting from a high bank where he can see the whole procedure his blood pressure is likely then to rise also at an alarming rate.

I remember once in the Wind where a deep pool hemmed in by steep rock cliffs held a school of steelhead. Standing on a ledge where I could see their every movement I kept floating a fly down over them. About the sixth time my fly made a pass, a lunker that looked all of 20 pounds

Summer-run Steelhead Taken on a Fly

These two steelhead caught by Sandy Bacon in the North Fork of the Stillaguamish River show the streamlined nature of these summer fish. Their long, slim form turns them into torpedo-like speedsters when taken on fly gear.

The runs of summer fish have been augmented in Washington rivers within recent years by the Game Department's hatchery program. While the majority of these summer-run migrants are planted in streams tributary to the Columbia, others go into Puget Sound rivers. The North Fork of the Stillaguamish has received numerous plants of Washougal steelhead. So have the North Fork of the Skykomish and the Tolt, a tributary of the Snoqualmie River. The best time to fish these streams is from late May into August.

A Typical Kispiox Steelhead

A number of British Columbia Rivers hold tremendous runs of steel-head; and the Kispiox, a tributary of the mighty Skeena, is one of the greatest in this hemisphere. It produced the world's record steelhead, a 36-pounder caught by C. B. Ewart, in 1953, on a spoon. The author, pictured here, shows a typical Kispiox Steelhead taken on a fly. It weighed 15¾ pounds.

The Kispiox, which is about a 950-mile drive northwest of Seattle, lies between Prince George and Prince Rupert. The Babine, which empties into the Skeena above the Kispiox, is another of these fabulous streams. It is best in October and is always clean as it flows directly out of Babine Lake. The Thompson, the large tributary of the Fraser River, is also an excellent winter stream, with fishing at its best from early October into December.

wove up from the bottom—paused an instant under the fly—and then turned back.

This left me weak from excitement, but when a few drifts later another steelhead rose in the same manner I about blew my cork. I struck so hard when the fish took that I not only broke off the fly but smacked the line back on the pool and scattered the school of fish down into the next riffle.

Another time in a small box canyon below the forks of Canyon Creek (which is now closed to summer fishing) I stood on a ledge thirty feet above a small pool. A fast riffle poured into the head of the pool but below me it was quiet and I could see almost to the bottom. My coachman danced out of the riffle and floated down over the glass-like surface of the pool. There was a flash of silver at the bottom and I could see a steelhead come up from the hidden recesses of the deepest water. It came up in slow easy curves, just dimpled the surface, and sucked in the fly.

Everything had been relaxed and easy up to this moment, like a slow-motion picture. But as soon as the hook was set, the quiet setting burst into tumultuous action. The fish went crazy, rushing hither and yon about the pool, leaping once and almost startling me off the narrow ledge. All that I could do was to attempt to keep the line free and hold onto my perch. Then the steelhead rushed out of the pool, around a curve in the canyon wall and cleaned me easily and efficiently.

Migration Pathways. In strange waters the angler should study his river carefully as he walks downstream. He should try to find the true run of the current as this will point out to him the upstream pathway that the steelhead will follow. As the current shifts from bank to bank there will always be a small portion of it that runs deeper and faster than the rest. This will normally be the highway that the steelhead use on their journey to their spawning grounds. Watch for lie spots in this highway—for long pools below and above rapids—for narrow chutes against a bank. Look over connecting pockets below and between rocks under the surface or the deep spots scooped out of the bottom below rocks jutting out through the water flow.

If the stream is one that can be waded at low water levels, like the "Stilly," the Skykomish or many of the Olympic rivers, then the angler can always cover the water from the best possible casting position. But in the larger streams he may know where the migration pathway goes but can hardly cast it or can, at best, cover it very poorly. In such cases he should fish this water from a boat or content himself with the accessible drifts or the smaller pockets.

Taking Winter Runs on the Fly. The Skagit, although one of the largest rivers in Washington, surprisingly enough provides some of the best fly fishing for winter runs along Puget Sound. February and March will usually be the best months, as the river should then be at its normal winter low and of the right color. As one cannot hope to cover such a wide stream with a fly, the caster looks for bars and runs where he can get his fly out to a lie spot or to a migration highway.

A stiff rod that can handle 70 feet or more is necessary for this kind of fishing and one usually needs plenty of backing as the ironheads have long stretches of water in which to do their cavorting.

The same fly patterns as those used for the summer fish will be takers in the Skagit or on any of the other winter streams. However they are customarily dressed in larger sizes, running from 4 to 2/o, with a heavier hook wherever procurable. A line that sinks readily is employed as the winter fish, especially during the cold weather, are not too active. A fly must be drifted right into their jaws before they become interested.

The Skagit has many good drifts for the fly fisherman all the way from Lyman up into the upper reaches above Rockport. Most of these drifts are easily reached from the bank although anglers must learn the means of access to the stream. Below and above the Lyman Ferry, particularly the Rancheree Hole, the drifts near Grandy and Pressentine Creeks, and the runs above Concrete are all considered prime fly water. Bank fishermen will find much better fly fishing conditions during week days, for on Sundays there are so many boats drifting the stream that many of the steelhead will be chased into the more inaccessible lie spots that are difficult to reach with a fly.

A fly on winter runs in the Puget Sound country is not too widely used. The main disadvantages to this method are the fact that the rivers are high and off color, which condition is prevalent during much of the season. Then during cold spells when rivers clear, guides are likely to freeze and lines become so ice covered that fly casting is extremely difficult. The steelhead themselves at such times are hugging the bottom and getting a fly down to them without a weight is often out of the question.

However, during February when rivers are often low and clear a fly can be very effective. And the winter fish, although not quite as fast as their summer cousins, average much larger in weight; and steelhead from 10 to 18 pounds are a worthy match for any fly angler. One of the main tributaries of the Skagit, the Sauk, is usually clear during the winter and at times produces big ironheads on the fly. Although the Skagit gets a run of summer fish it is usually so badly off color during the trout season that it is little fished.

The Skykomish River is another good winter fly stream, especially in the drifts near Monroe. Its North Fork was once also good but this tributary is now closed to all winter fishing, although it remains open during the trout season. The Green River has some good fly drifts that produce but it is fished so heavily with bait that the fly anglers have little opportunity to cast.

All of the Olympic Peninsula rivers have fine runs of winter fish and most of them should show some good fly fishing. While the fly is used very sparingly in these streams and some of the water is not suitable for the artificials, there exist long drifts where a fly would work. These streams present the only virgin steelhead fly water left on the West Coast and some Ike Walton can make himself famous by pioneering an exploration of their possibilities.

A few of the rivers that enter the Columbia below Bonneville Dam should provide winter fly angling. The most famous is the Kalama, which is a fine summer stream and which turns out fine fly fishing during April and May. However these are not strictly winter fish but very early summer runs as they are almost a year away from spawning.

Chapter Four

STEELHEAD RIVERS OF THE PACIFIC COAST

Even though virtually all of the coastal rivers from British Columbia to California hold steelhead runs of varying magnitude, they differ greatly in the sport fishing that they afford. Some of them are pounded steadily every day of the week; others are crowded only on week-ends, while a few of the more remote streams are fished only by the exploring angler. Some streams put out steelhead by the thousands, while others produce spotty and erratic fishing.

The "Big Four" of the southern coast—the Eel and the Klamath of

California and the Rogue and the Umpqua of Oregon—are nationally famous for their summer and fall fly fishing. In Washington, the Chehalis, Cowlitz, Green, Hoh, Nooksack, Puyallup and Skagit are all heavy producers of large-size winter fish. British Columbia has many streams that do not receive the heavy play of those below the border and their excellent runs have hardly been exploited.

The great reputation that Pacific Coast steelheading enjoys throughout the East and Middle West has been built up mainly on the fishing in a mere handful of rivers. Spectacular as the sport furnished by these streams is, there are hundreds of others equally good if not better that are hardly known outside of their own watersheds. Year in and year out these waters yield great numbers of large-size ironheads to resident anglers only.

The principal reason that the knowledge of this sport fishing is not more widespread is that the bulk of these fighting sea-educated rainbows are taken in winter when tourists are not traveling through the country. Moreover they are almost all caught not on fly but on bait.

There isn't any question but what a steelhead gives superlative sport when caught on a fly but this type of fishing may be practiced only under the proper conditions. Moreover bait gear may be made so light that it will require as expert and dexterous an angler to land fish with it as on a fly rod.

The fisherman should always remember that in all of these streams steelheading depends on runs and water conditions. When water levels are right and a new run has come in, the fishing will be excellent. A sudden rise in the level and off-color water conditions will put the same river down at the bottom of the list as far as catches are concerned. So in attempting to list the important Northwestern rivers and their best seasons for steelhead fishing one must consider that success in the final analysis will always depend on the weather.

Whenever possible, weather conditions should be checked with people living on the particular river you wish to fish. If this is not possible, you should study the weather reports for the district in which the river is located. It is well to postpone a trip for several days after extra-heavy rainstorms. Also, during protracted cold spells fish will not be traveling and no new runs will be coming in to the river. Generally speaking steelhead tend to travel during periods of rising water and will be active and afford good fishing until the stream becomes too high and turns badly off color. On the other hand it is easier to hook and catch steelhead in slightly murky water than when the stream is low and the water crystal clear.

While what follows is not a complete listing, it includes virtually all of the better-known rivers that produce either summer- or winter-run steelhead along the Pacific Coast:

British Columbia

The steelhead streams of British Columbia are divided into two general classes: first, those on the mainland draining into the Strait of Georgia; and second, those situated on Vancouver Island. In the listing they will be designated as (mainland) or (Vancouver Island) rivers.

Allouette Rivers (mainland). These runs are reached via Haney. South Allouette shows excellent steelheading when the water is right but levels are controlled by dams. It offers winter-run fish only, with best fishing from December through February. The fly is seldom used. North Allouette yields an occasional steelhead but is not considered a good fishing stream.

Ash (Vancouver Island). The Ash is reached via Alberni. It is 28 miles in length. This river has a good run during the summer, showing excellent fishing in July and August. The months of September, October and November are good while December and January are fair. Some large fish are taken here during July, August and September.

Brunette Creek (mainland). Brunette Creek is reached via New Westminster. It is 4 miles long. It yields only a few winter fish.

Big Qualicum (Vancouver Island). This river is reached via Nanaimo to Qualicum Beach. It has about 7 miles of fishing area. This river is good for winter fish but there is no good proof of summer-runs. Fish show in November and fresh fish may be caught as late as April. February and March are the best months.

Campbell (Vancouver Island). Reached via Nanaimo, it shows mainly winter-run fish. The best months are December, January and February. It also has a fair run of summer fish of small size ranging between 3 and 5 pounds, caught mostly between April and June in the Canyon and Island Pools.

Campbell (mainland). Reached via New Westminster, it offers winter fishing only with best months February through March.

Capilano (mainland). Reached via Vancouver, it has a 5-mile open area. The best months to fish this stream are November and May. Fish come in almost year round with best fishing during a rise in water. Fair fly fishing during the summer months.

Caycuse Creek (Vancouver Island). The Caycuse flows into Nitinat Lake. It has a run of summer fish with best fishing during the months of June and July. All of the west coast rivers of the Island are reported to hold summer fish which will take flies, but these streams are difficult of access.

Cheakaamus (mainland). Reached via Squamish, this river is 28 miles in length. Best fishing is from September to June. It is a big fast stream having several runs of steelhead.

Chehalis (mainland). The Chehalis is reached via Harrison Hot Springs. It has a length of 16 miles. It holds winter fish with best fishing during December, January and February. Steelhead are of good size.

Chemainus (Vancouver Island). Reached via Chemainus, it has a length of 32 miles. It is a winter-run stream with best fishing during December, January and February.

China (Vancouver Island). In the Alberni district, the China is a winter-run stream. Fishing is excellent during January and February, and good during March and April.

Coquahalla (mainland). Reached via Hope, it has a length of 33 miles. This stream is heavily fished and holds both winter and summer runs. Winter fishing is best from December through February and summer fishing best from June to September. Resident anglers use bait (salmon roe), copper spoon and devon minnow in winter, and single egg, devon and bucktail flies during the summer. It is one of the good summer streams.

Coquitlam (mainland). Reached via New Westminster, it is 9 to 10 miles in length. A fine river for winter-runs only. Like the South Allouette its waters are controlled by dams. Best months are from December through February, with fine results obtainable all through this period when water levels are right.

Cowichan (Vancouver Island). Reached via Duncan, it has a length of 28 miles. Winter fish are the main run with December through February best months. A run of smaller or first-run fish appears in February and March. Lures used are mostly spoon, shrimp and devon minnow, with an occasional fly.

Englishman's (Vancouver Island). This stream lies 20 miles north of Nanaimo between Parksville and Craig Crossing. It is 19 miles in length. It holds winter-run fish only, with the run beginning early in January and continuing at intervals until end of March. February is the best month. Steelhead weigh from 4 to 18 pounds.

Franklin (Vancouver Island). This stream is in the Alberni district and is a winter-run stream with steelhead tending to be of a lean variety. The months of January and February show excellent results, with March good and April only fair.

Gordan (Vancouver Island). This stream is reached via Port Renfrew at Port San Juan. It has a good summer run of steelhead. Best fishing is during the months of June and July.

Indian (mainland). Reached by Burrard Inlet via launch from Vancouver, it has a length of 3 miles. This winter stream holds large fish with February and March the best months for fishing.

Kanaka Creek (mainland). Reached via Haney, this creek is 11 miles in length. A few winter-runs are taken here but it is not considered good steelhead water.

Koksilah (Vancouver Island). Reached via Duncan, this is another winter-run river with best results obtained in January, February and part of March.

Little Qualicum (Vancouver Island). This stream lies north of Qualicum Beach and is 8 miles in length. A winter-run river, the fish come in from January until March with February showing the best results.

Lynn Creek (mainland). Reached via Vancouver, this stream is 10 miles in length. It produces a fair steady run almost the year round with November and May the best months. Steelhead up to 16 pounds have been taken here within recent years.

Nahmit (Vancouver Island). The Nahmit is in the Alberni district. The Lower Nahmit is mainly a winter-run stream with January, February and March showing excellent fishing. April and May are also good. These fish are inclined to be thin but are in fair condition. The Upper Nahmit, on the other hand, is primarily a fly stream with the best fishing from May through August. However the majority of the fish taken at this time are dark.

Nanaimo (Vancouver Island). This stream is reached via Nanaimo and is 36 miles in length. The run starts here about December 20 and the fish keep coming up at intervals until late in April. Fishing is fair to good all of the winter months, providing the water keeps at a low or normal stage. February is usually the best period. The fish run up to 18 pounds. There is no summer-run angling.

Nickomekl (mainland). Reached via Cloverdale, the Nickomekl is 19 miles in length. A winter stream, the fish come in from December 20 to March. Best results are obtained from January on. Most of the fish are taken on bait. There is no summer run.

Nimpkish (Vancouver Island). This stream can be reached via boat only to north end of Island. It is fished very little but is reported to have a good run of steelhead and exceptional runs of large chinooks.

Nitinat (Vancouver Island). The Nitinat flows into Nitinat Lake on the west coast and is about 40 miles in length. It is a seldom-fished stream that holds a fine run of summer fish. Best months are June and July with August, at times, also good.

Oyster (Vancouver Island). The Oyster lies 15 miles north of Courtenay, and offers about 15 miles of fishing water. Winter-run fish show here as early as November and fresh fish may be taken in April, with February and March best months. No summer-runs are available.

Puntledge (Vancouver Island). Reached via Courtenay and Comax, it is 25 miles in length. A winter-run stream from November to April, it offers its best fishing in February. Some of the largest steelhead in this district come from here. Winter-run fish that have spawned are at times taken on a fly in the Puntledge between Comax Lake and Stotun Falls.

Quinsam (Vancouver Island). Reached via Courtenay, it is 23 miles in length. A winter stream, December through February are considered the best months. No summer fishing for steelhead is available.

Salmon (Vancouver Island). Reached via Courtenay in Campbell River district, the Salmon is another winter river with December through February the best period. No summer-runs are seen although the occasional steelhead is taken on a fly in the summer at the junction of the White in the Samward area.

San Juan (Vancouver Island). This river on the west coast is accessible by boat. It has a good summer run lasting into the fall. Fish come in from March through April and again in August and September. They can be taken on the fly.

Sarita (Vancouver Island). The Sarita is accessible by boat and lies 10 miles from Bamfield. A winter stream with fish lean but in fair shape, fishing will be excellent from January through March and good in April and May.

Serpentine (mainland). Reached via Cloverdale, it is 16 miles in length. Offers winter fishing with best results had from December through February. Bait is customarily used.

Seymour (mainland.) Reached via Vancouver, the Seymour is 20 miles in length, four miles of which are open. It is one of the mainland streams where steelhead enter nearly the year round. The best months are November and May, with some fly fishing done. The fish run to good size.

Silver Creek (mainland). Reached via Hope, this Creek has a fine run of both winter and summer fish. The best winter period is from December through February and the best summer period from June to September. A good river to use the fly on during the summer months.

Somas (Vancouver Island). Reached via Alberni, it is about 5 miles in length. This is one of the best fly streams on the Island. Most of the fish are large and in fine shape and most of the fishing is done with a fly. December results are good; January, February and March are excellent; and April is good.

Sooke (Vancouver Island). Reached via Milnes, the Sooke is a river flowing from the southern tip of the Island. This is another one of the fly tackle streams. Best fishing with the fly is from March through April; fall fishing in August and September is best on troll.

Sproat (Vancouver Island). Also reached via Alberni, the Sproat is another noted fly stream, with all fish large and in good shape. Spring is the best period with fishing excellent on the fly in January; good in February and March; and fair in April. Biggest fish have been taken below the falls.

Spring Creek (mainland). Spring Creek is a tributary of Harrison Lake. It is a small winter stream with best fishing from December through February.

Squamish (mainland). To reach this stream, go via boat from Vancouver to Squamish. It has a run of steelhead all during the year with quality of fishing depending on water levels.

Stamp (Vancouver Island). The Stamp lies about 8 miles out of Alberni and is 10 miles in length. One of the best-known rivers in the Alberni district, it is famous for its fly fishing. Its run of summer steelhead are clean lively fish with good girth; the majority of them of good size. The best month for the fly is July with good fishing in August, September and October and fair fishing in November and December.

Stave (mainland). The Stave can be reached via Mission City or New Westminster. It is a winter-run river with fish coming in from November to March. Reports, however, indicate that although a few steelhead are still taken from this stream each year it is steadily showing poorer fishing.

Suicide Creek (mainland). Reached also via Mission City, it contains winter fish only, with December through February the best months. It is a clear creek that rises and falls quickly.

Trent (Vancouver Island). The Trent is also in the Courtenay district. As in the Tsable and the Tsolm rivers, this is a winter stream with the majority of the steelhead ascending during the months of February and March.

Tsable (Vancouver Island). The Tsable lies just south of Courtenay and is 9 miles in length. A winter-run river, the best months for fishing are February and March. There are no indications of summer fish.

Tsolm (Vancouver Island). Reached via Courtenay, the Tsolm is about 20 miles long. It is similar to the Tsable in that it holds only winter-runs with February and March the best months.

Vedder (mainland). Reached via Chilliwack, the Vedder is one of the best steelhead rivers on the mainland. It is principally a winter-run stream and is fished heavily from December to April. It turns out many fish, mainly on bait, spoon and devon minnow. It is also fished with a float and cluster eggs. From time to time a steelhead is taken on a fly when the water is clear.

Chapter Five

STEELHEAD RIVERS OF WASHINGTON

The State of Washington has well over 100 rivers that contain runs of steelhead at one time or another during the year. The listing that follows contains all of the major rivers and most of the smaller creeks. Wherever possible each stream will be located to its closest town or junction with a highway. Consult the Pacific Northwest Fishing Guide or other similar guides for more precise directions.

Abernathy Creek (Cowlitz County). The Abernathy intersects Ocean Beach Highway about 12½ miles west of Longview. It flows into Columbia River and is best fished for half a mile above its mouth. Winter-run fish are taken from late December through March. Fish are of fair size and are caught by both drift fishermen and plunkers. An occasional steelhead is taken on a fly while cutthroat fishing.

Asotin Creek (Asotin County). Asotin Creek enters Snake River at the town of Asotin. It holds winter-run fish only, with January and February the best months. It has a good run of steelhead that do not usually run more than 6 pounds. A new ladder now being constructed over the old intake dam should improve the run in this stream.

Bear River (Pacific County). To reach Bear River, take Ocean Beach Highway either south from South Bend or west from Longview to Johnson's Landing. This river enters Willapa Bay. It holds a small run of winter fish with January and February best months.

Big White Salmon (see *White Salmon*)

Bogachiel (see *Quillayute*)

Calawah (see *Quillayute*)

Canyon Creek (Snohomish County). Canyon Creek is a tributary of South Fork Stillaguamish and has its mouth above the bridge west of Granite Falls. It is open as far as Bear Logging Company Bridge above Canyon Creek Lodge during the winter season only. A fast stream with canyon pools, it holds a fine run of winter fish. The best months are December through January. It is hard to drift but a good producer to anglers acquainted with its lie holes. It has a run of summer steelhead but is closed at that time to protect young downriver migrants.

Carbon River (Pierce County). Carbon River is a tributary of the Puyallup with its mouth at the town of Orting. It has a fair run of winter steelhead, the majority of which are taken near the mouth or below Carbonado. The best period is usually January and February.

Cedar River (King County). Cedar River is the source of Seattle's water supply and flows into Lake Washington at the town of Renton. It is closed above Landsberg, but the lower reaches are accessible by road. Although levels are controlled by a City watershed dam the river is usually clear. It is very fast but has good holding pools. It has a fair run of steelhead with best fishing during late December into February.

Chehalis River (Grays Harbor County). The Chehalis River flows through Chehalis, Elma, and Aberdeen. It is a large sluggish stream which harbors an excellent run of steelhead—many of good size. The lower river is most heavily fished, with portions near Elma and at the mouth of the Satsop very popular. Due to its type it is fished mostly by plunkers who sit on the bank and await developments. It ranks right at the top of the state rivers in producing steelhead. It is the parent stream for the Satsop, Skookumchuck and Wynooche Rivers.

Cispus River (Lewis County). To reach this river from Randle, cross the Cowlitz and then drive to the Cispus which lies at the mouth of Camp Creek. It is a rather large mountain river which is usually clear in the upper portions. Has a fair run of steelhead which are taken between January and March.

Clallam River (Clallam County). The Clallam is reached by Olympic Highway north from Sappho. It is a clear stream which flows into the Strait of Juan de Fuca. It has flash runs of steelhead, when the fishing is of the "hot" variety in the reaches above the Strait. Best times for fishing are after December.

Clearwater River (Jefferson County). To reach Clearwater River, turn off the Olympic Highway about 22 miles west of Lake Quinalt to follow up the river after crossing the Queets. This clear stream enters the Queets on the reservation, and the long drift at its mouth is a famous steelhead hole. A good portion of the Queets steelhead run heads up the Clearwater, and while it is not as famous as the big river it produces some nice fish.

Cloquallum Creek (Grays Harbor County). This creek is a tributary of the Chehalis with its mouth at the town of Elma. The lower reaches provide some good steelheading during January and February.

Columbia River. This stream, the West's mightiest river, which once held the greatest runs of salmon and steelhead on the coast, is fast becoming a gruesome monument to man's folly. Power dams are rapidly destroying the runs of all migratory fish, salmon, steelhead and cutthroat, in the upper river. These species no longer go above Coulee. McNary Dam, almost completed, undoubtedly will destroy another segment of the run, as no migratory fish up to now have ever been taken up, over or down a dam of its height. The lower river is rather large for the steelheader. However there is considerable plunking done from the bank where the current swings in. Also steelhead are taken at the mouths of most of the tributaries that enter the stream. In the upper river there is some steelheading in the vicinity of Celilo Falls; and in the late spring or summer off the mouths of the Wenatchee, Entiat and Methow. The water at the mouth of the Snake puts out good fishing at Pasco in August and September. Occasionally a steelhead is taken on the fly off the bars at these points.

Coulter Creek (Mason County). To reach Coulter Creek, take Allyn Road out of Belfair and thence journey two miles to its mouth in Case Inlet. A small creek, it has only a small run of steelhead in December and January.

Coweeman River (Cowlitz County). The lower reaches of Coweeman River are accessible from Kelso. The upper reaches are reached via the

Rose Valley road which leaves the Pacific Highway five miles south of Kelso. This river is open to steelheading up to Gobel Creek. It has winter-runs mainly with fish averaging about 7 pounds. Fish come in throughout the season with March the best month. This is mainly a drift stream with its best water from Gobel Creek to the top of the tide water. Fish have been taken on the fly in this portion. Some plunking is also done.

Cowlitz River (Cowlitz and Lewis Counties). The Cowlitz flows east through Lewis and south through Cowlitz counties. The Pacific Highway runs along the full length of the stream in Cowlitz County. The mouth of the stream is at Longview in the Columbia. It is a large river which holds the lion's share of the lower Columbia River run of steelhead, virtually all winter-run fish. It is one of the few major rivers of the State that are open the year round, which it is up to the mouth of the Muddy Fork. Fish can be taken most of this time. Its steelhead run large, averaging about 10 pounds, many going up to 15 and some even nudging the scale at 25 pounds. It ranks third on the Game Department list. Best months are from December until April, with March usually showing a fine run. The river goes out of condition easily, and fishing will depend greatly on the condition it is in.

Due to the size of the Cowlitz much of the fishing is done from the bank by plunkers. Some of the fast riffles are fished by keeping the bait out in the fast water with a heavy sinker and off the bottom with a cork float attached just above the eggs.

Dakota Creek (Whatcom County). The highway to Sumas and Blaine runs along this creek which empties into Drayton Harbor. It has a good run of steelhead considering the size of the water. It is a late-winter run stream, with March one of the best months. Open only up to the Haynie-Custer Road.

Deep Creek (Grays Harbor County). Deep Creek is reached by taking Pacific Highway east from Copalis, cross the Humptulips and then upstream ¾ mile to where Creek enters. It is a small creek that has a minor run of steelhead in January and February.

Dosewallips River (Jefferson County). The Dosewallips flows into Hood Canal at town of Brinnon on Olympic Highway. A fast stream with brushy banks, fast runs, and small pools, it holds a fine run of steelhead that are hard to take unless the angler knows the river. It discolors easily from snow water but produces better fishing when a bit off color. When it is clear, it takes a light leader to hook fish, and these are hard to land in fast water. The fish run from five to eight pounds. The best months are January and February.

Duwamish, or Black, River (King County). The Duwamish is the lower portion of the Green River which flows into Elliott Bay at Seattle through

East and West Waterways. It is fished for steelhead in the vicinity of
Renton Junction virtually 100% by plunkers. When new runs come in
during periods of falling or rising water, they take many fish. The section
of this stream from Boeings down to the Bay is becoming rather badly
polluted.

Duckabush River (Jefferson County). The Duckabush crosses Olympic Highway to enter Hood Canal one mile north of town of Duckabush.
Is a large mountain stream, rather fast but with good holding pools. It is
clear in the winter when most other rivers are not. It has a good late run
of summer fish that are taken in the early part of December. A few winter-
runs come in through the season. The fish average between four and
seven pounds.

Dungeness River (Clallam County). The Dungeness is crossed by the
Olympic Highway about three miles west of Sequim. It is a fair-sized
stream which flows out of a rugged watershed and fluctuates in level and
condition rather rapidly. It has a good run of steelhead of which many are
caught early in the season—in December—mostly below the highway
bridge. It also gets a good run of summer fish which are taken after opening of the trout season in May and June. Virtually all of the fishing is
done with bait.

Elochoman River (Wahkiakum County). Ocean Beach Highway crosses
Elochoman River about 3 miles past Cathlamet near its junction with the
Columbia. Winter-run fish only are available with February and March
the best months. Fish average 7 or 8 pounds, and are taken both by
drifting and plunking. Most of the fishing is done in the lower tidewater
reaches and for about six miles upstream.

Elwha River (Clallam County). The Elwha is crossed by the Olympic
Highway about nine miles west of Port Angeles. Steelhead runs are found
from the mouth to a dam below Aldwell Lake, leaving only about seven
miles to fish. It has a good run of steelhead which come in from the
Strait in periodic surges. The river is silt colored much of the time, but
shows fair results in January and February when the water is in shape.

Germany Creek (Cowlitz County). Germany Creek is crossed by the
Ocean Highway about five miles west of Longview. It is a small creek
that flows into the Columbia, holding only winter fish of fair size. Lower
reaches above tidewater best with both plunking and drifting methods of
fishing used. Good months are February and March.

Goldsboro Creek (Mason County). Goldsboro Creek flows through
town of Shelton. A few winter-run steelhead are present with January
the good fishing month. This stream has been badly polluted from a pulp
mill but may now be improving.

Grande Ronde River (Asotin County). The Grande Ronde is a good-sized river flowing out of Oregon across the southeast corner of the state to enter the Snake at Rogersburg. It is accessible on Mountain Highway from Pomeroy. While not heavily fished, it puts out steelhead of average size.

Grays River (Wahkiakum County). To reach Grays River, take Ocean Beach Highway west from Longview to the town of the same name, where road follows the stream toward its mouth in Grays Bay in the Columbia. It is a late winter-run stream with February the best month in the special winter season. Below the town of Grays River, the stream is slow tidal water. Best fishing extends from this town upstream to the "Mackey Hole." The fish run large—some from 9 to 12 pounds. Fishing is spotty, but when the runs are in, this stream affords excellent catches.

Green River (King County). Accessible by highways through Renton Junction, Kent, and Auburn, Green River is the most heavily fished river in the Seattle area. It is open to winter steelheading from the Flaming Geyser Bridge to its mouth. Steelhead ascend to the headworks dam above Kanasket where they are held in a trap and spawned. This river produced about 2,000 fish in 1947 and 1,750 in 1948. Fish average 6 to 8 pounds with a fair number going 10 to 14 pounds and each year a few from 16 to 20 pounds are beached. Every possible drift is lined with anglers over a week-end and even on week days it is difficult to find a run devoid of fishermen. The lower river from Kent to Renton Junction is slower water suitable mainly for plunkers. There are many holes here where older anglers spend whole days beside a camp fire watching for their rod tips to start twitching.

The drift anglers fish virtually every foot of the river between Kent and Auburn, where a highway parallels both banks. Every drift is named, among them Orphanage, Lucky Hole, Carrot Farm, and Garbage Hole. The mouth of Soos Creek takes a heavy pounding, and the water below and above the Porter Bridge is also well fished. The water of the upper river from Porter Bridge to Flaming Geyser is usually the clearest and takes a lot of pressure. Between the Porter and Whitney Bridges it is a short hike into the runs around Circle Water, Newuakum Creek and the Dairy Hole.

Green River rises quickly but levels off rapidly and clears easily. It shows its best fishing when a bit off color. It is fished by many expert bait anglers, who can feel the slightest nudge of a steelhead. Of late years, anglers are using lighter leaders and lead so as to take fish out of the brushy spots where they have taken refuge from the excessive pounding of the current.

Although the river now opens in December the best fishing months are January and February. New runs come into the river all through

February but, during this month, dark fish will begin to appear in the catches.

A few steelhead are taken on flies here or on fly and spinner during the winter. During the summer the occasional steelhead will be taken, mainly above the gorge.

Hamilton Creek (Skamania County). Hamilton Creek flows into the Columbia 5 miles west of Stevenson and is crossed by the North Bank Highway. It is a short rugged stream that receives a fair run of steelhead. Best fishing is in late winter, or after the trout season opens.

Hamma Hamma River (Mason County). This river enters Hood Canal at town of Eldon and is crossed at its mouth by Olympic Highway. It is a large and rugged stream which receives a heavy salmon run and a fair number of steelhead. These are taken during January and February in the lower reaches up to the "Blue Hole."

Hoh River (Jefferson County). The Hoh is crossed by the Olympic Highway about 20 miles southeast of the town of Forks. Oil City road leaves this highway to reach the mouth of the river from the north bank. The upper river may be reached by going 19 miles by road to Jackson Ranger Station, which is 5 miles within the boundaries of Olympic National Park. The Hoh is a large glacial river discolored most of the summer.

This river receives one of the biggest runs of steelhead on the Peninsula and has never been fully exploited. The fish run in directly from the ocean and come in at each rise of the water level from December until spring. Good fishing will depend greatly on the condition of the river and on locating a run. There are cabins available at Bogachiel Park, Ruby Beach and Kalaloch.

The steelhead average good size, with an occasional lunker over 18 pounds being taken. In late season, the angler is apt to run onto dark fish in the upper reaches.

Hoko River (Clallam County). The Hoko enters Strait of Juan de Fuca at Clallam Bay and is bordered by a road south from the town of Sekiu to Ozette. A small stream, it is easily fished in its lower reaches which contain a fine run of steelhead. January and February are the good fishing months. Large runs enter the stream when the water is right and exceptional catches will be made if the angler hits the stream at that period.

Hoquiam River (Grays Harbor County). The Hoquiam enters Grays Harbor at the town of Hoquiam. It is a large river which forks just above tidewater. It has a good run of steelhead which are taken during January and February. The upper reaches are usually clear and may be drifted. It does not get the play from anglers that it received in former years.

Humptulips River (Grays Harbor County). The Humptulips enters North Bay of Grays Harbor and the Pacific Beach Highway out of Hoquiam crosses its lower reaches. The Olympic Highway, 21 miles north of Hoquiam, crosses the stream at the town of Humptulips below the forks. From this point, a road on the north bank follows the river south to the Beach Highway. The river is open to winter steelheading from its mouth to the forks.

The Humptulips receives a heavy run of winter steelhead and January and February are the best months. The lower river is too large to wade and many of its best bars are difficult to reach without a boat. It is a beautiful river to fish and contains ideal steelhead riffles with gravel bottoms that prevent hooking up. Fish are above average in size and on occasion will go to the 20-pound mark.

Johns River (Grays Harbor County). Johns River enters Grays Harbor at the town of Markham and is reached by the Aberdeen-Westport Road about 12 miles southwest of Aberdeen. It has a small run of winter steelhead and the river is open during the season from the mouth to the forks.

Kalama River (Cowlitz County). This river is crossed by Pacific Highway over a bridge north of the town of Kalama. Half a mile north of this bridge a road goes east 17 miles upstream. It is a beautiful fast, clear river which cannot be waded in its lower reaches and is brushy in the upper portions. The Kalama is a wonderful steelhead stream with a fine winter run and one of the best runs of summer fish in the state. It is open the year round from its mouth to the Puget Sound Power and Light Plant.

The best months for winter fishing are February and March; for summer fishing April and May in the lower river, and all during the trout season in the upper river with August probably the best month. The winter-run fish are of good size, some going over 18 pounds. The summer fish average about 7 pounds but there are numerous fish beached in the 10 to 12 pound class.

Winter fishing is done mainly by drifting bait in the runs from the power plant to the mouth. Much of the water is rugged and hard to reach. Best results are obtained by drifting in a boat. Boats and guides are available at Camp Kalama.

The very early summer fish are taken on flies when water is right in the lower river during late April and May. Occasionally one of these will go over 15 pounds.

During the trout season, the river above the power plant is restricted to fly fishing only. All of the water from this point to Pigeon Springs is heavily fished and, although a road conveniently parallels the river, the angler must learn just where to hit the good runs. There are fast riffles and fine holding pools where many steelhead rest until they are ready to spawn. When the fish move out of the pools they will take a fly readily in the riffles. They are hard to attract with the fly in the pools and a well-sunken wet fly is usually required to do so.

There is much good water above Pigeon Springs but this area is closed to anglers during the summer because of fire regulations.

Most of the fly patterns in use on summer steelhead in Washington will work on the Kalama. It is interesting to note that there are a few designed particularly for this river. Most of these are bucktails, in combinations of yellow, white and orange. In the deeper pools, an Optic fly will be effective at times.

Klickitat River (Klickitat County). The Klickitat is reached by the North Bank Highway along the Columbia, where an oiled road at the town of Lyle heads north for 25 miles along the stream. It has both a winter and a summer run. It is open during the winter season from February to May 1, and under summer limits from May 1 to September 15. During the winter, fishing is permitted only from the mouth to the first bridge below the Fisher Hill Bridge. During the summer it is unlawful to fish the river from a boat from this Fisher Bridge to the source.

The river is usually clear in winter and many fish are taken, with the best fishing found near the mouth.

The Klickitat has a fine run of summer fish and they are taken up to September. Being a glacial stream, it is usually discolored during hot weather when fishing falls off. However, whenever the stream clears, a fly will be an effective lure. One of the favorite types of bait here is the tail of a crawfish used in the same manner as cluster eggs.

Lewis River (Clark and Cowlitz Counties). The Lewis is crossed by Pacific Highway at Woodlawn just above its entrance into the Columbia. East of Woodlawn, 12½ miles, the Ariel Dam closes the river above it to the progress of migratory fish. The main river, the North Fork to just below the Ariel Dam, and the South Fork to the Daybreak Bridge are open to year-round fishing.

The Lewis receives a large run of winter fish from late January up to May, with February through March the best period. An occasional fish will be taken on the fly in the latter part of this season.

Both drift anglers and plunkers take fish and the South Fork receives most of the play.

Lyre River (Clallam County). The Lyre is crossed near its mouth by Joyce Road west from Port Angeles. It contains winter-run fish only. A usually clear small stream which does not discolor easily, it holds a good run of steelhead up to the falls below Lake Crescent. It is a difficult river to fish due to brushy banks but it puts out good catches.

Mashell River (Pierce County). To reach Mashell River, turn east on National Park Highway at Eatonville and go two miles to the stream. From there a trail goes to the upper reaches. It holds a fair run of winter fish with January and February the good months. The stream is rather inaccessible, and does not produce too many fish.

Mill Creek (Cowlitz County). Mill Creek is crossed by the Ocean Beach Highway about 12 miles west of Longview. This is a small creek that holds winter fish only. Such fish as are to be had are found mainly in the section about a half mile above its mouth or at the highest point reached by tidewater.

Morse Creek (Clallam County). Morse Creek is crossed by the highway about 3 miles east of Port Angeles. Although a small stream it has a good run of fish and fair catches are made when the run is going through.

Naselle River (Pacific County). The Ocean Beach Highway reaches the mouth of Naselle River south of the town of South Bend and then turns upstream to the town of Naselle. The river empties into Willapa Bay. It is a winter-run stream with best fishing during January and February. The local residents fish it hard and customarily use bass casting rods and plunk in the holes rather than drift.

Nemah River (Pacific County). The Nemah is crossed by Ocean Beach Highway near the town of Naselle, where the stream enters Willapa Bay. It has a fair run of winter fish, most of which are taken close to tidewater. January and February are the two good months.

Newaukum River (Lewis County). Accessible by main highway southeast from town of Chehalis, the Newaukum is a small stream which flows into the Willapa River. It has winter-run fish only which average about 7 pounds. The best months to fish are January and February. Fish are scattered all through its length and through its two forks. Mostly a drifting stream, some plunking is done nevertheless.

Nisqually River (Thurston County). Crossed by the Pacific Highway about 20 miles south of Tacoma, the Nisqually was once among the best winter steelhead streams. It is now almost ruined by a combination of power dams and netting Indians. The level of the stream fluctuates greatly, and is difficult to fish on the reservation. It is off color during the summer. Few fish are taken now but the stream might come back if levels became more regular and Indian netting stopped.

Nooksack River (Whatcom County). The Nooksack is crossed by the Pacific Highway north of Bellingham at Ferndale. Other roads north and east from Bellingham follow the lower reaches to where the mouth enters Bellingham Bay. It is one of the biggest rivers in the state, but is of the glacial type and is therefore off color during the summer.

This river has one of the largest runs of winter fish in Washington and ranks fifth on the Game Department list. They are prime fish averaging 7 to 8 pounds with a few taken in the 15- to 19-pound class. The runs are late, with good fishing during February and in the lower river during the March opening. Most of the fish are taken drifting. All three of the forks hold steelhead in their lower reaches and are fished consistently during the season.

The river empties through the Lummi Indian Reservation. However this tribe has been rather cooperative with the Game Department and has imposed short voluntary closures on itself. Given the proper protection, this fine run of steelhead should be maintained.

North River (Pacific and Grays Harbor Counties). The North River empties into Tokeland Bay and is crossed by the Aberdeen-Raymond Highway. It contains winter-run fish only of good size, many going 10 pounds. The lower reaches, where the best fishing is to be found, are rather inaccessible, and can best be fished from a boat. The banks are brushy and there are no trails. January and February are the best fishing months. This is one of the best coast rivers for sea-run cutthroats.

Palix River (Pacific County). The Palix River enters Willapa Bay and is crossed at its mouth by the road running south from South Bend. It is a short stream which contains a few steelhead in its lower tidal waters, which are taken mostly by local residents. It is another good sea-run cutthroat river.

Percival Creek (Thurston County). Percival Creek empties into Budd Inlet and is the outlet of Black Lake. It is reached by Black Lake Road out of Olympia. It has a small run of steelhead which are taken mostly by local anglers.

Pilchuk River (Snohomish County). The Pilchuk empties into Skykomish River at the town of Snohomish. The road through Machias to Granite Falls and side roads tap the upper river. It is a clear, small river, flowing through farming country, which has a good run of fish. It is closed during the summer season to all fishing. The winter fish average 6 to 8 pounds with an occasional one up to 14 pounds. It is a difficult stream to fish because it has brushy banks and many logs and snags. However there are many resting spots in the lower section below Machias and in the pools from there to Granite Falls. Careful casting with a light leader and small lead will take fish out of the shallow riffles or from under snags. It is not for the inexperienced angler.

Puyallup River (Pierce County). The Puyallup joins the Stuck River at Sumner and from that point is paralleled by the main highway south to its mouth where it enters Puget Sound at Commencement Bay. It is a glacial stream which receives a fine run of winter fish, and is pounded heavily by anglers all during the season. Proof that these get good catches is in the fact that it stands fourth on the Game Department listing.

The river goes out of shape easily, rising and discoloring badly with heavy rains. However it has fine runs during January and February. Below Sumner the stream is banked with concrete for much of its length and is fished mainly by plunkers. The pools at the confluence of the Stuck contain many steelhead.

The stream above Sumner has many fine riffles and most of the fish are taken by drift anglers. The fish average about 6 to 8 pounds with an occasional one above ten pounds.

Pysht River (Clallam County). The Pysht is crossed by the Coast Highway out of Port Angeles where it empties into the Strait by the town of Pysht. A small stream that remains clear during most of the season, it has a fair run of winter fish which are taken mostly by resident fishermen.

Queets River (Jefferson County). The Queets is crossed at its mouth by the Olympic Highway 26 miles east of Lake Quinault. Above the mouth at the Jefferson County line a road forks to the right to follow upstream about 12 miles into the Olympic National Park. Another road forks from here to cross the Queets and go up the Clearwater. The river enters the ocean on the Indian reservation.

This glacial stream is one of the most noted steelhead rivers on the Olympic Peninsula. It holds a tremendous run of fish and its count in the Game Department listing is way below its annual catch. It has an immense winter run as well as a good run of summer fish.

It is fished very heavily by the Indians, who stagger their nets closely all the way upstream on their reservation. The fish run very large, 12-pounders are not uncommon, and every season occasional fish ranging from 20 to 25 pounds are beached.

There are many wonderful bars for drifting all along the stream, but although it is paralleled by a road one must learn how to cut down to the good riffles through the timber. Much of the water around Salmon Creek is fished by drift anglers and when the run is on a limit can be beached within an hour.

Anglers may secure accommodations at Queets Inn or cabins at the mouth or at Kelly's Ranch at the end of the road upstream.

This stream is never really clear and always carries a certain amount of slate coloration. It is a stream with fast riffles and a decided drop with a strong current. Although it has a good run of summer fish, for these two reasons it is not a good fly stream in the summer. Much of the time it is off color and it is difficult to get a fly down in the rapid runs. However these summer fish may be taken on bait or on a spinner. During

August many summer-runs are caught and at the mouth of clear tributaries, such as Sam's River, fly fishing could be effective.

Any time from mid-December until the end of the winter season, the Queets can put out the type of steelheading that causes the Puget Sound angler to drool in anticipation.

Quilcene Rivers—Big and *Little* (Jefferson County). The Quilcene Rivers are crossed by the Olympic Highway near the town of Quilcene on Hood Canal where they enter Quilcene Bay. They contain a small run of winter fish and afford only fair fishing during the months of January and February.

Quillayute River (Clallam County). The Quillayute is formed by the Bogachiel, Soleduck and Calawah Rivers. It is followed by the Ocean Highway west of the town of Forks to the point where it enters the ocean between the Indian villages of Mora and La Push. These streams form a vast network of steelhead waters that hold one of the greatest runs of wild, ocean-fresh steelhead along the Northwest coast. From early December until late in April steelhead surge into the broad slow reaches and sparkling riffles of the Quillayute in one fine run after another. After traveling the four short miles of its length they divide to seek their appointed spawning homes in either the Bogachiel or the Soleduck. Then the Bogachiel run is separated later with a portion going into the Calawah.

From the beginning of the winter season in December through the 15-day extended season in March, one can find ironheads in this stream. Most of the fishing is done in the long, long riffle below the confluence of the "Bogy" and the Soleduck. This is a mixture of white and broken water with a fine gravel bar flanking it where an angler can dance along behind an 18-pounder if it starts back toward the ocean after being hooked.

The river below this riffle may be most easily fished with the aid of a boat to get from one riffle to another. The fish run from 6 pounds up to 20 pounds and all of them are as fresh-run as an ocean steelhead can be.

An angler may fish the Quillayute in the morning with never a strike, and then come back in the afternoon and hang onto one fish after another. Some anglers believe that the steelhead tend to come into this stream on an incoming tide and that fishing is best at such times. But whatever the theory, my experience is that fresh runs are likely to come up from the rocky beach at La Push at any hour.

The Bogachiel River is crossed by the Olympic Highway about 9 miles south of the town of Forks, and the portion below the junction with the Calawah is touched intermittently by the road to La Push. It is a large stream which is usually clear except after heavy rains. It contains long holding riffles, and deep pools, most of which can be drifted nicely without hanging up every minute. Except during protracted spells of cold weather when the river is way down and fish have gone upstream and are not moving, there will usually be a run of fresh fish somewhere along the "Bogy."

It follows the same pattern as its parent river, the Quillayute, with fish to be taken from December through February, but it does not have an extended season in March. Virtually all of the ironheads here are taken by drift fishermen, as it is a stream primarily suited to this technique. From the first riffles above its junction with the Soleduck to as far as you can hike along its upper reaches you can take steelhead if you locate the run.

Calawah River is crossed by the Olympic Highway about a mile north of Forks and may be fished from here either upstream or for three miles downstream until its confluence with the Bogachiel. This stream gets its run during the same periods as the Quillayute and the Bogachiel, but the runs are a day or so later than those coming into the Quillayute. Many of its riffles and bars are hard to reach except by a short hike-in from the various roads or branching skid roads.

The Calawah is a river with brush-lined banks and many of the good runs are difficult to cast into for the drift fisherman. But the fish are there if you can get your bait in front of their noses.

The Soleduck River is paralleled at varying short distances for most of the length of its lower stream by the Olympic Highway north of Forks. The Mora road touches the river at spots and crosses it by a bridge just above its confluence with the Bogachiel.

It is the third link in the chain that makes the Quillayute. It is a long river, branching into two forks before its south fork comes out of the noted Sol Duc Hot Springs. The lower reaches contain the steelhead. This is a difficult stream to fish for steelhead as much of it is brush-lined. However there are trails into many of the "hot" spots and in places the brush has been cut away to permit casting.

The three winter months of December, January and February are the ones for the best steelheading. It is reported that these three rivers all hold summer-run steelhead. However very little experimenting has been done by way of taking these fish during the trout season either on fly or bait. But as anglers have even now picked up occasional fish on a fly in the Soleduck and Calawah during August, this sport is undoubtedly waiting to be developed at a later date.

Quinault River (Grays Harbor County and Olympic National Park). The lower river of the Quinault is crossed by the Olympic Highway as it leaves Lake Quinault, and is reached at the mouth at Taholah by the Pacific Beach Highway from Aberdeen. Above the lake, the river extends for about 10 miles where it branches into an east and north fork. The road up the east fork goes through the village of Quinault and up to Graves Creek. A road goes along the north bank of the river, leaving the main highway north of the Lake Quinault Bridge, and extends to the North Fork Patrol Cabin on that stream.

The Quinault is the third member of the noted "Q trio" of the Olympics. The main river from the lake northeast to where it forks puts out some wonderful steelheading, and gets a heavy play all winter. It is both a winter- and summer-run river. It receives one of the earliest runs on the coast, often putting out limit catches when the season opens in December. Christmas week is usually good for a fine run. In fact, all through the season until it closes at the end of February the Quinault will be putting out fish whenever it is in condition. It rises quickly and turns milky, but also comes back into shape rapidly if the weather turns cold.

The fish run large—their average being around 8 pounds with many over 15 pounds and 20 pounders not too rare. The stream is fast and is too large to be waded but it shows many beautiful casting bars and riffles. This main river is accessible by the road along both sides although the south bank gets a majority of the anglers.

The river below the lake, which lies on the reservation, is not accessible by road and is fished only by Indian-manned canoe. These trips are taken during the summer, usually for trout. It is only on rare occasions that it is ever fished for steelhead, as the stream above the lake attracts all the steelhead anglers.

The fine run of summer fish in this river has never been fully exploited. These fish will be found in the main river from July on, and in the forks in August and September. Most of the fish are taken in the east fork in the canyon about a four-mile hike above Graves Creek from the middle of August into September. This water is more suited for bait or spoon than a fly. The main river during the summer is likely to be snow colored and permits fly fishing only during a cool spell.

Salmon Creek (Lewis County). The mouth of Salmon Creek is crossed by Pacific Highway south of the town of Toledo. This is a tributary of the Cowlitz which receives a nice portion of the steelhead run. It puts out good fishing during the latter part of the steelhead season.

Samish River (Skagit County). The Samish is crossed by the main highway about 6 miles north of Burlington and it enters Samish Bay at the town of Edison. It is a small clear river that produces fair fishing during January and February. This is one stream that has declined as a steelhead ground and it apparently spawns more silver salmon at present than it does steelhead.

Satsop River (Grays Harbor County). The Satsop is crossed near its mouth by the highway that runs between Elma and Montesano. It is one of the largest tributaries of the Chehalis. The main river below its forks puts out very good steelheading during the winter season. The best months are January and February, and the fish are of good size, running larger than in the average stream. It once was one of the premier steelhead rivers of the state. It subsequently declined badly, but now is coming back in fine shape.

Although a highway goes upstream, the angler must know the spots to cut across fields to reach the good riffles. Much of the bank is brushy, and it is a long way between the good runs. There are long bars and fine lie holes. The best way to case this stream is by boat.

Sauk River (Skagit County). The lower section of the Sauk is followed by the highway north from the town of Darrington to Concrete. This is a large tributary of the Skagit. It is badly off color during the summer below its confluence with the Whitechuck. However it clears nicely during the winter and puts out some fine steelhead during January and February. The angler must learn how to reach the good drifts as the stream is in a wild uncharted country.

The fish are of good size and run late. In fact a few bright fish are taken in this stream after the opening of the trout season. As this stream is rather far from any center of population, it does not get too heavy a play. A steelhead is occasionally taken here during the winter season on the fly.

Sekiu River (Clallam County). The Sekiu is crossed by Coast Highway near its mouth in the Strait of Juan de Fuca near Kydaku Point. It holds winter-run fish only. Although its run is spotty, this small river at times puts out some good fishing. It is fished mostly by local residents.

Skagit River (Skagit and Whatcom Counties). All of the steelhead water of the Skagit River from Mount Vernon to Marblemount lies within Skagit County and is available by highway for its entire length. The Skagit is undoubtedly the greatest producer of steelhead trout in the Northwest. It has top ranking in the Game Department Listing, with 3,712 caught in a four-month winter period in 1947, which was a rather poor year, and this count is probably way below the number actually taken. It is fished very little during December, but January is good, and the period from Washington's Birthday until the end of March is the best.

It is the best boat river in the state and the only one where a regular guide service is maintained. Although most of its fish are taken on cluster eggs, when it is in proper level and color, many big ironheads are taken on a fly. The fish run very large, rarely under 6 pounds and many in the 15- to 20-pound class.

Arrangements may be made for guides at Mount Vernon, Sedro Wooley, Lyman and Hamilton; but most of them are booked months ahead. A detailed description of fishing spots and methods used on the Skagit are given in the foregoing steelhead chapters.

Skamokowa River (Wahkiakum County). The Skamokowa is crossed by the highway near its mouth about 35 miles west of Longview at the town of Skamokawa where the river enters the Columbia. It holds winter-run fish only, and produces only fair fishing.

Skokomish River (Mason County). The Skokomish is crossed by highway from Bremerton near where it empties into Hood Canal near Union. From there, a road branches to the left to go up the south bank to the forks and part way up the north bank. The north fork's run of steelhead was killed off by a power dam at Lake Cushman. The south fork provides the bulk of the spawning grounds.

This river has the best steelhead run in the Hood Canal area, and the best months are January and February. It gets a fine late run in March and April of bright fish but the season is usually closed at this time.

The main river below the forks is a beautiful stream with fine casting bars and good holding pockets. The fish are above average in size. The lower section of the stream flows through an Indian reservation where the usual netting of steelhead is carried on by the Indians.

Skookumchuck River (Thurston and Lewis Counties). The Skookumchuck enters Chehalis River near Centralia. Its lower reaches are followed by a road from Centralia to Tenino. It enjoys a good run of winter fish, and January and February are the better months, the best of the fishing coming late in February. Most of the fishing in the lower reaches is done by plunking but there is some fine drifting water at Bucoda and above. This river may hold some summer-run fish and it would pay to investigate the possibility after the opening of the trout season in May.

Skykomish River (Snohomish County). From its confluence with the Snoqualmie, the Skykomish extends east to where it forks near Index. Virtually all of this lower river is accessible by road—the north bank by the Stevens Pass Highway and the south bank by side roads.

This is a clear large river, which, although heavily pounded, turns out fine catches of steelhead. Its best months are January and February. Some years there is a late run in March after the season closes. Although the river rises quickly during rains, it does not discolor too badly as it drains from a high country.

Some of the best drifting riffles are in the areas both above and below the town of Monroe: the section of the stream between Monroe and Sulton; the bars near the mouth of the Sulton River; off the mouth of the Wallace; and the area below the confluence of the north and south forks.

Although a good summer run goes up this river, the fish are not angled for until they get into the north fork. To reach the north fork leave the Stevens Pass Highway about a half mile east of the bridge over the south fork and go one mile to where a bridge crosses the north fork at the town of Index. A road from here parallels this fork up to Goblin Creek almost 18 miles.

During the winter season the north fork is open only to the railroad bridge at the town of Index. However many steelhead are taken in the waters from this bridge to the river's confluence with the south fork. The north fork has a fine run of summer fish. They will be found in the stream from the opening of the trout season until late September. Due to the fact that this is a fast stream with swift riffles, it is not entirely suited to the use of a fly during the summer. But many steelhead are taken on bait and spoon from Index to Garland Hot Springs from July to September.

The best spots in the river to take summer-runs are from Index to the entrance of Trout Creek; at the Galena Bridge; and in the waters from Bear Creek Falls to Troublesome Creek. When the river remains low for long periods during the summer there are several lie holes in the vicinity of Index that hold fish, and many are taken here on bait and occasionally on a fly.

The south fork of the Skykomish, which lies in King County, does not have a steelhead run, as migratory fish cannot ascend Sunset Falls a short way above the mouth of the stream. (For other tributaries of the Skykomish River, see Sultan River and Wallace River.)

Smith River (Pacific County). Crossed by Raymond-Aberdeen Highway near its mouth at Tokeland Bay, the Smith is a small stream which has a fair run of winter fish. Most of these are taken in the lower tidal waters of the stream.

Snohomish River (Snohomish County). A large river, the Snohomish is formed by the confluence of the Snoqualmie and Skykomish Rivers about 3 miles southwest of Monroe. It is bordered by roads all the way to its entrance into the Sound at Everett.

This stream is badly polluted by pulp mills at its mouth, but it does nevertheless receive a good run of steelhead. It is a big stream, the lower sections deep and slow moving, and is best fished from a boat. However there are good long bars below Monroe where plunkers gather and fish all day long. It is heavily fished and puts out good catches.

Snoqualmie River (Snohomish and King Counties). The Snoqualmie flows south through Duval, Carnation and Fall City to where it forks in three branches east of the town of Snoqualmie. Steelhead do not run above the Snoqualmie Falls at this point.

This is a large winding river, seldom wadable. It is paralleled by roads on both sides for most of its length. It puts out a good many steelhead, mainly in the upper reaches from Carnation to Fall City. Some fish are taken in the lower river when fished from a boat or by plunkers.

It holds winter fish mainly with the best period in January and February. Some of the better drifting riffles are in the Carnation area; off the mouth of the Tolt River; from this mouth to Fall City; and off the mouth of Raging River.

The river drains a low valley and rises to flood stage quickly during heavy rains, so that it is out of fishing condition during all bad rainfalls.

Squalicum Creek (Whatcom County). The Squalicum is the outlet of Squalicum Lake and is crossed by highway 3 miles from Bellingham. It is a small creek with a poor run of steelhead.

Stillaguamish River (Snohomish County). The Stillaguamish is a large river which flows from Arlington through Silvana to its mouth in Port Susan at Stanwood. It is accessible for almost its entire length from roads out of these towns. This river with its north and south forks is one of the noted fly streams of the state. The main stream from Arlington to Silvana holds a large run of winter fish that are taken from January to March. The riffles from Arlington to Silvana put out the largest number of winter fish and drift fishermen outnumber the plunkers. This stream is out of shape during much of the winter due to the presence of a clay bank on the north fork. However, it has one of the best runs of sea-run cutthroats in the Puget Sound area. The cutthroat are taken by bait, spoon and fly during August, September and part of October. It also has a nice run of silver salmon which will take spoon or fly. An occasional steelhead is taken on a fly at this time by cutthroat anglers.

The north fork of the Stillaguamish is crossed by the highway from Arlington to Darrington at Cicero and Oso. It is a winter-run stream as well as being one of the premier summer-run rivers of Washington. Although this stream gets a good run of winter fish, it is usually so off color from the clay slide at Hazel that it is rarely fished even with bait. However, the river is usually clear above the slide and at times some nice catches of winter fish are taken from the riffles above the town of Hazel.

Summer-run steelhead ascend the north fork from May until September and can be taken as soon as the river clears enough to permit fly fishing. It is the only steelhead river on the Pacific Coast which is open to fly fishing only during the steelhead run in the summer. The majority of these fish go up the north fork as far as Deer Creek, in which they spawn, and which is closed to all fishing. They are bright prime fish of good size. A portion of the run will average between 4 and 6 pounds, there are a large number of fish going from 6 to 8 pounds, and an occasional steelhead ranging from 8 to 10 pounds. A very few have tipped the scales at 11 and 12 pounds.

The river from the mouth of Deer Creek to the Cicero Bridge is intensively fished all summer. Whenever the river is clear, anglers will be working the riffles from the long casting bars. A fine spirit of cooperation prevails on this stream and consequently a dozen anglers can work the same riffle at once.

The proper flies and methods of fishing this river are detailed in the chapter on fly fishing for steelhead.

The south and north forks of the Stillaguamish join at the town of Arlington and the south fork is followed by a road to Granite Falls. The falls above this town prevent migratory fish from ascending the river to its upper reaches.

The south fork gets both a winter and a summer run of steelhead. The winter fish are taken in the greatest numbers, because for unknown reasons, few anglers fish this stream for summer-run fish.

This river is clear during most of the winter and summer as it is not bothered by the bad clay slides of the north fork. The best steelhead water lies between Arlington and the highway bridge that crosses the river below the mouth of Canyon Creek.

Stuck River (Pierce County). The Stuck is crossed by highway from Auburn to Sumner south of Auburn and followed by a road from here to its confluence with the Puyallup at Sumner. The Stuck is a glacial stream with most of its water being diverted through the power plant which dumps the water back at Dieringer. It is clear during the winter and affords good fishing. There are no summer runs and best months are all through the winter season. Some of the best drifting runs are below the Buckley Bridge; in the vicinity of the game farm; below the spillway at Dieringer; and at the river's mouth.

Sultan River (Snohomish County). The Sultan is a tributary of the Skykomish River and enters the latter at the town of Sultan. It has a winter run only. The stream, perhaps due to the Everett water supply dam, does not have the water flow of former years and not too many fish are taken in the river itself. However, many steelhead are taken in the "Sky" at the mouth of the Sultan. In the Canyon not far above its mouth, steelhead are taken when water levels permit access into its riffles.

Tahuya Creek (Mason County). To reach Tahuya Creek from Belfair go along north side of Hood Canal for 15 miles to the mouth of the creek. It is a small stream which has winter fish only but fair catches are made in the lower reaches.

Tilton River (Lewis County). The Tilton joins the Cowlitz near Silver

Creek, and the main river is followed by the Elbe-Morton Highway. It is a winter-run stream with a late run. Best fishing is from February to March. It is a rugged stream which may have gone down slightly within recent years.

Tolt River (King County). The Tolt enters Snoqualmie River just south of the village of Tolt; a road out of the village follows the north bank for about 4 miles. A trail goes into the Forks area.

This is a fine small river with good gravel bars. It receives a good steelhead run both winter and summer. During the winter, fish run up from December until the end of the season. The fish are of average size with rare specimens going up to 20 pounds.

The Tolt is open only to its forks. Both forks are closed to fishing during both the winter and the trout seasons. The drift at the mouth of the river at the Snoqualmie is a noted steelhead hole and is fished steadily all winter and summer. But it produces fish even under this intensive pounding. During the winter, all of the main river is good steelheading but many of the riffles must be reached by hiking.

A fine run of summer steelhead goes up the Tolt and into its forks, but as the forks remain closed the run is hardly touched by sportsmen. However the hole at the mouth puts out a good number of summer-runs. The main river also puts out fish although part of it is closed due to fire restrictions during the summer.

Touchet River (Walla Walla County). The Touchet enters Walla Walla River at Touchet and is paralleled by a highway most of its length. A late winter-run stream with a few fish taken during the winter season, and others during spring and summer. It is a fast stream, mostly one long riffle, with few pools. The steelhead run small, ranging from 3 to 5 pounds.

Toutle River (Cowlitz County). The Toutle River is crossed near its mouth on the Cowlitz River by the Pacific Highway north of Castle Rock. Its north fork is followed by Spirit Lake Highway to its source at Spirit Lake, which road also crosses the south fork near its mouth. It is open to the forks the year round. It receives a big run of winter fish and best fishing months are February and March. Occasionally an early run comes in around Christmas. The steelhead run large, sometimes going up to 20 pounds.

Although it is essentially a drifting river, it is difficult to fish because of its rocky bottom. Many anglers strip fish here with nylon lines and light leaders. It is one of the best winter streams and is apparently holding up well.

Union River (Mason County). Union River enters Hood Canal near

Belfair and is followed by Navy Yard Highway. It is a very small stream which has a fair run of steelhead. The fish are easy to hook within its small waters but difficult to land.

Walla Walla River (Walla Walla County). The Walla Walla is followed by highways from its mouth at Wallula on the Columbia to Touchet and Lowden. It has a good run of winter fish, with January and February the best months.

Wallace River (Snohomish County). Wallace River is crossed by Stevens Pass Highway near Startup. This tributary of the "Sky" puts out few fish. It is a short, very clear stream and the run has declined within recent years. However many fish are taken in the main river at its mouth.

Washougal River (Skamania County). The Washougal enters the Columbia and is crossed by North Bank Highway at Washougal. It is followed upstream by various roads. It has a fair winter run of fish and a better spring run. Best months are April, May and June after the opening of the trout season. Removal of dams in the lower river has improved the run. Fish taken are of good size, averaging 6 to 8 pounds, with an occasional one from 10 to 15 pounds. This stream is heavily fished by anglers from Vancouver and Portland, using spinners.

White Salmon—Big (Skamania and Klickitat Counties). The Big White Salmon enters the Columbia at Underwood and is followed upstream by a road past Trout Lake. It is a glacial stream that holds winter- and summer-run steelhead. Most of the steelhead are caught near the mouth. Many of them are taken in the backwater of the Columbia from a boat either by trolling or casting a spoon.

White Salmon—Little (Skamania County). The Little White Salmon enters Columbia 7 miles west of the town of White Salmon. It is a fast stream which holds summer-run steelhead. Most of the steelheading is done either in Drano Lake at the mouth or a short way above. Fish are taken in the lake on a troll and occasionally on the fly. August is the best month.

Willapa River (Pacific County). The Willapa is followed almost its entire length by Ocean Beach Highway west from Chehalis to where it enters Willapa Bay. It holds a fine run of winter steelhead, with January and February the best months. It is fished heavily by anglers from Aberdeen and Raymond. The lower reaches may be drifted or fished from a boat.

Wind River (Skamania County). The Wind River enters the Columbia River near the town of Carson 50 miles east of Vancouver along the North Bank Highway. A road follows the river upstream to Government Springs. The Wind holds one of the best runs of summer-run steelhead

Modern Steelhead Boat

Fifteen years ago most of the members of the steelhead clan who boat-fished the rivers of the Northwest did so with licensed guides, and their boats were constructed to carry parties of three to four anglers. Within the past decade, though, private boats have almost taken over the Skagit as well as many other streams that are suited to boat-type fishing. Shown here is a modern steelhead boat, privately manufactured in Seattle to be used by two anglers. One angler handles the oars while drifting down a river. The motor is used to go back upstream. Note the anchor rope which runs through a pulley in the bow.

Most of these boats are 12 to 15 feet in length and powered with 18 to 30-horse outboards. Capable of carrying two to three anglers, they may be constructed of wood, glass, or aluminum. They are transported by car trailers that can be backed into a river where the boat may be launched with little trouble.

Most of the larger rivers have launching sites, either gravel bars or concrete slabs that have been built by the State Game Department. Streams such as the Skagit, Skykomish, Kalama, Humptulips, Sauk, and the lower Toutle are drifted daily by private boats.

Steelhead "Plunkers" on the Alert

Most winter steelheaders drift fish; that is, they cast a lure out into a run and then allow the lure to bump down along the bottom until it has reached the end of the cast. However, there is a significant number of winter fishermen who are "plunkers." A plunker is a steelheader who casts out into a deep run or pocket and with the aid of a heavy sinker hangs up his lure on the bottom and then sits down and waits for a strike.

Most plunkers use a hollow, pipe-like receptacle that is inserted into the sandy river bank to act as a rod holder. Sometimes a small bell is attached to the rod so that it will sound off when a fish hits. At the sound of the bell, the angler grasps the rod and starts playing the fish. Plunkers generally use a winged bobber as well as a gob of cluster eggs. They hook up with a heavy sinker—usually the pyramid type—at the end of the line, then attach a winged bobber by a short leader above the sinker. Just above the bobber another leader carries a gob of bait.

In the accompanying photo, a long row of plunkers stand ready at their rods on a foggy morning. Minutes before, one of the anglers had a strike; now all are alert, hoping that the fish will hit again. Note the little bells on some of the rods.

in the State of Washington. These fish enter the lower river in April and May but usually do not jump Shepherd Falls until July. They are fished for intensively in the runs below the falls up to May 1 and then after the trout season opens. Best lures are cluster eggs, crawfish tails and spoons.

When the Columbia goes down to fall level the Wind River from the falls to its backwater affords some fine fly fishing. Fish may be taken here on wet or dry fly in the fast riffles from August into September. After July, when the steelhead enter the canyon above the Falls, they may be taken on fly, bait, or spoon in the canyon as far up as the junction with Trout Creek.

This is a rugged river to fish with a fly and the pools are the best spots. A sunken fly is the most effective. When the fish are moving they may be hooked in the fast water but an angler is lucky if he can make a score of 50% in landing them in this type of water. Fly fishing extends into the month of September.

A spinner or spoon angler can do well in some of the riffles in the upper canyon. The water in the Wind is crystal clear and fish are wary and hard to hook.

These summer fish are of exceptional size. I have fished during a week's vacation in August and had my fish average 8 pounds. Very few weigh less than 6 pounds and often an angler will hook his limit of two for the day, both going over 9 pounds. The Fourth of July in 1947 I landed two summer-runs in the upper canyon that went one ounce less than 26 pounds.

Wiskah River (Grays Harbor County). The Wiskah enters Grays Harbor at Aberdeen, and is paralleled upstream by a road to the city waterworks dam. It has a good run of winter fish and good catches are made in January and February. It is fished primarily by local anglers.

Wynooche River (Grays Harbor County). The Wynooche is crossed by the highway as it enters the Chehalis just west of Montesano. From this point, a road goes up the east bank of the stream for 28 miles. It is a winter-run stream, with January and February the best months. It holds a good run of fish that are of large size, with a few going between 15 and 20 pounds.

The runs of this river are best fished by drifting and most of the fish are taken by that method. Anglers in the Grays Harbor area go here to do their drift fishing while they use the main river, the Chehalis, for plunking.

Chapter Six

STEELHEAD RIVERS OF OREGON

Lying mid-way between the northern and southern zones, Oregon has several outstanding streams that hold both winter- and summer-run fish. Some of these are already word-famous, while others are very little known except by resident coast anglers. The listing that follows will give the larger streams without attempting to describe the smaller tributaries.

Alsea River (Lincoln County). The mouth of the Alsea is at Alsea Bay near Waldport. It is accessible by county roads which go upstream from its mouth. This is a large stream with a fine run of steelhead, mostly winter fish. The fish start coming in during late November with the peak months being January and February. In the lower river much of the fishing is done casting from a boat.

Chetco River (Curry County). The Chetco is crossed by Highway 101, but much of its upper reaches are accessible only by trail. Its mouth is near Brookings in Chetco Cove. This stream gets a fair run of winter fish and a few during the late summer.

Coos River (Coos County). The mouth of the Coos is at Coos Bay, near the town of that name which is on Highway 101. It is paralleled upstream by various roads. It is a good-sized river with winter-run fish. The runs start in early winter and continue into January.

Coquille River (Coos County). The Coquille enters the ocean at Bandon and is touched here and at the town of Coquille by Highway 101. It is a large stream with winter-run fish.

Deschutes River (Wasco County). The Deschutes is crossed by Highway 30 near where the river enters the Columbia near Moody and Miller. This is one of the long, very famous trout streams of Oregon in its upper reaches. The steelhead section is near its mouth.

These are summer-run fish and come in from August through November with September and October the best months. Most of these steelhead, due to the fact that they have come a long way up the Columbia, will have a rainbow coloring, but they are prime fish.

The best section is limited, and extends only about five miles up from the mouth, with parts of it hardly fishable. However the fish are truly giants—some going more than 20 pounds. It was here that ex-Governor Griswold of Nevada took his monster 26-pounder on a fly.

There are a few cabins available about a half mile from the mouth but accommodations are limited. Although not too many fish are hooked, this is a spot for the experts to try for a trophy ironhead.

Grande Ronde River (Union County). The Grande Ronde flows out of the northeast corner of Oregon into Washington where it enters the Snake. It has winter runs of average size.

John Day River (forms border of Sherman and Gilliam Counties). The John Day is another long stream which is fished for steelhead only in the lower reaches. It enters the Columbia near the town of Goff in Gilliam County, and is crossed by Highway 30. Has an average run of late summer fish into November.

Kilchis Creek (Tillamook County). Kilchis Creek empties into Tillamook Bay north of Tillamook near Daville. It is crossed by Highway 101 and has a road going upstream to its forks. A small winter-run stream with January and February the best months.

Miami River (Tillamook County). The Miami enters north Tillamook

Bay near the town of Garibaldi, and is crossed by Highway 101, with a side road going part way upstream. Although it is a small stream it has a good run of fish with many fine pools for drift fishing.

Necanicum River (Clatsop County). The Necanicum enters the ocean near Seaside and is crossed by Highway 101. Its upper reaches are paralleled by the side roads. It is a small stream with a nice run of winter fish taken mostly on bait in the months of December to February.

Nehalem River (Tillamook County). The Nehalem enters Nehalem Bay near Wheeler. The town of Mahler lies further upstream. The river is crossed by Highway 101 near its mouth and is accessible by many side roads above this point and along its two forks. It is a good winter-run river with December to February the best months. A tributary, Rock Creek, flows into the upper river near Veronica and gets a big run of fish in February.

Nestucca River (Tillamook County). The Nestucca enters the ocean near Pacific City. It is crossed by Highway 101 and may be reached via Cloverdale and Hebo. A big river in the lower section, it offers good boat drifting from Beaver downstream, and many fish are taken by this method. A large tributary, Three Rivers, comes in near Hebo. December through February are the best months, with fish above average in size.

Nestucca River—Little (Tillamook County). The basing town for the Little Nestucca is Medea near its mouth at Nestucca Bay. It is accessible via country roads from Hebo south. This is a small stream with a fair run of steelhead and many nice holding pools.

Pistol River (Curry County). Crossed by Highway 101 near its mouth at Pistol City, the Pistol is a fair-sized stream with a fair run of fall and winter fish.

Rogue River (Curry County). The Rogue is crossed by Highway 101 near its mouth at Gold Beach, and by Highway 99 at Grants Pass. It is followed to its upper reaches by Highway 62. This is the most highly publicized steelhead stream of the Pacific Coast. It has been celebrated in tales by Zane Grey and should receive the full credit for introducing the nation to the sport of taking a steelhead on a fly.

It is a long rugged river with a long steelhead season, for these fish may be taken from July into December by following the various runs upstream. Generally speaking, the river is divided into two areas— the lower area out of Gold Beach and the upper area out of Grants Pass.

In the Gold Beach area, the first real runs enter the lower river during July and some fine fish which run from 5 up to 7 pounds are taken on flies. However, these runs depend greatly on water levels which are controlled by a dam at Trail. In early September, the so-called "half pounders" begin to arrive. These are small fish actually going from a pound to 3 or 4 pounds, and will hit only small flies—eights and tens. The fishing improves through September and October is usually quite good, but the best periods are after the first heavy fall rains when the fishing is hot after the river clears. Good accommodations are to be had at Weddeburn and Agnes, Oregon.

In the Grants Pass area, fishing usually starts in September and lasts into December, with October the best month. The best fishing will be had drifting downstream in a boat. One can make the full trip down to Gold Beach—a wild ride of 125 miles. During the late fall, this section of the river puts out some wonderful fly fishing. Later in the winter, many of the steelhead will be taken on bait or spoon.

The Rogue is a great salmon river for the sport fisherman. Off Gold Beach the chinooks come in during the spring in April and May and the fall run in September. The silvers come into the river during September.

Salmon River (Lincoln County). The Salmon enters the ocean near Cascade Head and is crossed by Highway 101 near Otis. This small river gets a heavy play and provides its best fishing in December and January.

Siletz River (Lincoln County). The mouth of the Siletz is in Siletz Bay near Kernville. It is crossed by Highway 101, and followed upstream by county roads. The lower river is too large to wade, but some fine holes may be found in the upper reaches. It gets a good run from November to February.

Sixes River (Curry County). The Sixes is crossed by Highway 101 at the town of Sixes above where it enters the ocean. A fair-sized stream, it has runs from November into the winter months.

Smith River (Douglas County). The mouth of the Smith lies near Reedsport where it is crossed by Highway 101. A county road at Gardnier follows the river upstream for about 40 miles. This large stream gets a fine run of late steelhead, with the best fishing during the fall, both on bait and fly. It is also noted as a very fine fall stream for chinooks and silver salmon.

Suislaw River (Lane County). The mouth of the Suislaw is near Florence where Highway 101 crosses it. It is followed upstream by county roads. It has a fair run of winter steelhead.

Trask River (Tillamook County). The Trask enters Tillamook Bay near where Highway 101 crosses it at the town of Tillamook. Its upper reaches are accessible by county roads. This stream is a heavy producer of winter fish through the months of December to February.

Umpqua River. The Umpqua enters the ocean at Reedsport. It is paralleled upstream by Highway 225. Side roads leading off Highway 99, which runs to Roseburg, follow the North Umpqua upstream via Glide and Steamboat. Another steelhead river famed in many a story, it is a noted fly stream for the big ironheads. As an angling friend said once, "When I think of summer-run steelhead I think of the North Umpqua."

This stream, like the Rogue River, is also divided into two main areas. The lower river up from Reedsport is considered winter water and most of the fish there are taken on bait. Runs will come in from October until May but the months of January and February are best. There are closed periods here from early March until late April. The North Umpqua from Roseburg to Steamboat is the fly water. It is a rugged tough stream to wade but not too difficult to fish for the experienced steelhead angler. However one must be able to handle a long fly; know how to cover fast deep water; and be able to keep one's feet in deep fast runs.

The fish start to appear in June and while these early runs are light, they include a good number of jack salmon that go from 10 to 20 pounds and will take the fly. The best months for steelhead are July, August and September. October at times is very good, but one cannot depend on the October fly fishing as weather is apt to put the water out of shape. These steelhead are above average size, going from 6 to 8 pounds and an occasional one over 10 pounds.

There are many good cabin camps, among which are those at Williams Creek, Canton Creek Forest Camp and, of course, Gordon's North Umpqua Lodge.

Wilson River (Tillamook County). The Wilson enters Tillamook Bay and is crossed by Highway 101 near Tillamook. It is paralleled upstream by Highway 6, and is closed above Jordan Creek. The fish caught are of average size, and from mid-December through February is the best fishing period. This stream gets a heavy play from Portland and is considered a fine bait winter river.

Yachats River (Lincoln County). The Yachats empties into the ocean near the town of Yachats, and is accessible by county roads up most of the territory drained by its three forks. It has a fair run of steelhead during November to January as well as a fine showing of sea-run cutthroats.

Yaquina River (Lincoln County). The Yaquina enters Yaquina Bay near Toledo, and is followed upstream by Highway 20. A fair run of winter fish which extends into February can be found here.

Chapter Seven

STEELHEAD RIVERS OF CALIFORNIA

What follows may not be as complete or as detailed a listing of the California rivers as has been made of the Washington and Oregon rivers; it includes, however, the most important steelhead waters of the southern section of the Northwest Pacific Coast.

Albion River. The Albion is reached via the town of Albion and is crossed by Highway 1. It is a winter-run stream with no lagoon at the mouth.

Bear River. The Bear River is reached via Ferndale and is crossed

153

by the Coast Highway. It has winter runs. There is an open lagoon but the stream may be fished offshore.

Big River. The Big River is reached via Fort Bragg. It is another of the northern rivers with winter fish and no lagoon.

Eel River. The mouth of the Eel is at Leota, and Highway 101 follows the main river and then up the South Fork. The best basing points are Fortuna, Scotia, Eureka, and Garberville. It is one of the most famous steelhead rivers of the West, especially noted for its large fish which come in after November. Steelhead of large size are taken just before Christmas and this run continues until the season closes in February.

When the river is not out of condition for the fly in late December, the large steelhead can be taken by this method. These fish run from 8 to 12 pounds; with a good sprinkling of 14- to 17-pounders and an occasional 18-pounder. Many *Field and Stream* winners have been taken from the Eel around Christmas week.

However the whole winter season is good in this river whenever it is in shape and spinners and cluster salmon eggs are the preferred lures.

Garcia River. Empties near the town of Point Arena. The Garcia is a short stream with a large lagoon that gets a winter run. Its mouth is near the town of Point Arena and it is crossed by a branch highway.

Gualala River. The Gualala is another one of the short redwood streams which is crossed by a side highway near its mouth at the town of Gualala. There is a bar and a lagoon which open after the first heavy rains.

Klamath River. The Klamath flows into the Pacific between the towns of Klamath and Requa, where it is crossed by Highway 101. The upper river is crossed by Highway 99 near Yreka. Most of the steelhead fishing with a fly is done below Copco Dam and down to Happy Camp and Weitchpec. A road parallels the river along all of these points.

Steelhead usually reach Weitchpec by the middle of August, and then progress upstream to Happy Camp by the latter part of September. Fly fishing should be good during October and November.

While the Eel River has the reputation for the biggest steelhead the Klamath is undoubtedly the premier sea-going rainbow stream of California. It puts out great numbers of fish; enjoys a long season; and it is noted as a fly river. It has miles of canyon water with beautiful riffles which may be waded efficiently by the experienced river fisherman. Most of these spots are accessible from paved roads or side forest roads.

Mattole River. The mouth of the Mattole is near the town of Petrolia. This is a short coastal stream with a bar that is not opened until the fall rains.

Novarro River. The Novarro is paralleled by Highway 28 and its mouth is near the town of Albion. There are accommodations at Novarro. It is closed by a bar but affords boat fishing. It may be fished upstream from the bank during the winter.

Noyo River. The Noyo enters the ocean near the town of Fort Bragg. Its lagoon and bar are constantly open.

Pajora Creek. Pajora Creek enters the ocean near Watsonville and is crossed by Highway No. 1.

Paper Mill Creek. Paper Mill Creek flows into Tomales Bay—a long tidal lagoon which also affords steelhead fishing. These winter fish then are taken up the creek.

Pescadero Lagoon. Pescadero Lagoon lies about fifty miles down the Peninsula. It is quite a large lagoon and steelhead are caught there on fly, spinners, and salmon eggs.

Redwood Creek. Redwood Creek is crossed by Highway 101 near its mouth at Orick. This is a good-sized stream heading north which has a good run of winter fish ranging up to those of large size.

Russian River. The mouth of Russian River is near the town of Jenner-by-the-Sea and its upper reaches above Healdsburg are paralleled by Highway 101. It is a large stream blocked by a lagoon which has a good steelhead run. It has a winter run of steelhead which are fished for intensively by anglers from the bay region.

Salinas River. The mouth of the Salinas is in Monterey Bay near Castorville. It is one of the streams with a bar that remains closed until after the fall rains.

Salmon Creek. Salmon Creek joins the ocean just north of Bodega Bay. It has a run of winter fish which enter the large lagoon but cannot get over the bar until after a heavy rain. Fish may be taken on fly and bait.

San Gregorio River. Enters the ocean south of San Francisco. It has a large lagoon but its bar will not open until after a heavy rain.

Santa Clara River. The Santa Clara enters the ocean south of Ventura. Fish are taken in the lagoon during the winter after the heavy rains. Some of the fish run to large size.

Santa Lorenzo River. The Santa Lorenzo enters the ocean through the city of Santa Cruz. It has a large lagoon with a bar that does not close. Its winter run is best in January and February both in the lagoon and in the stream itself.

Santa Ynez River. The Santa Ynez enters the ocean near Surf, and is crossed by highway 101 near Buellton, as well as by a highway that follows down to the lagoon. It has a good run of fish which are taken in January and February along thirty miles of the stream.

Smith River. The Smith is a short stream which enters the ocean near the village of Smith River. This is the most northern of California's streams, lying only about eight miles below the Oregon border. It has a late fall and winter run of good fish which are taken mostly on bait in the lagoon and in the lower river.

Trinity River. The Trinity is a large tributary of the Klamath, which enters its parent river near Weitchpec. The basing point for the upper Trinity is the town of Weaverville. The river may be fished above and below this point. From Willow Creek the highway follows down the lower river until it joins the Klamath. Although the Trinity is discolored from mining operations during the summer it clears after August. From then until October this stream puts out fine fly and bait fishing for average-size fish.

Chapter Eight

THE SEA-RUN CUTTHROAT AS A SPORT FISH

Like the rainbows of the West Coast which go to sea and develop into steelhead, the cutthroats of the coastal streams also make an ocean migration. Those that do are called sea-runs. Rainbows are the other fresh water game fish which make this migration.

Both the rainbows and cutthroat are native trout which have become ocean rovers due to their presence in anadromous rivers. As a consequence of their trips to the ocean, both attain a much greater growth than their landlocked brothers. This is, of course, due to the larger quantities of food available in the salt chuck. Both the steelhead and the sea-run afford a unique type of sport found only in the coastal rivers of the West.

Although the coastal cutthroat is not as completely addicted to salt water journeys as the steelhead, most of his kind do migrate from time to time. Some will remain resident in rivers for long periods but usually they drift out to sea when they reach a size that requires them to find more food than their river affords. A few of them do get up into the small tributaries and from thence into old abandoned mill ponds or creeks dotted with beaver ponds. Here food is often fairly plentiful and the trout may remain resident for a year or two before going back to the sea.

But in most of the coastal streams, food and resting spots, especially within recent years, have become scarce. When the watersheds of the Pacific waterways were clothed in heavy timber, moisture was held in the forests, and streams had a gradually tapered run-off. But due to the intensive logging of the past fifteen years, rivers flood easily now, and their beds tend to become straight channels that provide neither resting pools for fish nor quiet spots for water-borne insects to hatch. The lower reaches of many rivers spread out into wide rock-strewn beds over which the waters rush with great force during flood periods.

As a consequence food is scarce in these tumbling rivers of the Pacific slope. Moreover in virtually all of the Northwest streams the young of at least two species of salmon—the silvers and the chinooks—share the available food supply with the migratory trout. The young chinooks migrate at a few months of age but the silvers remain for a year or more and they compete directly with the trout for their daily diet.

Then, usually in late spring and through the summer, the millions of young chinooks, silvers, cutthroats and steelhead are crowding down the rivers together in their common irresistible urge to reach the sea. Some of these will be four to seven inches in length while others will be only "flippers" or fish two to four inches long. With the opening of the river season in Washington coming late in May, a large percentage of the downstream migrants will fortunately have reached salt water. But there is a steady movement in the coastal rivers toward the sea all summer long, and many immature fish are caught by anglers. The greater proportion of the fish caught will be so injured that they cannot be released unharmed.

For this reason there is a considerable loss of these small migrants every trout season. In many rivers they constitute almost the entire trout population and anglers cannot hope to take many "keepers" unless they fish for the trout when they are on their return trip—back from the ocean. Considering the fact that a 6-inch steelhead can return after one year in the sea as a 3-pound steelhead, that a fingerling cutthroat may come back as a pound and a half sea-run, and that a silver salmon in four years may return as a leaping 6- to 20-pound cohoe, it is certainly a needless waste to catch these young migrants before they have matured.

The cutthroat of the West, the best-liked native trout to the old timer, is a friendly sort of fish. It does well in little creeks, beaver ponds, mountain lakes, and rushing rivers. It occurs in various forms all through the Northwest. The Montana black-spot, the Yellowstone Trout, and the Crescenti of Lake Crescent are all cousins of the Pacific sea-runs.

The coloring of this trout varies greatly depending on its environment. The native "cut" is usually heavily covered with black spots which taper into smaller sizes as they disappear into the white of the belly. The back is dark green with an olive undertint. The underside ranges from creamy white to yellow. At times a small yellow spot the size of a pea may appear on the belly. The ventral fins may be rose-pink, green, or yellow.

Other cutthroats may be dark, almost black, when they have been resident in dark boggy ponds. Still others will be very light, their whole bodies having a yellow cast. Sometimes they will be all gleaming silver like the trout in Pass Lake. But there is always that distinguishing mark, the red slash on either side of the head below the jaw; the blood-like mark which gives the trout its name.

When this trout makes the decision to take to the sea, it enters on the different color phase that denotes the sea-run. For then it assumes a radically different dress. By the time it comes back to fresh water it has lost its color and, like a steelhead, has become all bright silver. The spots are hardly distinguishable, and there is a very evident median line discernible. The red-slashed throat mark has become dim and at times has almost disappeared.

Although the cutthroat wanders out to the salt chuck when just a "little cuss" it saunters back a heavy solid trout 12 inches up to 4 pounds in size, full of vim and vigor. It has meandered along the shore line, never far from the mouth of a river, seldom losing all touch with the fresh water it calls its home swimming grounds. Unlike the salmon or steelhead the cutthroat does not journey to distant waters or seek the depth of the ocean. It is content to remain in its river estuary, waxing fat on crustaceans and other foods so bountifully available at the salt water table. It seldom reaches the size of a steelhead or salmon. A 2-pounder is a good specimen and those weighing more than 4 pounds are exceptional.

Cutthroat are beautiful trout, streamlined in conformation and having solid hard meat that never turns soft and is usually pink or red in color. When fresh run out of the ocean, the scales are often loose and tend to slough off on the hands when the hook is being removed.

With the State of Washington having over eight hundred named streams and with equally numerous other watercourses scattered from

British Columbia to the High Sierras, trout fishing conditions in the Northwest will, of necessity, be too complex to be encompassed by uniform season dates. In fact, although the various game departments continue to open trout seasons by the calendar, there are other opening dates over which a game commission has no control. These opening dates, scattered throughout the year, are controlled by the trout themselves, with man having very little to say in the matter. These opening dates occur when the various anadromous fish come into streams on their annual migrations. They institute their own seasons, and if an angler can travel up and down the coast he will encounter a series of staggered fishing dates that will run from spring until late fall.

Taking Sea-runs in the Salt Chuck

During the spring and early summer, usually from April until July, sea-going cutthroats tend to gang up along the gravel beaches near the rivers or creeks that they will ascend in a couple of months. At such times, in contrast to the steelhead which are caught rarely in salt water, the sea-runs may be taken readily by sports anglers.

Back in the 1930's there were many fishermen with an expert knowledge of the good beaches who made excellent catches of these scrappy trout on a troll. But this type of fishing has fallen off greatly, perhaps because of the very human desire to "catch a big salmon" when trolling the salt chuck. These old-timers trolled a jigger spoon—a number 1 or 0 F.S.T.—offshore in water 4 to 15 feet deep. They used fly rods, a buckshot or two for sinkers and throttled the outboard down. When they located a school they usually had fast action. The shores off the Tualip Indian Reservation north of Everett is one location where this type of fishing is still practiced every April and May.

These sea trout may also be taken on a fly at the right beaches when they are feeding near shore. The best spots are usually near the mouth of a slough or river where a gravel beach slants down to a firm bottom. Priest Point near the mouth of the Snohomish River is a good example.

The best catches are generally made during the period starting an hour before low slack until an hour or two after the tide has turned. When this period occurs in the early morning or at dusk, so much the better. The trout feed in the shallow water as the tide turns or they may follow the tide in to feed on insects or bits of food washed off the beach.

You should use a single wet fly on a 7- to 9-foot leader. Cast it well out into the tide, allow it to sink and then strip in slowly. If a feeding trout is rising try to anticipate the direction it is traveling and cast to it. If you are casting "blind," cover the water in a quarter circle to your right and then to your left. These are traveling trout and you can profitably cover the same water repeatedly.

Any of the Northwest hair or streamer type of flies will prove to be takers—with royal coachman, yellow hammer or shrimp popular patterns. Combinations of red, orange or yellow bodies with white or reddish hair wings seem to be enticing. The "cuts" will usually fight under the surface in short sharp runs but at times they will come out of the water in clean leaps like a rainbow.

Fall Migrations. Although, like all of the migratory trout, sea-runs may be found in some of the coastal rivers nearly every month of the year, early fall is considered the best period for the sport fisherman. At this time, when the trout are making their spawning migration, they are most readily available to the angler, for they tend to school up in the lower rivers before they scatter out in the upper reaches.

In the heavily fished rivers of the coast which hold few resident trout these salt water migrants provide the main sport for the angler. Rivers paralleled by main highways are pounded so heavily that even the baby 6-inchers become frightened to death, and after the first few weeks of the season there is little left to catch. But after the hay and oat fields become fragrant and brown, and an early seasonal rain has raised the rivers a bit, then the cutthroat addict gets busy. He knows that harvest time brings in these sea trout, which are actually known as harvest trout down around the Columbia River area. He remembers a sweet mile of water on his sea-run stream that even the tin-can tourists have deserted, claiming it had been completely fished out. But the "cut" expert knows better. He is aware that these harvest trout are not disturbed by the clamor of civilization. They don't live here—they are just passing through—and farm buildings, cabin camps, or even small towns mean nothing to them. They will stop a while in resting pools or in the snag holes wherever they find them—the majority seeming in no great rush to get upstream.

Drifting the Lower "Stilly." So not being able to resist the pull of autumn any longer, Charley King and I make our first drift of the season down the lower Stillaguamish. We load the light boat onto the trailer and launch it into the stream at the gravel pit below Arlington. The balance of our party drive the car down to Silvana to pick us up there after they have fished the river down to tidewater.

It is a week-day and heavily overcast and we hope that the stream will be fairly free of other anglers. Charley is using a light 9-foot rod and I a two-piece 8-footer, both rods having good backbone but light flexible tips. We have double-tapered lines with about 75 yards of backing on the reels.

Backing isn't really necessary for the sea-runs but one never knows what will rise to a fly in the "Stilly" at this time of the year. I recall once when I was drifting the river alone in a rubber boat, I had taken a nice cutthroat and was covering the water along a rock revetment. The fly had sunk well and, as I stripped in slowly, there was a strong strike and I was fast to a salmon. It ran down the whole length of the steep bank and was into the backing immediately. I pushed over the anchor to keep from drifting into a brushy snag. My leader was tapered to 1x and 1 had my hands full trying to control the salmon softly and keep it away from a sunken stump. Finally it tired and stopped taking out line. The boat, however, was so buoyant that with the light leader I could not put on sufficient pressure to bring the salmon close enough to be landed. So taking a chance I rested the rod in the boat with the reel free, hurriedly pulled up the anchor, rowed into shallow water, shoved over the anchor, jumped out, and then was able to beach a nice bright 6-pound cohoe. Without backing, I would never have held the fish on its first run.

As is customary with most of the sea-run anglers, we are using tapered 9-foot leaders down to 2x and 1x, and number 6 flies. I win the toss and stand up in the stern of the boat ready to cast my Conway Special. Charley is at the oars and allows the boat to drift backwards slowly downstream. In this manner both of us can clearly look over the run, and the rower can carefully back the boat up to a good casting position for any desired piece of water.

We pass up without a single cast the fast riffle below our launching spot. This is a beautiful rainbow riffle but it isn't cutthroat water. For some unknown reason the harvest trout do not school up in the fast current. They seem to prefer the slower-moving water that has both shelter and cover. A rainbow or steelhead utilizes turbulent water with a broken surface for cover. A cutthroat, by contrast, lies in the quiet water and seeks the aid of brush, snags, or rocks for camouflage.

Just below this riffle the river swings against one bank in a slow run where willows hang well out over fairly deep water. This is an ideal sea-run spot but hard to cover. Charley holds the boat about 30 feet from the bank and I with a horizontal cast flip the fly under the overhanging brush, so that it lights almost on the bank. No trout will rise to a fly that drops like a handful of shot, so the Conway must be dropped gently.

I allow it to sink slightly and then twitch it in with slow even jerks. Nothing happens; again I slip the fly under the brush and begin the retrieve. There is a flash but I do not feel a touch.

"I teased one out," I say, "now watch me connect this time—I hope."

I flip in once more, allowing the fly to rest a bit longer before slowly pulling it out along the same pathway. This time I am ready and set the hook at the same instant as the rise, and my rod tip bends in a full arc.

Charley backs the boat out from the bank so that I can fight the trout well away from the lie hole. It is a strong fighter, taking out line, twisting downstream for a snag and once jumping into the air. But finally a prime 15-inch sea-run, as shiny as a new silver dollar, is brought to net.

"You have one more to catch before it is my turn," remarks Charley, as he quietly rows me back into position.

"That will only need a cast or two," I reply confidently, "I got 'em located now."

My first cast is right back in the groove but it produces nothing. Then I become over-eager, raise my back cast, and hook my fly into a willow branch.

"Aw hell," I mutter in disgust, "row me over so that I can get my fly."

"No you don't, "yells Charley, "You don't get by with that. You know the rule—when you hang up—you gotta' take the oars, and this looks like a real good spot for me. So bust off your fly, I don't want the hole disturbed."

After a short bit of grousing, mainly to keep up appearances for I know that I have already lost the argument, I get on the oars and put Charley into position. And with great care he puts his fly under the brush and in short order hooks and lands two cutthroats, both over a foot long. Then the hole goes dead. We row over to the bank, secure my brush-hooked fly and drift downstream.

Sea-run Water. Anglers who have drifted a stream such as the Stillaguamish for many seasons learn how to know the good waters. They remember stumps and deadheads near a bank that never seem to get washed out and that always shelter trout when the run is on. They know the deep hole under the highway bridge where sea-runs hide in the shade of the heavy timber piling. They recognize the spot where a fallen tree anchored on the bank extends over the stream to form a resting spot for the harvest trout. And although the majority of these migrant trout are coming up the river for the first time, they never fail to stop in the same old familiar lie holes. These spots are like waiting rooms in a railway station: the travelers are always changing but they always sit down and wait in the same old seats.

Such a typical "waiting room" is a small area around a sunken deadhead out in a flat in the main "Stilly," where the water is about three feet deep. It looks like dead water and a stranger wouldn't waste any time on it. But through experience I know that the cutthroat find it to their liking. In season there should always be trout resting there. And they are always big ones. Little trout cannot seem to hold such a favored lie spot.

So whenever I reach this spot I start floating the fly down well upstream from the dead head. Caution is necessary as the trout will be frightened easily in the low clear water, and, if the spot has not been disturbed for a day or so, I know my chances of taking a fish are excellent. As the fly swings gently down along the near side of the log, I see a wake like a submarine's following it. There is a swirl near the surface and I have set into the trout. It runs in short savage jerks; tries to get back under the log; but with the right pressure I keep it clear. Then under the tension it comes up into the air and makes a fast dash out into the current. I follow it down the bar, allowing it to fight out its energy in the fast water below. I finally pull out onto the gravel a 2-pound sea-run, fat and firm, as beautiful a wild trout as one can take these days anywhere in heavily fished water.

"Harvest" trout also like the deep, quiet pools, the bottoms of which are littered with rocks—not gravel—but rocks ranging from man-size to room-size. Such bottoms provide hiding places galore and cutthroats often rest here for long periods.

Where the Wind River flows into the backwater from the Columbia River, much of the upper section of this water is of that character. During the month of September, the harvest trout will come into the head of the pool, and lie there just below the rapids. When the sun leaves the water one can get out onto its quiet surface and successfully entice the cutthroats into hitting. These fish average two pounds and go readily for a wet fly.

A "Hot" Day on the Wind. Under certain conditions, cutthroats, steelhead and salmon may all occupy the identical section of a stream at the same time. When they do, the sport is superlative and of the nerve-shattering variety. One September day Frank Headrick and I hit this ideal condition in a stretch of the Wind River.

We had gone down to the Wind for a week of steelheading around Labor Day in 1945. While we were there, a sudden severe rainstorm put the river out of shape and stopped our fly fishing at the point we had selected. However the next morning we visited the mouth of the Wind and found to our delight that the stream at this point was dropping and was clear enough for a fly.

We started covering the lower section of the riffle and Frank almost at once was tied onto a fish that danced all over the flat and finally broke off around a sharp rock. Then, just at the head of the flat pool, I had a savage strike and found myself fighting a leaping steelhead gone beserk that came out of the water like a jumping jack. It was absolutely fresh-run and its silver sides shone like molten aluminum in the rays of the rising sun. Exceedingly active for its size—it went only about 6 pounds—it pranced from one end of the pool to the other before I was able to bring it into the shallows and release it.

I then went back to the foot of the riffle, cast to the opposite bank and allowed the fly to drift across the pool until it was directly below me.

I stripped it in slowly, and, in no time at all—or so it seemed—I had another strike. This fish hit solidly, but without the electrifying jolt of a steelhead, and then made a long straight run. The "feel" of the fish indicated it was a salmon and after a prolonged tug-of-war I brought to beach a jack chinook weighing about 10 pounds.

Directly after that, Frank hooked another jack that took off in a screeching run that melted line off his reel so fast he had to get out of the river and follow his salmon down the river at a dead run before he could control it and then bring it into the bar to be landed.

Then I had another steelhead on that I handled too roughly, and it broke loose. I kept right on casting in the same spot and later, when I was stripping in slowly, there was another hit. This time the fight took the form of a series of swift jabs and short runs. With a 9/5 tippet I could control the trout, and I brought in a shiny sea-run that would easily have tipped the scales over the 2-pound mark if I hadn't released it.

And so it went for most of the day. We never knew after a cast whether we would just drift along without a hit or whether we would sock into a chinook or a trout.

When we finally quit in the mid-afternoon, I had killed only one steelhead and a cutthroat and had given two salmon to non-fishing campers who were an appreciative audience. But a careful recounting showed that I had in the course of the day hung onto six steelhead going 5 to 8½ pounds, four jack chinooks weighing 6 to 12 pounds, and three cutthroats averaging 2 pounds each.

Still more amazing, as I took down my rod I realized the same fly was still on the end of the leader that I had bent on that morning. It was a Brad's Brat dressed on a heavy number 3 hook with chenille body and had had rather bushy bucktail wings. But now it was a bedraggled specimen, with the body and a few shreds of hackle remaining but with virtually every shred of deer hair broken off. To hang onto so many large fish on one fly without losing it was a record for me. I still have the chewed-up fly and have not broken the record.

Frank had done about as well as far as the fish were concerned, although he had used a number of different flies.

Fly Patterns for Sea-run Cutthroats. One marked difference between sea-runs and the other river migrants of the Pacific coast—the steelhead and salmon—is that the cutthroats are feeding fish. After ascending a stream the steelhead feed but seldom until after they have spawned, when they eat in order to build up their depleted strength. The salmon, according to the experts, never eat.

But the cutthroats feed the same as any other trout. They take insects, small trout fry and whatever food may be washed down to them by the current. Consequently, any good trout fly will interest them when they are in a hitting mood. At times they will be lying close to the surface and will rise to a floating fly. At such times a small gray hackle, a black gnat, or a flying ant when the hatch is on will be taking patterns.

It is wonderful sport when you hit a piece of water where the cutthroats have moved in and you find them taking a dry fly. They are rugged trout and although they do not possess the fire and jumping technique of a rainbow they are determined fighters. They have the stamina and tenacity of a bulldog rather than the dash of a greyhound.

Most of the coastal anglers use "attractor" patterns to take these trout. These are usually patterns dressed in the same combinations of yellow, white, red or orange that are effective on steelhead. Although this is only theorizing on my part, I believe that these attractor flies are "takers" for two reasons. First, they are readily seen in the turbulent rivers of the coast, the waters of which are often foam-flecked and bubble-filled. They display a flash of color that can be seen at some distance even if the water is cloudy from snow water or murky after a rain. These trout are interested in big morsels of food and these flies look like something.

Second, to the large cutthroats or to steelhead a small fry or minnow is a tempting morsel—especially when it is twisting and turning as if crippled. These attractor flies, usually dressed with wool or chenille supplemented with bucktail or polar bear, should resemble such a fry. According to Preston Jenning's theory of refracted light, these color combinations under the surface of the water look like the flash of a struggling minnow. It is only natural therefore for a sea-run to rise and investigate such a prize.

This may be one of the reasons that the Conway Special is such an effective pattern; or the Yellow Hammer, from which the Conway was adapted, dressed with bucktail for wings. The royal or California coachmen, with either hair or feather wings, are also good patterns.

In Washington, a type of fly called "shammy-tail" is a taker on harvest trout. The distinguishing feature of this pattern is a tail $\frac{1}{8}$ to $\frac{1}{4}$ of an inch long made from a narrow strip of chamois. This chamois has an enticing action in the water. It may be used on any of the bright-colored flies. A Shammy Royal, a coachman dressed with black chenille instead of peacock herl, has been a favorite pattern. Another is the Shammy Bee made with red or yellow chenille body. Both have white bucktail wings.

Other flies that appeal to cutthroats are some of the British Columbian patterns. The best known of these "cut" dressings are Nation's Fancy, Black O'Lindsay, Teal and Red, or Haig-Brown's Brown and Silver. Then, too, many of the steelhead patterns dressed lightly on size 6 or 7 hooks are effective.

In many of the rivers, such as the Skagit, that carry runs of cutthroats, there may also be large runs of humpbacked salmon in the odd years. These young "humpys" go back to salt water as fry one to three inches long. Often there will be a downriver movement of sea-runs on their return journey to the ocean that coincides with the humpy fry migration. This is usually in late spring when "cuts" are through spawning and they follow down with the salmon fry feeding on them. At such times the minnow fly, a simple pattern of tinsel and peacock herl, will be a killer. Earlier in the winter these same sea-runs may be found resting in the pools of the river or in the many slow-moving sloughs where they can be taken on the regulation cutthroat patterns.

Spinner and Bait. Next to a fly, perhaps one of the most effective lures for these trout will be a small spinner. Any spinner the size of a dime that may be worked with a fly rod will do. It should be stripped through the water in which the cutthroats are supposedly lying with as little disturbance to the water as possible. This spinner technique works well also when used in the faster water where the sea-runs are moving either upstream or downstream.

Bait may be used on the sea-runs and when they are schooled up in a deep pool it is an effective method of taking them. The experienced angler with a single egg or angleworms should take trout when they can be located in such spots.

Feeding Migrations. Although the greater bulk of the upriver migration of cutthroats occurs because of the spawning urge, these trout may enter a stream during the early summer for a feeding journey. Entrance for this purpose is usually confined to the lower section of the waterway. Rivers such as the Skokomish, which flows into Hood Canal, will hold fresh-run cutthroats during the tag end of the steelhead season and this run will hold over into early summer. It is entirely possible that these trout wander up or back the lower "Skok" from tidewater to the forks any time from spring until low water in mid-summer. Similar feeding excursions undoubtedly occur in the lower sections of most of the Olympic rivers that flow directly into the ocean.

The lower Quinault is famous for its cutthroat fishing but as it is entirely on an Indian reservation one must fish here under reservation regulations. However the Quinault Indians will take fishing parties either up or down the stream in their large dugouts powered with outboard motors. It is a thrilling trip both for the fishing and for the boat ride through the rapids.

Most of the coastal rivers in British Columbia have good runs of cutthroats. Those on Vancouver Island, for example, are particularly adapted to sea-runs and present virtually untrammeled fishing opportunities for the angler who likes to try out-of-the-way spots. The "cuts" in these waters grow larger than those in the States—some even attaining 12 pounds in weight.

The principal upriver journey of these sea trout is, of course, the trip to the spawning grounds during the period from July to early winter. This often coincides with a salmon run and when this happens the trout have a food item added to their bill of fare—fresh salmon eggs. But the old legend that cutthroats and Dolly Vardens, which are to be found in most coastal streams, have depleted the runs of salmon through feeding on their spawn will hardly bear up under investigation. These species of fish have existed together without one destroying the other ever since such fish have been coming into fresh water from the sea.

Sea-runs do eat salmon eggs but not to the detriment of a run. A large portion of the eggs devoured by the trout are either infertile ones floating free or others washed out of the spawning redds to roll downstream. These may often be found when an exceedingly large run of salmon piles into one section of a river at the same period. Good gravel bars suitable for spawning may be limited in area, and the anxious female salmon may be forced to use the same spots of gravel repeatedly. Under this condition eggs previously buried may be dug out to drift down with the current.

I have observed the upper Stillaguamish on an odd year when the river was filled almost from bank to bank by spawning "humpies." From a bridge over a shallow gravel bar one could see the sleek female humpback salmon digging their spawning beds. The bar was small and had undoubtedly been used already a number of times for the same purpose by earlier arrivals. On a shallow flat below the spawning redd was a sheet of red caused by a thin layer of eggs that had been pushed out of the gravel above. In the fan of the pool below the bar was a school of fat, husky sea-run cutthroats ranging up to 16 inches in size. They were lazily fanning their fins in the shadow of a huge rock just out of the current. As a pair of overzealous salmon dug hurriedly into the gravel, a thin trickle of eggs floated down into the pool. And as they sank into its depths several of the trout would lazily separate from the school and, with a sudden dart, pick up an egg. They were obviously not harming the spawning operation, but were simply getting an added tidbit for dinner.

The Dolly Varden as a Sport Fish

The third migratory trout of the Northwest, which only within recent years in Washington has graduated to the status of a game fish, is the Dolly Varden.

This remarkably handsome member of the char family, the western cousin of the eastern brook trout, has been largely neglected by the

Northwest angler. It is rather difficult to determine exactly why this has been the case. While it may not possess the acrobatic ability of a rainbow, or the dashing abandon of a brookie, it is a sporty fish to take on light tackle. Caught in cold waters it is a fine table fish. It often grows to large

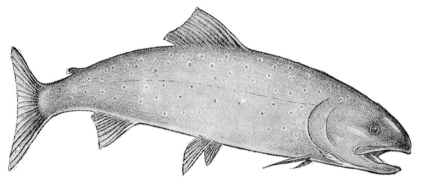

Dolly Varden Trout

size in rivers and usually does in the larger lakes. These characteristics should be sufficient to make it a popular member of the game-fish tribe.

Wherever the Dolly is found in our coastal streams, particularly from the Columbia north to Alaska, it will navigate into salt water. However, like the sea-run cutthroat, its ocean journeying is not carried too far away from its home estuary. It tends to lose some of its brilliant spots after a sojourn in the salt chuck, and will come back to fresh water with the same silver body tints possessed by all of the Pacific coastal migrants.

In the larger lakes of Washington and British Columbia, Dolly Vardens are likely to be found as resident trout. When the lakes are of sufficient size to provide a rich supply of food these "Dollys" may grow to enormous size. Six-pounders will be common; others go up to 10 pounds; and lunkers of 20 pounds or more are taken each year. Lake Chelan in Washington and many of the British Columbian lakes produce this char in the larger sizes.

The Dolly Varden is usually taken on bait—salmon roe, or on a trolled spoon. In a lake it will tend to hit the bait of a still fisherman or strike the flashy turning of a spoon dragged over the shallow sections. But these "Dollys" will also take the fly. In lakes they will strike a wet fly readily when it is worked across the mouth of a tributary creek or stream. Or a fly cast out over a drop-off along the shore and allowed to sink and then stripped in will often take good-sized fish.

In rivers, Dollys are often taken on steelhead tackle baited with salmon eggs or a spoon during the winter season. In the Skagit, steelheaders often take fish from 4 up to 7 pounds while they are drifting for the steelhead—

particularly in the upper river. Many are also caught in this manner in the ocean streams of the Olympic Peninsula.

When casting a fly for steelhead during the summer in certain rivers the angler may hang onto a Dolly. I recall one August when I was trying to locate summer-run steelhead in the upper reaches of the Sauk near Bedells. I had been covering a fast riffle, when I had an unusually heavy strike. And I had fought the fish for five minutes before I discovered it was not a steelhead. It was only after 15 minutes that I was able to beach the prime 6-pound Dolly that had hit my bucktail.

I have often taken Dollys on the fly during the summer in the north fork of the Skykomish River above Index. Those only going two to four pounds put up a good fight in the fast water on a fly and a 9-foot rod. So don't sell the Dolly short; he's a sporty fellow on the right tackle in the proper waters.

PART THREE

Chapter One

PACIFIC SALMON: THEIR CHARACTER-
ISTICS AND SPECIES

The Pacific Salmon is without question one of the most widely known fish in these United States. It reposes in cans on the shelves of grocery stores all over this country, and is a prized delicacy in many foreign countries. During the first world war it was such a common part of the soldier's diet that it was disparagingly referred to as "goldfish." It is the raw material for one of the leading industries of the Northwest and is a leading factor in the economy of West Coast residents from Oregon to Bristol Bay in Alaska.

As a sport fish, the salmon is highly valued by the anglers of the Pacific Coast, and it is in this role that he is most important to the readers of this book.

In the spring, every trout angler catches large numbers of "silvers" along with the rainbows, but few know the difference. But the fact is that the family pan fish of the Puget Sound country, the silver trout that is caught by the hundreds of thousands in lakes, is simply a land-locked sockeye salmon.

From August through December river anglers witness the surging miracle of the spawning migration. Riffles up in the hills far from the sea, at the appointed time, will be occupied by monster fish, wiggling their huge bulk through the shallows—their backs often out of water. Deep pools are filled by tier after tier of hefty "kings," by active silvers, by odd year "humpys," by calico-colored "dogs" in late fall, and, in a few watersheds, by red-orange "sockeyes."

When wading across the fan of a riffle in the fall, an angler is apt to disturb the chinooks resting there, so that they wallow from under his feet like huge pigs, spattering water in every direction. Or he can sit on the bank along a quiet pool and watch the salmon roll to the surface or rise to swing their dorsal fins and huge tails out of the water.

The winter steelheader sees the salmon during the unpleasant part of their spawning cycle. For during that time their dead carcasses litter the shallows and, following a drop in water levels, are to be found up on the bank in the roots of brush or behind logs. Partially decomposed, the odor of these bodies is sometimes so strong as to partly gag the newcomer whose olfactory nerves are unaccustomed to it. Some rivers, due to their type of watershed, become so filled with dead salmon each fall that they have been named accordingly. For example, the Hama Hama, which flows into Hood Canal on the Olympic Peninsula, is Chinook for "stinky-stinky."

But out in the salt water the salmon is a creature of beauty—a fish whose symmetry is a design for power. When bright and virile after feeding on the ocean's bounty it cannot be surpassed for fighting qualities when taken on the proper tackle.

Toward the end of their life cycle, when salmon are approaching their parent river, they tend to become very active. When in the estuary, they will often come leaping out of the water for no apparent reason. They are not feeding, and old-timers watching then say, "they are jumping to loosen their eggs," or "they are trying to get rid of the sea lice," or "they are just playing and won't hit any lure right now." Silvers are inclined to be particularly active and often dozens of them may be seen in the air at once.

The life cycle of the Pacific salmon should by now be fairly well known to most anglers. They are spawned in a river that permits a journey into or out of salt water. After leaving the river and remaining a period of time in the ocean, they always return to the parent river in which they were born to perform their own spawning function and then to die. Salmon have been marked and released in a river and except for an occasional stray the same fish always seem to return to their home stream.

After spawning, all Pacific salmon die. They do not feed after entering a river as their gullets and stomach have shrunk at this time to the point where they could not digest food even if they should swallow it. When salmon school up in a bay or river estuary waiting for a rise in water to draw them up the river, they have usually stopped feeding. These are the salmon which anglers call "spawners." Salmon which are not yet ready to make their spawning run are known as "feeders."

Young salmon spend the first few months of their lives in a river and then start downstream for the ocean. The age at which they migrate depends on the species and there is much fluctuation in age between species. Their whole life cycle varies from two years for a humpback salmon to seven years in the case of a certain race of Chinook. Although the ocean wanderings of each species is charted to some extent, with the greatest volume of information available on the chinook, there are still many blank pages in the story of the migratory journeys of each variety.

The Five Species of Pacific Salmon. Of the five species of salmon—the chinook, silver, humpback, dog, and sockeye—only the first two are commonly taken by sportsmen. These two hit lures readily and form well over three-fourths of the total catch; while the other three species are taken from time to time, they will rise to a lure only under certain conditions. "Humpys" will take lures and, when they are running, are occasionally caught by trollers and spinners but not in great numbers. The dog salmon will hit a troll or hang onto a cut spinner but they come into rivers so late in the fall that comparatively few are caught by sportsmen. The sockeye, which at one time were erroneously said not to hit any kind of lure, are nevertheless seldom sought by sportsmen.

An experienced commercial fisherman can tell at a glance to what species a salmon belongs. But to many sportsmen, particularly those new to salt water, all salmon will look more or less alike. The young immature fish, locally dubbed "salmon trout," are puzzling to nearly everyone. And when it happens that a steelhead or sea-run cutthroat is taken along with the young salmon in salt water, the difficulty of distinguishing one from the other is very great.

Positively identifying a fish without having the actual specimen to examine is always difficult. But there are various characteristics peculiar to each species that can be detailed by description or in an illustration.

In the first place anglers should remember that salmon are caught in three phases of their life cycle: first, when salmon first come into salt water and during much of the following year when they may grow up to 18-inches in length, all five species look pretty much alike. The only sure way of identification when they are small is to make a count of the rays in the anal fin or the number of scales along the median line. Second, when the salmon are partly grown, which is from their second to third year (except for humpys), they are nearly all fat, prime, chunky, silvery-colored fish. Third, just before they enter their spawning rivers, when they tend to darken up and the male of most species develop a hooknose.

In general all salmon have three characteristics in which they differ from trout. First, their tails are forked, deeply for "dogs" and slightly less for the other species, while steelhead and cutthroats tend to have "square tails"—that is, their tails run in a straight or gently curved line across the base. Second, with all Pacific salmon, the anal fin, the one under the belly nearest the tail, joins the body at an oblique angle. With a steelhead or cutthroat the same fin adjoins the belly at almost a right angle. Third, all of the salmon differ from trout or char by having thirteen or more rays in their anal fins, while the trout have 12 or less. In counting these rays separate them with the point of a pin or sharp object. Count only the fully developed rays: those at least 2/3 as long as the largest ones.

King Salmon (oncorhynchus tschawytscha). The king salmon is variously known as king, chinook, tyee, spring, or tule. It is the largest of the Pacific salmon, ranging in size from 10 to 60 pounds in Puget Sound. The largest specimen on record weighed 125 pounds and was taken in a trap near Petersburg, Alaska.

Kings usually start their downriver migration at three or four months of age, although they may remain in rivers for a year. Their life cycle is generally four years, although it may extend to five and occasionally to seven.

The body of the king is deep and powerful, with a small head, the back a deep olive green color and the belly silvery. There are many large black spots along the back, on the dorsal fin and on both lobes of the tail. The color of the flesh ranges from "salmon" pink to orange red, although the meat of a few kings is white. These white kings bring a lower price for canning but are just as tasty when fried as steaks.

The anal ray count is 15 to 19, commonly 16. The scale count in the lateral line averages 146.

Silver Salmon (oncorhynchus kisutch). The silver or cohoe resembles the king, although the body is not so deep. Its color is a very bright silver with only a few spots along its dark green back and occasionally a few at the base of the tail.

The silver ranges in weight from 4 to 20 pounds. A 25-pound fish is extremely large. They usually remain in rivers for at least a year and their life cycle is three years.

Most large male silvers are called "hooknose," due to the shape of their

King Salmon (above) and Silver Salmon (below)

nose, but this is to some extent a characteristic of all male salmon. The flesh is medium red, although less vivid than that of the sockeyes.

The anal ray count is 13 to 16 commonly 14. The scale count averages 127 in the lateral line.

Humpback Salmon (oncorhynchus gorbuscha). The "humpy" or "pink" salmon, although spawning every year in Alaskan waters, runs only on the odd years in Puget Sound. Its head is small and sharp and its tail relatively large. Its back is a light olive green and it is rather heavily spotted on the tail and along the back. The spots are oval rather than round. The scales are very small and numerous, and the skin feels smooth like that of a Dolly Varden rather than rough like that on a king.

The flesh is pink and delicate in flavor.

The male develops a decided hump on its back before spawning, although the female remains comparatively streamlined.

The young fish leave fresh water at about two months of age or when they are very small. Their life cycle is two years. These are the smallest of the salmon and run only from four to eight pounds.

The anal ray count is 13 to 17, commonly 15. The scale count is 170.

The Dog Salmon (oncorhynchus keta). The dog or chum salmon comes into the sportman's catch from September through December. It resembles the silver salmon when bright and specimens between six and ten pounds are easily confused with a cohoe.

The tail of the dog salmon, however, is deeply forked as contrasted with the silver's gentle curve. The caudal peduncle—the "handle" between

PINK or HUMPBACK SALMON – SPAWNING MALE

the tail and the body—is slender and almost round, while in the case of the silver it is wider and flatter. When these two means of identification fail, there is one sure, infallible test—counting the pyloric caeca. These are small white worm-like appendages in the digestive system. The dog salmon counts 150 to 180 of these, while the silver has only 50 to 80.

Dog salmon range in weight from 8 to 12 pounds—a 20-pounder is a lunker. Like the silver, it has few spots. It remains in fresh water about two to four months and its life cycle ranges from three to five years, with four years the average.

The anal ray count is 13 to 17, commonly 13. The scale count is 150. The flesh is light pink or yellow and turns white when cooked.

Sockeye Salmon (oncorhynchus nerka). This salmon is called sockeye, red, or, along the Washington coast and the Columbia, blueback. It is one of the most highly prized salmon for eating but is seldom caught by anglers.

It averages 6 to 8 pounds in weight. The body is trim, compact and rather slender with a small round pointed head. The back of the head and body is a deep clear blue; the other parts are silvery without spots or markings.

It always runs up a river that has access to a lake. The fish spawns in the stream and then the young drop down into the lake where they remain one to two years before going out to the ocean. Its life cycle is four years.

Arne Goett with His "Monster"

Any king that weighs 50 pounds or more is a monster salmon, and Arne Goett is the only angler on record who has boated two kings weighing 60 pounds. Here he is with a 63½-pounder caught at Hope Island, July 26, 1963, on a Canadian Wonder spoon.

Hope Island has for many years been the magnet for anglers eager to boat a lunker king. The first of the 60-pound-plus lunkers was Maury Miller's 66-pounder taken at Hope in 1951. That same year Arne Goett and Earl Thayer both caught 60-pounders there.

In 1953 the first woman entered the race when Mrs. Ray Shy boated a 65-pounder. John Mindt followed with a 60-pounder—but the star year was 1954 when Mrs. Howard Little brought in a 70-pounder. That same year Carl Gepner took a 61-pounder and Moore McKinley a 66.

The author's unofficial record of kings weighing 50 pounds or more, that have been caught in Washington waters since the early 1950's, shows 203 lunker kings, including 43 from Neah Bay and Sekiu; 41 from Hope Island; 28 from Westport, and 9 from Ilwaco. This record also shows 21 kings boated in state waters that have weighed at or over the 60-pound mark. The largest of these—and of course the state record— is Chet Gausta's 70½-pound king boated at Sekiu, September 6, 1964. This monster salmon beat out the former record maker—the 70-pounder caught by Mrs. Little at Hope Island.

Westport Harbor—Charter Boat Capital

Westport, the small village at the mouth of Grays Harbor, Washington, is the charter boat capital of the Pacific Northwest. It berths 200 charters, which is more than is provided by all the other state areas combined. During the height of the season, from July into September, virtually every charter is booked solid on weekends. Even on week days reservations are hard to come by, and motels are crowded to capacity.

The charters usually drift mooch; that is, the engines are shut off and the boat is permitted to drift with the tide through a likely stretch of water. Or, the skipper may decide to "rev up" his engine and motor mooch through the salmon grounds. The catch is cleaned by the skipper or his helper and is ready to be taken off when the boat docks back at the marina. At the end of the day the lucky fishermen, as shown here, pack their gear and salmon from the dock, heading for their cars and the trip home.

The sports catch at Westport averages about 200,000 a season, with 35 per cent of the boatings being king salmon.

The anal ray count is 13 to 16, commonly 14 to 16. The scale count is 133.

Jack Salmon. Jack Salmon enter into the sport catch both in salt and fresh water. But although many anglers may refer to catching a "jack," the exact meaning of the term is not commonly understood.

A jack salmon, according to the ichthyologists, is a precocious male

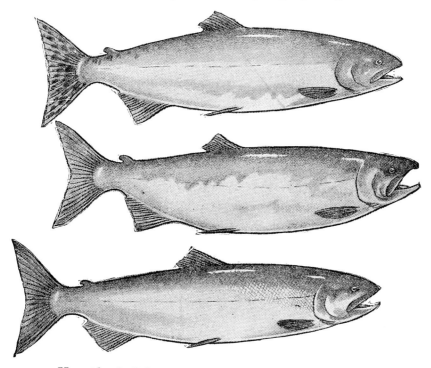

Humpback Salmon (above). Dog Salmon (middle)
Sockeye Salmon (below)

salmon of any species that has returned ahead of its cycle year. It is always a male and is always smaller than the accompanying migrants of the same species. In appearance, it will look the same as another of the same species except for size. Jacks are mature sexually and may contribute to the fertilizing of the eggs of a female when there is a scarcity of fully developed males.

When hooked either in the ocean or fresh water, Jack Salmon are usually very active. They will hit a fly or spoon readily in a stream and will put up as lively a scrap as a steelhead. However they are not as fast nor do they possess the leaping ability. Many jack kings or silvers are taken by sportsmen in rivers during a salmon run.

Jacks also occur among trout, and the mature steelhead running between one and three pounds caught in rivers during the winter are usually jacks.

Spawning Coloration. Both salmon and steelhead assume a very distinctive coloration when they put on their spawning dress. Since sportsmen frown upon ever disturbing any fish in such condition, it is important to be able to know the various color phases that distinguish the fish when they are on the spawning beds.

In the first place all male salmon become hook-nosed before spawning. At times this hook is so pronounced, bringing the upper jaw so far over the lower one, that it would be impossible for the fish to feed even if it wanted to.

Kings usually lose their silver color and turn dark verging on black. In the river they appear an ashy white and reddish green. Silvers range from a pink to a dark red with a touch of green on the back. Humpback males become dark green and black with a decided hump on the back that make the fish look deformed. Dog salmon color up in shades of yellow and pink that run vertically across the body in a "calico" type of coloration. Sockeyes turn a bright orange red somewhat like the color of a reddish goldfish.

All salmon become badly scuffed and battered by the time that they reach the spawning beds. In addition, fungus growths appear on them, especially around the tails, head and fins.

When salmon are waiting to spawn they become very pugnacious and will hit any lure dragged before them. For that reason it is now illegal to catch salmon in many of the rivers of Washington. Many people residing near rivers and creeks formerly gaffed many salmon in poor condition and smoked them afterwards. This is also illegal in most of the rivers. However on the Indian reservations, the salmon in all stages are taken by the Indians and dried or smoked for food.

Chapter Two

TROLLING FOR KING SALMON

The lordly king salmon, whether they are called kings or chinooks, belong to the royal family of game fish. They are really big, occasionally going up to 75 pounds, and 40 pounders are not uncommon. The "half-century" lunkers have the vigor and energy of 12-horsepower engines—rocketing off with the line on smoking runs like a porpoise or sounding like a submarine. They strike like pile drivers with a display of power that will not be believed until it is experienced.

They are beautiful to see with their clean rugged lines and powerful bodies that suggest the sweep of the ocean waves. From their rugged heads which taper from the trigger-like jaws onto wide torpedo-like bodies and into wide spreading tails, their every inch suggests dynamic energy.

Ocean Migration of the Chinook. In mid-summer of their spawning year the Chinooks seek the branch highways of the sea that will lead them to their final destination: the home river. This is a general movement of hundreds of thousands of prime kings. From the cold Bering Sea they fan into Bristol Bay where, with the sockeye run, they are caught by commercial men and canned. Sportsmen seek them but little here. Then from the Gulf of Alaska they surge into the many short rivers and the few great streams that run off the ice-rimmed coastal range from Cook Inlet to Yakatat. Further east they leave the Gulf to thread through the many channels of the Inside Passage to reach the rivers of Southeastern Alaska from Skagway to Ketchikan. Here there are many fishermen, mostly trollers, who catch the kings that are on the average larger than these further south. Then still further south the tyees swing into Hecate Strait and through Queen Charlotte Sound, around Vancouver Island, to enter the lonely coastal rivers of British Columbia. Here is a vast sport fishing territory which is little touched by anglers except by those who journey north by private cruiser. The west coast of Vancouver Island also empties many rivers into the sea that present almost virgin fishing territory. Along the east coast of the Island, sport fishing is well-developed. Every angler in the West knows the famed fishing off Campbell River and its noted Tyee Club.

Down to the State of Washington the kings surge in from their feeding grounds off Swiftsure Bank, to swing past the rock-ribbed cliffs of Cape Flattery and finally the Strait of Juan de Fuca. From here they fan out over all the waters of Puget Sound, going north to the San Juan Islands; south to Whidbey Island and the mighty Skagit; still further south to spread out over the lower Sound in the streams near Seattle and Tacoma.

The chinooks that are destined for the greatest salmon river of them all—the Columbia—travel by Flattery, down along the Olympic Peninsula and Grays Harbor, and then over the bar into the Columbia. Here, before dams such as Coulee were built, they went to their spawning grounds in Canada and Idaho. This great salmon run faces virtual destruction if and when the series of proposed dams in the Columbia and Snake are completed.

King salmon usually leave their parent river in late spring of their first year, when they are three to four months old, and then return as mature fish in four to six years, with jacks coming back as two- or three-year fish. It is believed that most kings of more than 30 pounds are at least five-year-old fish, while those weighing 20 pounds or less usually are four-year-olds. The young kings when descending their rivers are usually 2 to 4 inches long but occasionally a few remain an entire year and grow to 6 inches.

The kings of the Puget Sound area reach the Pacific through the Straits, while those of most other streams go directly into the sea. From the time that they reach salt water, their paths through the ocean are governed mainly by a search for food.

The Sea Highway of the Puget Sound King. The principal feeding grounds of the Puget Sound kings are spread out along the continental shelf, a strip of water going down to 100 fathoms and stretching out from shore for about 35 miles. This shelf extends north along Vancouver Island up past its northern tip.

From Cape Flattery north to Queen Charlotte Sound the kings drift with a current that works northward all year. Then as they approach maturity the mating urge turns them south and they head back for their parent stream to spawn.

One of the most popular spots on this continental shelf for salmon is Swiftsure Bank—a place northwest of Cape Flattery off Vancouver Island. Here the kings pause to feed on both their outward and homeward migrations. Fat, oil-drenched, virile fish, they drift away from Swiftsure, swing over to the Washington side of the Straits and swim past the cliffs at Neah and Clallam Bays. They pause here in their leisurely journey to pick up a few extra rations of herring, and then they head past Port Angeles either to swing northeast to enter the Nooksack or the Skagit or to head south to the tributary streams of lower Puget Sound.

By June, these salmon have gathered in the narrow slots off Hope Island, waiting to go up the Skagit. Later—about the first of August—other schools swing past the southern tip of Whidbey Island. By mid-August kings are schooling off Mission Bar or in the waters of Elliott and Shilshole Bays at Seattle. They remain in these spots until a rise in water brings them up into their home rivers. It is in these "waiting spots" that anglers encounter the sport that they have anxiously awaited since last year's run.

Trolling Tackle. The majority of the kings taken by sportsmen are caught by trolling an artificial lure. The king, except when it is feeding, is seldom found near the surface. It is a deep-water fish and in most waters it is necessary to use sufficient lead to take the lure down. This accounts for the use of rods and lines in the Northwest that are perhaps too heavy considering the average size of the salmon taken.

However the use of mooching gear—a light tackle hook-up—for the big kings is becoming more widespread each season. Although it is a form of trolling, we shall consider the whole allied subject of mooching in the next chapter.

The preferred tackle for the salt-chuck trollers has become fairly well standardized. A rather heavy two-piece split bamboo rod, varying from 6 to 8 feet in length, will be found in every Pacific salmon angler's fishing outfit. It should be capable of handling from 4 to 20 ounces of lead. The butt usually has a cork handle and the rod is divided so as to make carrying it in a car not too difficult. The new beryllium copper rods are also fine trolling sticks as they combine lightness with strength, but they will tarnish in salt water.

A substantial star-drag reel is almost universally used. Pfleuger, Penn and Ocean City have models well suited for these waters.

Monel metal or wire lines are in general use as they sink readily and will attain the proper depth on a shorter line than if cuttyhunk were employed. This is a distinct advantage in areas where boats are apt to concentrate, as trolling with a short line will prevent many entanglements. A popular size of wire line is .022 gauge Monel metal and 500 to 800 feet of length is about right, with backing, where necessary, to fill up the spool on the reel.

To the end of the metal line the angler should attach with a cinch knot about 20 feet of 45-pound-test cuttyhunk line in the dark-green color. A swivel is tied onto the end of the cuttyhunk. The use of the cuttyhunk permits easy attaching of a slip sinker which is usually fastened about five feet from the end of the wire line.

The slip sinkers developed in this area, and pictured in the accompanying drawing (page 184), are rapidly slipped onto the line at any point after the leader and lure have been attached. They may be easily taken off and replaced with a heavier one without taking the set-up off the rod. They slip down the line when a salmon hits.

A wire leader 4 to 6 feet long is generally used for plugs or spoons, in the number 4 or 6 size, testing from 38 to 54 pounds.

Trolling Lures. Four main types of lures are used at present by Northwest trollers—plugs; spoons; dodgers with herring or spoons; and cut herring with mooching gear. Spoons were the first type of lure to take kings successfully and still are the main standby of the commercial fishermen. Spoons may be of pearl, brass, or nickel or a combination of the last two. They are of many makes and designs and usually are used in the 2½ to 6 sizes. Generally speaking a spoon will be the most effective lure if used on feeding salmon.

Plugs were first used in Puget Sound waters around 1931, a shiny scale Heddon Basser being the most popular at that time. At present, virtually all the salmon plugs fished in the Northwest are locally made, with many of them manufactured in the Seattle area. Among those made at present are the Martin, Lucky Louie, Hanson, Rosegard Wallace and Hook Bros. They vary in color from white through various shades of red, pink, gray, green or yellow. In mid-sound waters, sizes 4½ to 5 appear to be most effective. In the outside waters, the larger plugs up to 6 inches are the most commonly used.

The dodger—a brass or silver or enameled oval-shaped rectangle 8 to 10 inches long—developed at Tacoma, became popular shortly after 1930. The dodger acts as an attractor for the kings and its turning flash may be seen at some distance. It is usually hooked up with a herring or a spoon. It is not as easy to handle or to fish as a plug or spoon but it is a killing lure.

The King Run of the Straits. The first Puget Sound kings to be taken in numbers each season are hooked near the entrance of the Strait of Juan de Fuca. Each year around June 10, the first schools of big early-run kings come down along the northern shore of Washington's Olympic Peninsula east of Cape Flattery. From then until September recurring surges of these salmon, "fresh in" from their feeding table in the ocean, are boated by anglers off the noted trolling grounds at Sekiu and Neah Bay.

The fortunate angler who hits into the midst of such a run will have sport of the spine-tingling variety. And for the inland fisherman who is accustomed to inner-sound beaches and a gently rocking row boat, the surroundings will be spectacular and breathtaking. He will be bucking ocean swells and heavy winds and at times venturing out into the Pacific. During the summer, both Neah Bay and Sekiu are thronged to capacity with anglers from all over the Coast.

Should the angler set his course for Neah Bay, he will find himself in an Indian village situated less than 10 miles from the Cape. This village straggles along the quiet harbor hemmed in by the long backwater. Here at anchor, between sorties, lies the fishing fleet. There will be purse-seiners and trollers who, in season, daily search the Strait and ocean for swimming gold—the kings and cohoes.

Three of us reached Neah Bay late one July evening, and before dawn the next day were rounding Wadah Island and breasting the open waters with our small inboard boat. There had been a strong wind the previous night and the long 30-foot swells lifted our boat to their crests and then raced it down their steep sides to their hollows, making it difficult to handle the boat.

Even if the water was a bit rough for good trolling we set up our rods. I strung the cuttyhunk through the guides of my rod and then fastened the loop on the wire leader attached to my plug to the snap swivel at the end of the cuttyhunk. I allowed about 20 feet of cuttyhunk to play out through the tip and then fastened on a slip sinker. See illustration on this page.

This sinker has a cut along the rounded side running almost all the way through. The line is run through this cut and is then held in place

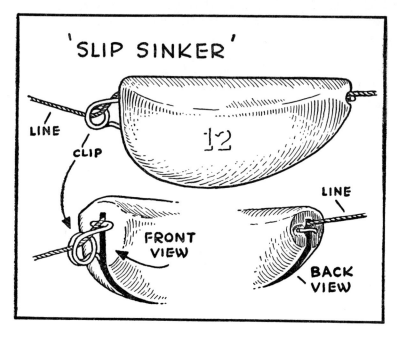

by wires at each end of the lead. The heavy strike of a salmon will slip the line out of the coiled-wire fastening at one end of the sinker and allow it to slide freely down the cuttyhunk to the leader.

I had selected a 6-inch plug in a white finish and used 6 ounces of lead. I let out about 50 feet of line, set the star-drag on the reel so that it was just right to hook a salmon on the strike, and sat back to await developments. As we rode through the swells, I could feel the heavy throbbing of the rod and see the bobbing of the tip as the lure felt the pull of the undertow. Then there would follow a period when the tension was released, and the plug's action would be free and unhampered. Our destination was Midway, a jagged reef of rocks which lies about half-way down the nine-mile stretch of coast from Neah Bay to the Cape.

As we reached Midway the swells seemed to become higher and longer. There were a number of boats trolling off the reef but they could only be glimpsed momentarily. These reefs are a series of black ugly-looking rocks sticking dangerously out from the heavily timbered shore, with waves washing against them and breaking whitely against their sides.

There is a hole off the reef and boats circle through and around it. This is a resting and feeding spot for the kings and will usually produce one when the run is on.

As we breasted a wave, there to our left we saw an Indian in an 18-foot dugout calmly paddling his frail craft down the swells.

"That's old Pete," said our boatman, Elmer Douglas, a full-blooded Makah; "he paddles out here nearly every day."

"What do you mean, old?" asked Eddie Vine. "Why it takes a young man to do that kind of navigating. Even our motors don't seem to be breaking any speed records out here."

"Pete's about seventy," said Elmer impassively. "He's been coming out here for salmon since he was a kid, and mebbe he's good for five, six years more."

Just then the old Indian carefully placed his paddle in the dugout and started pulling in his hand line, slowly but evenly. We shot down a hollow about that time and when we came up on another swell, Indian Pete's boat was dangerously close to the reef and he was gaffing a struggling king salmon into his dugout.

"Good gosh," I cried, "look at him handling his boat in these rugged waves; doesn't he ever crash into the reef?"

"Nope," said Elmer, "we Makahs know these waters like we do our own cabins. We never wash up on the reef. Catch fish nearly every day."

"What does Pete do with all the salmon?" asked Ed.

"Eat 'em," answered Elmer. "We live on salmon the year round. You heard what old Joe Sly said last night. 'White man crazy, he eat trout. Indian know better, he eat only salmon.' When we have any left we sell 'em to fish buyers."

The wind had been gradually rising, the swells were running higher and trolling was not only deucedly unpleasant but fruitless as well. So we headed back for the harbor and put in the rest of the afternoon resting and talking to the Indians.

Coast Indians as Salmon Fishermen. Wherever there are good runs of salmon in this north country, there will usually be Indian villages or a reservation close by. The coast Indians are fish-eaters and live where they can catch salmon or steelhead easily and in large numbers.

When the salmon runs are on, the Indians catch and smoke them for their winter food. Along the Strait, and wherever ocean rivers cleave the coast, Indians from time immemorial have lived and become excellent boatmen as well as adept fishermen. Some of these rivers are now devoid of fish, but the Indians remain. There are still Indians along the Nooksack, once a premier salmon river. There is a large village near LaConner at the mouth of the Skagit which runs a salmon trap. The Tualips off Mission

Bar once ate from the large runs of the Snohomish before pollution deci-mated it to almost nothing. Further south at the Nisqually there is another reservation, the inhabitants of which now live mostly on memories of former unlimited salmon runs.

But the ocean rivers of the Olympics, untouched by pollution and man-made dams, are still yielding their thousands of fat kings, silvers and bluebacks to the Indians. They fish the Quillayute out of Mora and La Push; the generous Hoh; and the bountiful Queets; and the almost virgin Quinault with its kings, its dogs, its sockeyes, and its silvers. And in all of these Olympic streams the steelhead as well are taken like salmon by the Indians to be eaten and sold commercially to out-of-state buyers.

Protected by ancient treaty rights, the Indians are allowed to fish on their reservations in their traditional manner. Although steelhead are game fish and cannot be sold in Washington, they are not so regarded in Oregon or many other western states. And through this loophole the steelhead reach the eastern market. In sealed containers the steelhead are shipped direct to the East and no local laws can prevent this.

Conservationists here feel that it is a needless and dreadful waste to allow such a superlative sports fish as the steelhead to be sold over a meat-market counter, especially when these game fish, due to intensive fishing and destruction of habitat through logging and industrial pollution, are rapidly becoming fewer. The bounty of the ocean rivers, the gift of the fighting steelhead as given by the sea, should be carefully preserved in-stead of decimated through the commercial channels of trade.

In bygone days, before the white man introduced chain store buying and outboard motors and nets to the Indians, these coastal tribes trolled the turbulent waters of the Pacific with primitive fishing gear. Their cranky dugouts were hollowed out of cedar logs, varying from 20 to 30 feet in length. They were so well constructed that many of them still in use are over 50 years old. Ninety-year-old Joe Sly, one of the tribal patriarchs of the Makahs, showed us his boat as it lay pulled up on the beach—the same boat he had paddled up into Alaskan waters in his venturesome youth. It was 24 feet long, with a 3½ foot beam, a depth of 2½ feet, and seven crossbeams. Its weight was approximately 300 pounds. The Quillayutes use similar dugouts to ride the surf out of La Push and once killed seal from them off the Olympic coast.

Before the white man came these Indians caught salmon in the sea, without the use of our fancy spoons or hooks. Sly told of the time when "the Makahs all time fish, but all time for eat and not for sell."

Their old-time hooks were made from "lucky wood," our white man's language for the Indian name of a hemlock bough of the right grain and shape. The heart of the bough would be fashioned into a hook 4 to 6 inches long. For a line the Indians would utilize the cord-like roots of kelp, soaking them in fresh water before splicing them into a strong durable line about 75 feet long. With nets of reeds they would catch small herring to use as lures to be trolled on their hemlock hooks behind a paddled dugout. At times they would catch sea bass with a small herring-like plug made from the root of the devil-club bush.

Boating a Big King. The wind died down that night and the stars came out. The bay was like a mill pond as we stumbled in the dark through the sand to pile our gear into a rowboat to take it out to the small cruiser. And while day was just breaking we were already well out on the Strait.

This was an ideal trolling day: a light breeze to ruffle the surface but no swells. I started out with a shiny scale Rosegard, number 6. We were out for big fish and wanted the tiddlers to keep off. Again I used 6 ounces of lead and ran out about sixty feet of line. Eddie had on a "hot" plug and was really confident. It was a rather battered red-head Martin that looked no different from any other. But, as Ed remarked as he twisted on a new leader: "This is my old standby. It always works. Didn't I take two kings with it last month at Hope—one going 45 pounds?"

A "hot" plug is one that apparently because of some unknown quirk in the composition of the wood catches fish more easily and readily than another exactly similar one of the same pattern. This slight difference in the wood gives the plug an action that salmon can't resist.

These plugs can't be made to order, they just happen. Whenever an angler falls heir to such a lure he guards it as if it were made of gold; never lending it to anyone. A veteran may go several seasons without finding such a plug, and a "cracker" may stumble onto one the first time that he goes trolling.

We hadn't reached Midway when Ed's rod-tip dipped down and he hung onto a salmon. It wasn't big however and he soon brought it to gaff, a nice king of about 15 pounds.

We had our rods in holders and I sat there with my eyes glued on my gently throbbing tip when it jerked a couple of times, bent over, and the reel started to sing. I grabbed the butt of the rod and was fast to a fish that put up a nice fight but did not take out line. When it was gaffed it proved to be a twin of Ed's.

We were approaching the hole off the reef and both of us were alert and watchful. Ed was watching his rod like a hawk when the tip bent slightly, hesitated a second and then swerved down, and line started screaming off the reel.

"I got him," yelled Ed, "he's a big one. Oh, boy! Watch him go! Who says that isn't a hot plug."

The metal line was running out in a steady direct pull as Elmer shut off the motor. Ed was standing erect, reeling in furiously, but his rod tip had stopped jerking. He gave several heavy pulls on the rod, held it steady and then let out with some good strong fishermen's curses.

"Hung up," he exclaimed with disgust, "and with my hot plug too."

He yanked, with all the force he had. Something had to give and as he couldn't pull up the bottom his line came in minus the plug. When he reeled in, the wire leader was broken near its center where it had kinked. Ed rummaged through his tackle box for another plug; the motor started up; I let out line; and we were fishing again.

One of the fascinations of salmon trolling is the electrifying suddenness of the strike. Kings, except when they roll on the surface, nearly always are down deep and there aren't any swirls or leaping fish to indicate their presence.

We were past the reef now, heading toward the Cape with Tatoosh Island just ahead. The dark rock-ribbed cliffs covered with thick stands of deep green fir along their tops led us on to the broad Pacific. At their base the cliffs were weathered by wind and tide into cave-like hollows and sharp promontories. They probably look just the same today as they did a century ago when the Indians paddled quietly by with their dugouts, with never a staccato explosion of an outboard motor to awaken the echoes.

We turned back toward Midway and for a change I held my rod with its butt next to my ribs and the tip extended over the side. There was a cluster of boats nearby and we could see an angler standing up playing a fish. The sun struggled through a mass of low gray clouds as I watched a flock of gulls to our left diving and screaming over the water, probably fighting over a school of surfaced herring.

Suddenly, without the slightest notice, my rod sprang into life with a dynamic wrench that started the reel singing, the tip madly jerking and the line melting off in irresistible pulls.

I clung to the bobbing rod, scrambled up, bracing my feet against the side of the boat, and yelled unnecessarily, "Fish on!" For by this time the motor had been shut off and Ed was busily reeling in his line.

"This fish feels awful heavy," I panted. "Watch the line melt away. Mebbe he's a good one."

I tightened the drag and started reeling but the salmon still dragged off line in 25-foot chunks. I shut down a bit more on the drag and brought in a few feet of line. Then suddenly the pull slackened, and the line came in freely. My heart sank.

"He's off, I think," I muttered as I reeled furiously. Then the reel suddenly started growling again and line was running out pell-mell through the guides.

"Like heck, he's off," hollered Ed. "You'd better handle that baby right. He's probably a big one. Don't set the drag too tight or the hook will pull loose."

There was all of 350 feet of steel line boring into the deep green of the Strait when the king started to give ground a bit. I reeled slowly and he came slowly and line was building up on the reel. Then he sounded, heading straight down with a rush. Now I had really to get to work. The rod bent dangerously as I pumped in line with just the right pressure and the salmon came up slowly but surely.

"Keep a-pumping," said Elmer. "You gotta keep that king a-moving or he will sulk like so much dead weight."

"Yes, but don't jerk his head off," came some more free advice from Ed. "Although we ain't got all day we can afford to waste a few minutes if you really want to land that youngster."

My wrist was tired and my knees were wobbly from the tension of bracing myself against the bobbing boat. But I steadily gained a few feet of line at each upward pull. The salmon must have been brought closer to the surface than I realized, for abruptly it broke water about fifty feet from the boat, surged on the surface, and sounded again.

"He's a nice one, all right," hollered Ed, all excited now, "handle him easy. He'll go fifty pounds sure."

Knowing that Ed's fish always looked twice as big in the water as they did on a scale, I did not get too agitated. The king now came up rather easily and started swimming around the cruiser. He wasn't through by any means. And he still possessed enough power to shake the hook on a slack line or tear loose if I bore down too hard.

Then I got cuttyhunk through the rod tip and Elmer released the sinker. The king was near the boat, twisting and turning in the clear water; his white underside and belly gleaming like spun silver. I brought him alongside, Ed made a neat swipe with the gaff and held the fish against the boat's side. I knocked it a couple of times back of the head and slid it aboard.

It was a prime salmon which went a bit over 35 pounds when weighed at the dock later that afternoon. It was absolutely fresh-run, fat and thick, dark green on the back. The sides were dull gleaming silver with a sort of salt water iridescence over the entire body. The king was a feeder, for when I cleaned it eight good-sized herring were crammed down into its gullet and a couple even down its throat.

Popularity of Plugs. It is an easy matter to see why the plug fishermen are so enthusiastic about their type of lure. There isn't any question but what plugs take plenty of salmon in every type of water—deep or shallow, strong tidal runs or calmer estuaries. A plug's action may be varied, it may be fished at all depths, and those lunker chinooks that tip the scales around fifty pounds often prefer a plug to anything else.

Moreover there are almost as many fancy patterns to choose from on the shelves of the sporting goods stores as ever greeted a bass plugger.

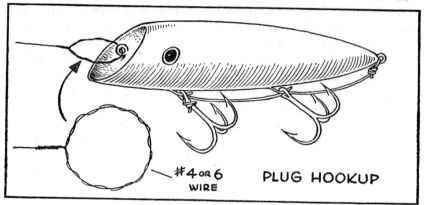

#4 or 6 WIRE   PLUG HOOKUP

The salmon troller has red, yellow or white, blue or pink pearl, shiny herring scale in various sizes and makes to mull over. Like a fly fisherman who gets such a kick out of changing flies, the troller can keep himself happily occupied all day long just snapping on one plug after another.

There are anglers who have been trolling for years behind a "kicker" boat who pride themselves on being able to make a plug perform. They claim that plugs as they come from the factory do not always work exactly right. One cannot tell how well a plug will troll until it is in the water. If it doesn't swim in just the right way, plug experts indulge in all sorts of tinkering to alter the action.

Such an expert is Herb Mills who is a past master at working over a wooden lure. One of his favorite fishing grounds is in the narrow slots at Hope Island. These spots are famous from June to August for monster kings, those broad lunkers that run from 35 to 50 pounds. Herb knows every rock in the channel at Hope and every quirk of the current.

Early last August we spent a day fishing together with host Paul Wagner. Herb carried a tackle box as large as a sea-chest and when he opened it and started dumping plugs out on the seat, he automatically started talking in his easy Oklahoma drawl.

"See this Lucky Louie plug? Boy! Is that a hot number at Neah Bay! It sure swims nice for me there, but I never hang onto anything even a silver with it here at Hope. Here I like a Rosegard; for me it has the best action in this fast current."

As he laid aside a yellow scale plug he expertly cut off about 6 feet of number 4 wire leader from a full coil. He ran one end through the eye of the plug, tying a simple knot. Then he slipped the loose end of the leader back through the eye again, making a loop circle about half an inch in diameter. He then threaded the loose end back and forth through the loop until it met the main length of leader. Then this end was twisted over the main length of wire in the regulation manner. See illustration on page 190.

He fastened a swivel onto the other end of the leader with the same simple knot and snapped it onto the swivel at the end of his cuttyhunk.

We expected to drag three lines and for the rod directly astern we put on a Canadian Wonder spoon, half silver and half copper, with 8 ounces of lead. We were all using the same make of reel and ran off 22 turns for the center rod. Then with the side rods we put on 4 ounces of lead and let out 30 turns of the reel. In this way the spoon and plugs were working at different depths and distances and were not likely to tangle.

Then, as we trolled along between Whidbey and Hope Islands, Herb set up a fourth rod and immediately snapped on a plug and dragged it alongside the boat to observe its action.

"I like a plug," he drawled, bending over to see the working of the lure, "that weaves from side to side in a narrow pathway 18 to 20 inches wide. It should not swing out only to one side. It oughta weave back and forth. Its action should be neither slow nor dead-like. It should swim along as if it were in a hurry to catch up with another fish. That's the action that those big ol' hog kings like to climb onto."

"Now this plug swings over to the right all the time," continued Herb. He reeled it in and held it between us. "See, I bend the eye in its mouth a bit to the left, which should start it swimming over toward the left. If you push the screw eye down it will make the plug wiggle faster; pushing it up like this will slow it up a little."

He cast the plug over once more, and then as it sank below the surface, sure enough this time it swam in a left-to-right pathway with a particularly enticing wiggle.

"That's about right," said Herb, pulling in the pink pearl Martin and snapping on the worked-over plug. "I know if there's any kings out there they can't resist it."

"Another way to vary the action of a plug is to retie the cord on the hooks or make bigger knots," continued Herb, as he snapped a Hanson plug onto his testing rod, and started dragging it along about ten feet off the side of the boat. "Another way to change the cords is . . ."

Just then Paul yelled "Fish on!" and pointed to the center rod. I took the wheel and he grabbed the rod while Herb was busier than a bird dog in a covey of quail getting in the other two outfits. Paul had a nice king on his rod which put up a fast quick fight. Much of the time it was near the surface. However it was not over 25 pounds and finally came to gaff.

"I like 'em that way," Paul said, as he slid the salmon into the fish box. "No sulking on the bottom. And if you notice, he took that beautiful spoon, completely giving all your plugs a cold fin."

"Probably just an accident," drawled Herb, who went on talking as if he had never been interrupted, "As I was saying, a different way to change action is to vary the length of the cord holding the hooks. Or, with a Martin, you can bend the cord clips either forward or back."

"Now, here's my 'ace in the hole' trick," he continued, "for a plug that just doesn't swim right. I unscrew the eye in the head and then plug up the hole with a picnic toothpick. Then I make another hole either to one side, above, or below the former spot with an ice pick and replace the eye. Sometimes this will make a hot plug out of a no-good one."

"Here's a couple of things I have learned to watch for when fishing. Always check your plug immediately when the rod tip stops working. The least bit of weed caught on one of the hooks will spoil the action. After you catch a king, throw the leader away and bend on a new one. Wire is cheap and you would hate to lose a king because in a hurry you had used a leader with a kink in it. Plugs nowadays seem to soak up water faster than they did formerly. So even if you have on a hot plug, check its action after an hour's trolling. If it has slowed up any put on a fresh one."

We trolled all the rest of the afternoon but never boated another king. However we did have one savage strike but the plug was unpinned while the salmon was making its first strong run. But salmon trolling is like that. Some days you have action and then on others you can't find a single fish of any kind.

Although the plug is still the most favored artificial lure among the king trollers, far surpassing the spoon, the dodger-and-herring combination is fast approaching it in popularity. Moreover, when it comes to trolling for silvers, the dodger is rapidly outstripping all other lures.

In the salmon derby conducted annually by the Seattle *Times* in Elliott Bay and at Ballard a careful count has been kept of the lures that have taken qualifying salmon during the past three derbies. These derbies start either in February or March when only the blackmouth are in the two bays and then run until the end of September when the king run is on. Here are the figures:

STATISTICS OF LURES USED IN SEATTLE TIMES DERBY

1946	Mooching	Dodger Herring	Plug	Spoon	Spin-ning	Fly
First period—blackmouth	54	8	1	7	—	—
Second period—early kings	181	133	317	—	—	—

Alan Pratt holds up a 40-pound king from his limit catch taken off
Spike Rock out of Neah Bay. These ocean-fresh kings, which congregate along the entire length of their feeding grounds from Oregon
north to British Columbia, are in their prime of life. Because of their
tremendous power, long runs, and rugged fight on sports gear, they
provide some of the most thrilling experiences that accrue to salt-water
anglers in the Pacific Northwest.

Official Inspection of a Day's Catch

Shown here is the charter-boat moorage at Ilwaco, where an inspector for the State Department of Fisheries checks over a day's sports catch of salmon. He measures each fish and checks for fin clips. Most of these fish are feeding kings.

Ilwaco on the Washington side and Astoria and Warrenton on the Oregon side are the three marinas that accommodate sports fishermen off the mouth of the Columbia River. This fishing area—where the salmon congregate before ascending their parent stream, the Columbia —is consistently one of the outstanding salmon grounds along the Pacific Coast. It ranks either one or two in sports landings of salmon annually in the states of Oregon and Washington.

The area is served by about 90 charter boats out of Ilwaco, about 50 out of Astoria, and around 20 out of Warrenton. These boats accommodate 8 to 12 fishermen each. The charter fleet is made up of regular charter boats, converted commercial craft, and cruisers. Kicker boats also ply the waters. On calm days the area may be fished by any type of craft, but when the ocean kicks up off the Columbia Bar, then an angler should arrange to fish off a licensed charter.

Depending upon where the salmon are schooled up, the charter will either head straight out from the Columbia mouth or move north and drift-mooch off Long Beach. Frequently the salmon will be feeding in shallow water only a short distance off the beach.

Indian Fishermen on the Quillayute River

Here are three Indians from the Quillayute Reservation on the Olympic Peninsula heading out in their native dugout to net salmon. James Island is in the background. Sports fishermen use the same route to reach the salmon feeding grounds. After passing James Island on the right, they will be out on the ocean and will probably head for Skunk Buoy, one of the better salmon areas at La Push. It is especially good when the kings are waiting off the river's mouth before going to their spawning grounds.

Farther out, the area around the Whistler Buoy provides excellent mooching grounds, particularly when the silvers are in. Cake Island lies north of the Whistler. About a mile south of the river's mouth, the Needles—a rugged formation of rocks—juts out of the ocean. The entire area between these landmarks holds salmon.

La Push, a combination Indian and sports-fishing village, is situated on the south bank of the Quillayute River in the midst of the Indian reservation. The region roundabout is one of the most picturesque and spectacular sections of Washington's west coast.

Eight charters operate out of La Push, with kicker boats also for rent. The salmon grounds may be easily reached by small boats or outboard cruisers, weather permitting. Boats headed out salmon fishing must follow the river's channel to get to the fishing grounds.

La Push had one of its best sports seasons in 1967, when the catch approached the 40,000 mark. The season runs from May into September.

King Salmon Boated West of Neah Bay

The salmon grounds out of Neah Bay are strung out along the northern coast of Washington State. They extend along the shore of the Strait of Juan de Fuca out to Cape Flattery and then south to Father and Son Rocks. King salmon usually come into these waters in late June, and from then until middle August king fishing is at its height. Silver salmon school up outside Tatoosh Island in July and by middle August start their spawning journey east through the strait toward Puget Sound.

There are a number of named fishing holes located along the south shore of the strait from Waada Island out to the cape. First is the Garbage Dump, only a short distance from the island. Then about five miles out is Midway Rock, which shelters small boats and commercial kelpers. It also holds salmon. Farther westward are Slant Rock, Ole's Hole, Mushroom Rock, and then Cape Flattery, which is a nine-mile run from Neah Bay.

Pictured here is an outboard cruiser whose two anglers have boated a pair of husky kings off the kelp bed at Ole's Hole. Just around the cape is the Hole in the Wall, a good spot to lie over in should rough water occur as you approach Tatoosh Island. After rounding the Cape, you can motor mooch south to the ocean feeding grounds. First stop will be at Skagway Rocks; then comes Mukkaw Bay. Spike Rock, six miles down the coast, can offer top king fishing.

Charters are a sure way to get to these spots, but outboard cruisers make the trip easily when the ocean is smooth.

1946	Mooching	Dodger Herring	Plug	Spoon	Spinning	Fly
Third period—kings	96	75	320	—	—	—
Total	331	216	638	7	0	0
1947						
First period—blackmouth	204	50	10	5	15	—
Second period—early kings	92	190	122	12	10	—
Third period—kings	226	375	345	15	9	—
Total	522	615	477	32	34	0
1948						
First period—blackmouth	116	11	2	8	8	1
Second period—early kings.........	106	101	70	9	7	—
Third period—kings	426	266	230	9	13	1
Total	648	378	302	26	28	2
1949						
First period—blackmouth	115	29	2	1	3	—
Second period—early kings.........	260	118	47	6	9	—
Third period—kings	485	425	205	10	9	1
Totals	860	572	254	17	21	1
Grand Total	2,361	1,781	1,671	82	83	3

These figures bring out a number of interesting facts. First, when fishing for immature salmon, the herring either as a cut spinner or plug cut will be by far the most effective lure. However, with the spawning kings artificial lures are more generally used with the plug and dodger and herring taking the most fish. Although the dodger has appeared to be gradually edging up on the plug, the moochers are also creeping up into the top bracket. As more anglers become experienced in the use of this light gear hook-up more of the mature kings will be boated by this method.

The Use of Dodger and Herring as a Lure. One reason for the widespread effectiveness of the dodger-and-herring hook-up is that it combines both an artificial attractor and a genuine bait. Secondly, its success has been so bruited about that new anglers are likely to start using it. Thirdly, as a trolling lure for silvers it far outstrips all other set-ups and in the 1947 *Times* Silver Derby it accounted for more than 70% of the fish caught. It is used by many of the family trollers who fish in Puget Sound waters any time from early spring until late fall.

Dodger fishermen claim that, considering the diversity of water conditions on the Pacific coast, this lure is the most consistent taken when used on mature salmon. They feel that it works in all waters—shallow or deep—as it is equally good in ten feet of water at Dungeness or in the depths off Cape Flattery. It will take kings in fast tides or quiet water. It has plenty of action and can be seen at long distances.

One disadvantage of the dodger is that it is not adapted to the use of a light rod. When the heavy thrust of the dodger is combined with a sinker it takes a heavy tip to handle it well. When hooked onto a small salmon, the strong pull of the lure will often offset the fighting qualities of the fish.

The dodgers formerly came in full silver or brass finish or in half silver and half brass. Now, however, they can be purchased with an enamel finish with white and yellow being the two popular colors.

Harry Jeffs, who has been a dodger fan for many years, was one of the first advocates of the enameled flashers. He experimented by dropping painted insulators onto a sandy bottom in Elliott Bay in about 50 feet of water. He then hired a diver to go down and observe what color could be seen at the greatest distance. After much experimenting he found that a white enameled was more noticeable on dark days and a canary yellow the best for bright days. Accordingly, he usually starts off with a white dodger in the dim light of early dawn and when it brightens up or the sun comes out he changes to a yellow one.

The Dodger-and-Herring Hook-up. The rod and reel generally used by dodger anglers is the same as utilized by the plug anglers except that too springy a tip is not practical. The Monel metal line is customary in 20 or 22 gauge, with a backing of 18-thread cuttyhunk. About 35 feet of cuttyhunk testing 45 to 63 pounds are attached to the wire line with a bead swivel and then a snap swivel is fastened to the end of the cutty-hunk. The dodger is attached directly to the snap swivel. A wire leader in number 4 or 6 weight is attached to the herring with 24-inch length for o size, 27 inches for size 1, and 30 inches for the number 2 dodger.

One should use as light a sinker as possible with the dodger as too much lead will tend to spoil the action of the lure. Regulation slip sinkers are used and two or three ounces will do in most waters for early morning fishing for silvers. When the kings are in and it is desirable to get down deep, up to 8 ounces can be slipped on. The closer the lead is placed to the dodger the faster it will turn. Distances varying from two to four feet according to the size of the lure will work correctly.

A good plan is to attach the lead and then drag the dodger alongside the boat to observe its action. Do not put out line until the lure is turning at the correct speed for the water you are fishing. The lure should dodge or turn fairly fast from side to side without spinning or turning over.

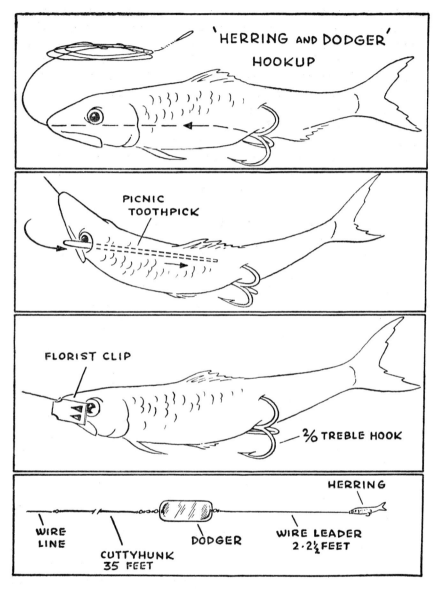

'HERRING AND DODGER' HOOKUP

PICNIC TOOTHPICK

FLORIST CLIP

²⁄₀ TREBLE HOOK

HERRING

WIRE LINE

CUTTYHUNK 35 FEET

DODGER

WIRE LEADER 2·2½ FEET

After you have let out sufficient line to get down properly, watch the rod tip to see that the line is still working. The tip should move steadily in short jerks.

Attaching the herring that goes with the dodger is the most complicated part of this hook-up. However by following the directions given below and referring to the sketches on this page you should be able to thread a herring so that it will spin naturally as if it has been wounded.

There are three steps in the process. First thread a 10-inch length of brass wire with a hook at its end through the mouth of a herring and then out the vent. Then the leader loop is hooked onto the end of the wire that extends out of the vent and the entire leader is pulled through the herring and out of the mouth. The eye of the treble hook (a 2/0 Mustad is a good size) is pulled into the vent. Then the prongs of one of the hooks is concealed in the outside bend of the herring with the other two extending freely below as shown in the illustration.

Now, using a picnic toothpick, thrust it through one eye, bend the herring in a slight arc and then push in the pick so that the fish will hold the proper bend. Do not pierce the skin on either side with the pick. Now snip off the protruding end. Finally snap an ordinary florist clip over the mouth of the herring and clip it down on both sides so that the mouth will be completely closed. This will prevent aeration. The herring should spin in the same manner as a cut spinner (explained in the chapter on spinning). The bright flash of the dodger is a great attraction for salmon. It is probable that they follow it and then notice the spinning herring. If the bait is working properly it should produce a strike.

Dodger and herring will work equally well for any species of salmon. The only difference in tackle is to vary the lead so as to get down to where the salmon are located. Generally speaking, a king will be found at a greater depth than a silver, dog or humpback. Many anglers feel that kings like a slowly spinning bait, while the cohoes will strike more readily at one with a fast, snappy action.

In place of the herring a spoon, small plug, or even a large hair fly may be substituted. The length of leader will be the same and the angler should make sure that both of his lures are working properly before releasing line.

Although now at the bottom of the sportsmen's list in popularity, the spoon was the first artificial lure used to take kings. Spoons were used almost exclusively by commercial fishermen and the sport anglers naturally followed suit. Today most commercial trollers still use spoons. However they also utilize large-sized plugs developed for this purpose by Seattle firms. These food fishermen usually troll with outriggers, using up to 10 lines with 2 to 10 pounds of lead on each. For boating large kings their lines will be drawn aboard with a winch.

Sport anglers troll spoons in the medium sizes, 4½ to 6, seldom going over 24 ounces of lead. Rather than use heavy sinkers they attempt to get down with a wire line or by varying the speed of the motor. Not more than twenty years ago most sportsmen would have a large assortment of spoons in their tackle box with only an occasional plug. Nowadays plugs are all the rage and only a few spoons will be found in the tackle trays.

Hope Island is one exception. Here the Canadian Wonder spoon, perhaps due to the fast water, has been very successful. Its use there is spreading and many week-ends it outfishes the plugs.

Spoons may be brass, silver or a combination of both. The pearl wobbler too has been a consistent taker of silvers and salmon trout. The spoons come in many makes and designs but virtually all of them are of the jigger type: that is they weave from side to side instead of turning over and over. When fishing strange waters, if you wish to use a spoon ask the local anglers what makes have been producing.

The same kind of hook-up that works well for plugs is customarily used for spoons. Generally speaking, a spoon will be most effective when trolled on feeding salmon.

One disadvantage of the spoon is the rapid discoloration of the metal that occurs when the spoon is taken from salt water. A spoon should always be rubbed clean or washed off with fresh water before it is put away in the tackle box. As the flash of the surface of the spoon is its main attraction, these lures must be polished to their pristine brightness each time they are used. Therefore, a soft cloth that will not scratch and a can of metal polish should be in every tackle box. Give the spoon a good polishing before it is snapped onto the line. (This advice goes for dodgers too.)

Many anglers polish up the spoons before laying them away as well. Wrap the spoon in a piece of tissue paper or cloth with the hook held away from the spoon before placing it in the tackle box.

Fresh Water Salmon Trolling. Although the greatest salmon angling on this continent will be found in the area extending north from the Columbia River into Alaska, there is a considerable amount in the coastal rivers of Oregon and California. The anglers to the south, however, take their salmon under very different conditions than do their neighbors in the Puget Sound district.

Virtually all of the salmon caught in Washington, British Columbia and Alaska by sportsmen are taken in salt water. All through this area there are hundreds of miles of protected waters of the Pacific where fishing may be done from a small boat. The salmon runs go through these waters on their last journey to their home rivers when they are at the height of their physical development: prime, lusty, full-of-fight specimens. The sportsmen have grown accustomed to the boating of these bright clean fish in the salt chuck and only in isolated cases do they seek these migrants in fresh water.

There are a few rivers where prime silvers are taken by fly fishermen during the summer-run steelhead season. In streams such as the Stillaguamish or the short rivers of the Olympics there will be runs of bright silvers in the early fall that will take a fly or a spoon. In the past, anglers sought the spring runs of chinook and caught many of these husky fish on a spoon in fast water. But within recent years such fishing has been banned in many of the northern rivers in order to protect the fast-dwindling spring run of this type of chinook.

In a few spots, such as Lake Washington, silvers or kings will be caught by anglers after they have come into the lake and are waiting to run up the spawning tributaries. However, many of these fish have already started to darken and are losing their salt water silver color.

On the whole sportsmen north of the Columbia frown on the taking of "dark" salmon. They feel that the ocean-fresh fish possess much greater fight and power and are more desirable as food. They claim that under the intensive fishing of the present day, combined with dams, pollution, and the deforestation of watersheds, that the salmon are so terrifically handicapped that they should not be caught after they have penetrated up a river and are approaching their spawning grounds.

The Columbia River Sport Fishery. However, in the Columbia River drainage and in many of the rivers south to California, slightly different spawning conditions prevail. The Columbia and its tributaries were once the greatest chinook spawning area in the world. Due to its length, huge kings came into its mouth still prime, so as to be set for the 1,000 mile journey ahead. These fish are taken at present in the lower river both commercially and by sportsmen. There is some sport and commercial fishing in the river above Bonneville Dam, particularly by Indians. But with dams that are already built and others such as McNary under construction or planned above Celilo Falls, it appears that the run in the upper river and the Snake, if not doomed, will be reduced to a pitiful remnant of its former size.

The peak of sport fishing in the Columbia is during a closure in the commercial season early each fall for about 15 days. This usually occurs about August 25 to September 10. At this time, during the height of the fall run, all types of commercial gear are banned and only sportsmen can take the husky prime fish. Virtually all of the salmon are caught by trolling and the commercial fishermen rent their boats to anglers and act as guides. The river from Astoria to Ilwaco is dotted with thousands of boats of all types: the large commercial trollers; private power boats; kicker boats; and even rubber rafts.

Anglers use the same trolling gear that they use for kings in salt water. Usually this will be a husky rod with a star-drag reel and plenty of cuttyhunk or metal line. Plugs are the popular lure with spoons second. The salmon run large, 20 to 50 pounds, and the fishing at times is fast and furious. When two scrappy kings are hooked at once from the same or adjoining boats the anglers must be not only lucky but expert enough to play their fish right up to the boat. And the man who handles the gaff must be certain of his aim.

The Lower Tributaries of the Columbia. Some of the large tributaries of the Columbia below Bonneville receive good runs of salmon, which are taken by sport trollers. The lower Willamette, although it is badly polluted, puts out some wonderful fishing, especially on spring-run chinooks. Most of these fish are taken in the months of March and April downstream from Oregon City, with sportsmen catching as high as 20,000 of these salmon in a single year. Most of these are prime fish in fine condition. The fall run, however, has been killed off due to the effects of pollution during low water levels.

On the Washington side of the river the Cowlitz is the big producer. It too is a spring chinook stream, with April and May the best months. These "royal" Chinooks are fine fish, occasionally ranging over 50 pounds. Much of this fishing is done from an anchored boat above a riffle where the current works the lure—a spoon or a plug.

The Kalama River is another fine salmon stream, which enjoys the peak of its run during the fall in September and October. These are large fish going between 35 and 50 pounds. Most of them are taken in the lower river or at its confluence with the Columbia.

Fishing the Oregon Streams. Most of the large steelhead rivers that flow into the ocean along the coasts of Oregon and of northern California have salmon runs. As the open water of the broad Pacific off these rivers is not too well suited for the sportsman angler, most of the catches are made after the salmon enter the stream itself. In the larger rivers, there are usually both a spring and fall run of kings. But in some of the smaller streams, especially in California, the salmon, like the steelhead, do not make their runs until the bar at the rivers' mouth has opened with the fall rains.

The angling techniques utilized in the lower sections of these coastal streams are virtually the same as those used on the tributaries of the Columbia. However in the smaller rivers lighter rods may be used especially during the silver runs or for the jacks of both the kings and silvers. When trolling from a boat in the broad still reaches of the lower rivers, sufficient lead is used to get the lure down near the bottom. Spoons are customary, both those of the jigger type and revolving type—the latter used with a red feather-covered triple hook trailing behind it being popular.

In rivers such as the Rogue, Umpqua, Smith or Klamath, many salmon are taken in the tidal waters of the lower stream or in the estuaries. This is boat trolling, with spinners, spoons or plugs the popular lures.

When the salmon have moved out of the tidal reaches and are headed upstream much of the angling will be done with casting outfits. Regulation steelhead gear or a stiff action bass rod will be the customary tackle. A good casting reel equipped either with silk or nylon line will do the work nicely. The new spinning tackle is excellent for covering the water but one will need the newer heavier lines instead of the "thread lines" formerly used. However such tackle or a fly outfit will be sporty gear when used on silvers or jacks.

In the upper reaches the usual casting lure for kings is a spoon, spinner or bait, the last generally salmon roe. Salmon, like steelhead, will take bait and hit cluster eggs readily when they are in the shallow water or riffles. They strike at such times out of anger and not to take food, as they are not capable of eating at such times.

When casting into water that is filled with snags or drifting over uneven rocky bottoms, it is well to tie on the lead with a light line, as with a steelhead hook-up. In this manner the lead will break loose when snagged and the angler will not of necessity lose the lure.

Chapter Three

SPINNING FOR BLACKMOUTH
AND SILVERS

When Paul Bunyan, according to the logger's tale, dug Puget Sound as a corral for mother whales to provide milk for his ailing Blue Ox, he builded better than he knew.

For this quiet inland waterway, seldom touched by ocean swells or storms, is not only a vast yachtsman's paradise, but the greatest holding basin for salmon to be found along the Pacific Coast. During the winter season, the adult salmon are "somewhere at sea" feeding on the ocean banks and of course do not figure in the sportsmen's catch. But all winter long large groups of young king salmon, locally known as blackmouth, which as yet have not ventured out into the ocean depths, are always cruising about the Sound. In addition, during the early spring and until the fall run arrives, schools of silver salmon will be found at the various "bait" grounds of the Sound. Both of these species, blackmouth and young silvers, form an important addition to the year-round salt-chuck fishing. They comprise the bulk of the catch of the ever-growing group of spinners and moochers.

It is a well-known saying among trout fishermen that spoon anglers look askance at bait anglers; that fly fishermen look down on the spooners; while the dry-fly purists speak only to God.

A comparable caste distinction appears to exist among the salt-chuck fishermen. The trollers disdain the hand-line fishermen; the plug expert looks down on the user of any other lure; the moocher gives a cold shoulder to the trollers and, in company with the spinners, communes only with Ike Walton himself.

Yes, the spinners are rightfully proud of their technique, even though this form of angling may not have had the attention given to trolling. In the first place, it takes a great deal of experience and training to become a good spinner, while, on the other hand, a troller with a bit of luck can hang onto a fish with very little advance briefing.

Tourists to the Northwest, who are salt water minded, always ask how they can "catch a big king salmon." They have heard so much about the size and rugged power of this noted fish that they can't wait to get one onto the end of a line.

Many of them do boat a king on their first trip to Puget Sound. For it is not too difficult to sit a newcomer in a kicker boat, place a trolling rod in his hand, with the plug or spoon working correctly and a proper set on the star drag, and have him hang onto a king. But it takes more than a rabbit's foot to be able to handle a fast-moving heavy fish on light tackle, and one doesn't learn the knack of cutting spinners the first trip out, or the second one either.

The Origin of Spinning Technique. The modern method of spinning was developed in lower Puget Sound waters among the salt-chuck fishermen in the Seattle-Tacoma area. They were rabid salmon anglers who fished the year round and were as enthusiastic about taking a salmon in the winter as they were when the spawning run was at its height. The quiet waters of the Sound provided an ideal testing ground for developing their technique.

In the first place, at the various "bait" grounds, there were ideal areas in which to anchor a boat and find salmon. Moreover the feeding silvers and young kings were in the Sound the year round. It wasn't too difficult to learn the periods when the fish would customarily school up in these spots.

Once this knowledge became general the anglers commenced the trial-and-error method of perfecting their "stripping" technique. A salmon on its return to the parent river to spawn tapers off on its feeding and while it lies off the river estuary it virtually ceases feeding. It will hit a lure, it's true, sometimes with abandon, but it does so either because of a lingering appetite for food or just because of an ornery scrappy instinct.

But the young salmon are still growing and feeding voraciously. So instead of trolling an artificial lure before them, the spinners utilized one of the salmon's main items of food—the herring—and devised the means of presenting this bait to them in the most life-like manner. As the herring bait could not be cast properly with trolling gear, a different type of outfit was developed, and salmon anglers found that they were taking fish successfully on tackle once deemed far too light for the smashing rugged fight of the salmon. Each year sees new refinements and advances in the use of this fishing technique.

The West Coast "Stripping" Technique. Although spinning at first was used mainly on silvers and blackmouth, anglers gradually learned that any salmon could be induced to hit a cut herring. So this type of angling called spinning was practiced the year round and in its modified form of "mooching" will take kings wherever they may be found. Some anglers "spin" summer and winter, rarely resorting to any other type of tackle. The main exceptions are at the height of a king run off an estuary, where trollers predominate, or at the ocean banks, where trolling is perhaps the only practical method of fishing.

Spinning is practical in any waters where a small boat may be anchored and where tidal currents are not too strong to prevent getting a lure down to the fish. Today there are spinners all through Puget Sound using rowboats or kicker boats. They cruise off the San Juans, using kicker boats near the resort islands or cruisers in the more remote waters. Then north in British Columbia waters, spinning will be a taking method wherever waters permit. A knowledge of local currents and tides will be a great asset to the angler.

Then in the salmon-crowded waters of southeastern Alaska from Ketchikan to Juneau, spinning is an effective technique. The Inner Passage presents hundreds of miles of protected water where spinners or moochers can work their lures. And although trolling is still the predominant method of fishing in Alaska at present, the stripping tackle is becoming more popular. When the runs are on in the Inner Passage the salmon are so numerous that they provide unexcelled sport. The angler who is accustomed to stripping all day for a dozen strikes will be amazed at the rapidity with which he can hang onto a king or silver in the less-fished waters up north.

The entire technique of spinning was built up on one fact: that salmon often "cripple" a candle fish or herring before gulping it down as food. After salmon reach a certain size they feed on fish whenever possible. In our local waters herring and candle fish form the bulk of this food, with herring generally considered to have the preference. These herring spawn in the Sound and salmon feed on them at all stages from the fry period when they are only 2 to 3 inches long until they grow to be 6- or 10-inch fish. When schools of herring appear at various locations, schools of feeding salmon are sure to follow. When the herring spawn in late winter, the blackmouth gang up off the spawning beaches and gorge themselves on the fat prime fish. The spinner takes advantage of these banquet tables.

A salmon when feeding is said to swim quickly through a school of herring, slashing as it goes at the small quick fish, or slapping them with its tail. It then comes back and picks up the crippled herring that are moving along in a twisting irregular progress far different from their usual quick dart through the water. It is the weaving motion of the hurt herring that the strippers imitate with their "cut spinners."

The really difficult part of this type of fishing, and the only phase that requires much practice, is "cutting a spinner." The "cracker" who is going stripping for the first time should either buy his bait already cut or inveigle an old-timer to take him out and show him how it is done. These experienced salt-chuck anglers, who fish so often that they have trouble washing the salt spray out of their whiskers, have cut thousands of spinners. They know the correct size of herring to use for spinner or plug cut.

They know the right angle to cut their spinners so that they will work properly. They cut their herring easily and deftly with a few swift strokes of the knife and rightfully feel that a properly cut spinner will take fish when a sloppy one will only give the fisherman exercise. It is only on rare occasions that salmon will go on such a feeding spree that they will slash at most any piece of herring dragged before them.

Cutting the Spinner. Most herring are cut right in the boat just before being hooked on, so as to keep the bait from becoming too soft. A cutting board about 15 inches long is placed on a seat of the boat. The preferred cutting knife is one with a single blade about six to seven inches long. This blade should be rather narrow, not too thick, and kept razor sharp.

The herring should be laid flat on the board. Some anglers first scale the fish on both sides; others do not. This seems to be a matter of personal preference. Next make a slanting cut back of the gills at a 45° angle beveled from the scale side toward the tail. Then, holding the fish firmly, a second cut should be made evenly along the back from the first incision to the tail. This incision should go down to the bone; be done with a quick even stroke so that the edge is clean and not ragged. It should come to a point at the base of the tail.

Then a third incision should be made along the belly side again from

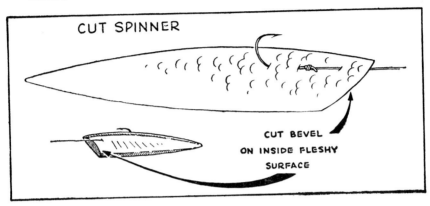

CUT SPINNER

CUT BEVEL
ON INSIDE FLESHY
SURFACE

the head to the tail, meeting the top cut so as to form a slice out of the fish's side shaped like a pennant. Then turn the fish over and make a similar series of cuts on the opposite side of the herring.

To remove the spinner from the whole fish place the knife blade in the bevel cut at the head and cut down to the bone. Then slide the knife in on an even slant along the backbone of the fish from the head to the tail, thinning off very slightly as the tail is reached. The pennant-shaped spinner may then be lifted off. A correct spinner should come off beveled along the top edge, while the cuts on either side should be straight and not ragged. The under surface should follow the contour of the backbone, being thicker in the center and tapering off toward the edges.

Herring in sizes ranging from 6 to 10 inches long will make the best cut spinners. But at many seasons of the year this size herring is difficult to obtain either fresh or frozen. At such periods the herring going only 4 to 5 inches long may be used to make "plug cuts."

The Plug Cut Herring. This type of spinner has come into general use only within recent years but it is now a popular and effective bait. Under many conditions it is as efficient as a cut spinner and many moochers seem to prefer it. When the small herring are the only ones available, it forms the only way of using bait.

To make the plug cut hold the herring between the thumb and forefinger of the left hand on the board with its back up. Insert the point of the knife about one inch back of the gills and then cut down at an angle toward the tail. Slice evenly until you have cut through the backbone at about a 30° angle. Then at this point slant the knife 10° more and cut all the way through. This will give a bevel edge to the cut that will cause the herring to twist through the water very like a crippled fish.

If the herring is very small, at this point simply pull out the insides.

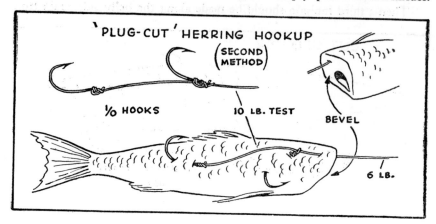

If it is larger, it may be necessary to cut off the extreme edge of the belly before taking out the entrails. In most cases do not tamper further with the flesh in any manner, as if cut correctly your herring is all set to be used. Occasionally, where herring become soft and flabby, part of the belly may be cut off so as to have a firmer spinner. Another advantage of this plug cut is that unlike the cut spinner it has the silvery scale sheen on both sides.

It is highly important that herring be well preserved, so that they do not become soft or flabby. This necessitates that they be iced even in winter, and during a hot day it is very difficult to keep them in top condition. Moreover herring just out of salt water will not cut up well. They will form firmer spinners if they have remained in a trap or tank for several days or at least overnight in a live box. This gives them an opportunity to clean themselves out. Herring full of food tend to burn when defrosted as well as softening up badly.

Hooking up the Spinner. Spinners cannot seem to agree whether the herring should be used with one or two hooks. Some always resort to the double hook-up while others stick to the single hook. And both seem to take fish. The rule that one hook works best on blackmouth and a double hook is better for silvers does not seem to be followed too closely.

In using a single hook on a cut spinner the hook may be inserted on the short flesh side of the spinner near its point and pulled all the way through. Then, with the point of the hook toward the tail about the distance of the length of the hook's shank, it is pulled through and out again. Then the leader is pulled tight so that the eye of the hook either enters or is close to the first hole that was made.

When a double hook is used, both hooks are pulled through the same hole. Then the top hook is inserted as in the case of the single hook. The end hook will be fastened in a similar manner near the point of the pennant-shaped spinner. When ready to use, the eye and shank of the hook should always rest against the scale side of the spinner or plug. Moreover the point of the hook should point in the direction of the head of the plug or the broad end of the spinner, with the bend of the hook toward the tail.

With the plug herring, the hook is first inserted through the flesh side of the bevel cut near its top on one side. It is then pulled all the way through and, if it is a single hook, it is fastened as with a spinner on the same side of the plug. If a double hook is used then there are two methods in vogue. One is to fasten the top hook as above. Then the end hook is crossed over to the opposite side of the herring, inserted into the lower half above the tail, and the leader pulled tight. This will place a hook on both sides of the plug.

The second method is to insert the top hook about halfway down on the flesh side of the bevel and pull it all the way through on the scale portion. The second hook is then pulled through the same hole. Then bring the two hooks down along the body, spacing them equally apart. Then with the point of the hook toward the tail, run it through the upper half of the herring below its dorsal fin, allowing the point to extend out beyond the fish. Then fasten the top hook near the upper end of the herring, turning the point of this one down. The eye of this hook, as in any of the other methods, should be buried in the hole through which the hook has first been inserted.

When only the small herring minnows are available, or as a contrasting type of bait, the whole herring may be used. In spinning usually the minnows will be used in this manner. Using a single hook, first insert the hook through the lower lip of the fish, bringing it out through the tip of the upper jaw. Then insert the hook into one eye and pull out through the other. When the leader is pulled tight the mouth of the herring will be tightly closed—a necessary adjunct to the whole-minnow spinner. The hook then should be inserted down the side of the minnow just above its fin and pulled snug with the bend to the tail and the point forward.

The proper action of a spinner, no matter of what type, should be one in which it wiggles from side to side as a hurt, struggling herring would swim. It should never turn over like a revolving spoon; and it should not be "dead," that is, it should not move through the water without any action. The ideal action will be neither too rapid nor too slow, but good spinners of course will vary between these two extremes.

Spinning Tackle—Rods and Reels

A spinner likes a rod very similar to one used for steelhead except that the tip may be a bit heavier. However this tip should be fairly springy, with a good live action that will "feel" a strike easily, yet capable of setting the hook well into the salmon's hard jaw. It should be stout enough to be able to handle up to three and one-half ounces of lead.

Lengths of rods vary from 8½ to 10 feet, with tips usually 7 feet long. A cork-handled butt with a double grip is preferred. Split bamboo is the common type, although a few old-timers still resort to the cane pole with guides and reel seat taped or wound on. The newer metal rods with light tips also make excellent stripping outfits.

The level-wind reel of large capacity and rugged construction is best for stripping. It should hold 200 to 300 yards of line. A free-spool reel without the level wind is sometimes used. As the reel is used mainly in the playing of the fish, a smooth-working reel that does not clog up or backlash is necessary to handle the fast-running blackmouth.

The reel should be well oiled to protect it from the salt water. The belt type of reel has found some favor because of its great line capacity and the ease it gives to handling a large fish on a long line.

Lines and Leaders. At first the Japanese raw silk lines were universally used for spinning. But since the past war monofilament nylon has become the spinners' standby. As blackmouth and kings make long runs, 600 feet of line is considered a minimum requirement and 1000 feet is recommended if the size of the spool will permit. The backing should be 15- to 20-pound test, either nylon or cuttyhunk, depending on the capacity of the reel.

Most strip anglers today utilize 6- to 10-pound test nylon for the terminal end of the lines. Some of the experienced anglers hook up 100 yards of either 6- or 8-pound-test nylon and then change it as soon as it shows the least sign of weakening. The 6-pound-test nylon is not too expensive and it is cheaper always to have a true-test line rather than run the risk of breaking off a good fish.

The lighter nylon line of 6 or 8 pounds sinks readily, is easy to cast, and camouflages well in the water. It does have one drawback, a tendency to kink when stripped into the boat, but this is not too much of a disadvantage unless one is fishing in very deep water.

Leaders are customarily at least 7 feet long or they may be the same length as the tip of the rod. They are made of clear nylon of the highest quality. Test of 6 or 8 pounds are the usual leader strengths, and they may be used with a line of the same test. If a salmon pops off a hook it is likely to break the leader at one of the knots instead of the line. Six-pound-test leaders are ample for blackmouth; one can go down to four-pound for silvers if desired or up to 10-pound-test for kings. A lighter leader than four pounds is rarely necessary as salt water is seldom clear enough to require that gauge.

Sinkers and Hooks. The crescent-shaped sinker is the lead universally used for stripping. It casts easily and due to its streamlined shape slips easily through the water. These sinkers come in regular rough lead finish but a few anglers like them chrome plated as they feel that the shiny flash of the sinking chrome helps to attract the salmon.

These leads come in sizes ranging through 1½, 2, 2½, 3, 3½ ounces. The lighter weights are used when spinning for silvers, which are usually near the surface. The heavier leads are necessary when fishing for blackmouth at greater depths or to carry down the spinner when there is a heavy, fast, tidal run-off.

Hooks vary somewhat according to the size of spinner used and the type of salmon sought; but most of them range between 2, 1, 1/0, or 2/0. These hooks are similar to the ones used for steelhead; and the Seely or Mustad are the popular brands. The point of the hook should always be kept sharp.

The Spinning Hook-up. The spinning hook-up does not differ too widely from that used in trolling in its essentials. A loop is made at the end of the nylon line in the regulation manner, except that after the doubled line has been looped over the finger this loop is twisted to the left and then the end is brought through. This makes a figure-eight type of knot to pull tight, one that will not slip or cut into the leader. This loop is then fastened to the end of the swivels at the top end of the crescent-shaped sinker.

A swivel has been fastened onto the end of the leader and a snap fastener may be attracted to this swivel. This fastening is then snapped onto the swivel at the other end of the crescent lead. These swivels are necessary to prevent the leader or line from tangling or knotting up from the action of the cut spinner when it is stripped in.

Old-timer Gus Zarkades has popularized an excellent method of attaching hooks with a double-hook tie-up. Hold up the hook between left thumb and forefinger—the point up and the eye between the fingers—and insert the leader through the eye. Loop the leader over the hook and under twice, then stick the leader end through the loops and pull tight. Then bring the leader back through the eye of the hook. Allowing about 2½ inches between hooks, hold the second hook in the same manner as the first and insert the leader through its eye. Then place three loops around the hook and bring the end of the leader through the loops back through the eye and snip off, leaving about ⅜ inch of leader as a loose end.

These double-hook ties may be made up at home with various sizes of hooks that can be used with either large or small herring. Then when a hook is popped off by a fish it is a simple matter to fasten a new one onto the leader. The same type of knot is made to attach the hooks to the leader and the three loops on the end hook act as a cushion for the three loops of terminal end of the leader that are thrown over them.

One may tie two hooks together with ten-pound-test nylon even if they are to be used with a six-pound-test line. The heavier nylon between the hooks stands up extra well when the spinner is hit by cod, dogfish or other bottom fish or by a lunker salmon.

Spinning at Gig Harbor. A spinning trip always involves a lot of gear. And when one gets out in mid-winter, even in our mild Puget Sound climate, the pile of duffle grows to monstrous proportions. There must be an outboard motor and cans of gas, and a good anchor, and plenty of rope. A large net with a long handle, and a box of herring are both necessities besides the fishing tackle. Then to ward off the weather one needs to wear long-handled underwear, woolen pants and shirt. Water-proof pants as well as rain-proof parka and a rain hat should always be part of the clothing issue.

It is a raw December day the week before Christmas when a group of us board the Harper Ferry on our way to Gig Harbor. The blackmouth have been reported in—large ones up to 20 pounds—and we are anxious to hang onto one of these rampaging, long-running young kings.

Although we arrive at the boat house in the pitch dark and no one can get out onto the water for several hours, there is a great deal of activity. A good boat must be picked out, which requires some deliberation, even if there are only two types, kicker boats for the spinners and row boats for the moochers. The anchor must be inspected to see if it is all shipshape since the last trip.

A workable anchor is a highly important part of the spinning gear. It must be one that is light enough to pull up from 125-foot depths without breaking one's back and still it must be heavy enough to hold in a tidal current. Nothing is more discouraging to a spinner than to get all set over the "lucky hole" and after a few casts notice that he is fast drifting along with the tide, as his anchor has failed to take hold.

Any of the modern folding type of metal anchors will do and they should be equipped with 200 to 300 feet of Manila rope ⅜ inch in thickness. This sort of anchor should hold even in a blow, especially if it is equipped with a holding chain. This is an ordinary lightweight chain 10 to 20 feet long fastened to the rope just above the anchor. It will help to prevent dragging and will keep you in the desired spot.

Although it has lightened considerably in the lower horizon the water is mysteriously murky as we put-put out of the quiet waters of the harbor, through the narrow channel, and smack into a heavy tide running off the bar. We buck the run-off along the steep cliff-like shore until we have reached the white house built right on the beach. We jockey around until we are opposite the lone madroña tree jutting out from the hillside. I let the anchor rope run through my fingers as Gus shuts off the motor. We head into the current as the rope slips over the gunwale. Then the anchor catches and we swing steady into the run of the tide, riding over about 95 feet of renowned spinning water.

The cutting board is placed on the middle seat and soon we have a half dozen freshly cut spinners ready to cast. We bait up and trail the pennant-shaped strips alongside the boat to observe their action. They are working fine and Gus to port and I to starboard make our casts out into the breeze-ruffled salt chuck.

Casting a spinner requires an entirely different technique than casting a plug. First the angler must strip into the boat the length of line that he expects to cast. He must do this in loose, even coils. It is perhaps well to start off with 50 to 60 feet so as to moisten the line before the full length required for the depth of water he is fishing has been stripped off the reel.

Then the sinker is pulled up to within an inch of the tip and, holding the line with thumb and forefinger on the upper part of the cork butt, the spinner is swung to the rear. It is allowed to come to rest just above the water. Then with a clean, easy side sweep of the arm, the bait is cast well out from the boat.

The line is released by the thumb as the sinker pulls on the tip, and the loose line in the boat whips out through the guides. The herring spinner should light on the water the length of the leader away from the lead so that both will sink well apart. Otherwise they may become tangled on the way down. The surplus line that was not carried out by the force of the cast can now be whipped out through the guides. The bait should be allowed to sink until it has reached bottom.

To strip in the line the angler, if he is right-handed, should grasp the butt of the rod in the upper section of the cork grip with his right hand and place the end of the butt between his body and his right arm. He should hold the line between the thumb and forefinger of the right hand. The city angler whose hands have not become calloused by heavy work may find that stripping the line—wet with salt water—through his fingers is apt to cut into his skin. In such cases, it is recommended that he wear a leather or wool finger stall or protector pulled over the middle joint of the forefinger of the right hand so as to prevent line abrasion.

Now the angler must reach up with his left hand and strip line over his right forefinger into the bottom of the boat. He should do this with a straight downward sweep, releasing the line as the hand reaches the six o'clock position. Strip in lengths equal to the easy reach of the left arm. It will help if the first several strips are thrown to one side and then subsequent strips are dropped into a loose circle directly to the left of where he is standing. He should be very careful not to step on a coil of the nylon and equally sure not to loop it over any projection within the boat.

This stripping action should be done slowly and evenly. It should not be too hurried or jerky. One trick to help slow it up is to open the fingers of the left hand at the lower part of the strip and pause for an instant. Occasionally several strips in faster tempo may be made; or one may pause and wait for a second or too. The angler should remember at all times that his cut spinner is supposed to act like a crippled herring and he should do his stripping so as to impart this action to it.

After all of the line on my first cast had slipped out through the guides and the bait had settled, I allowed more nylon to run off the reel until it hit bottom. Then, reeling up a couple of feet, I leaned my rod carefully against the gunwale, set the drag on the reel, and sat down to await developments.

This is called "dead-spinner fishing" and is a highly effective part of the strippers' technique. It is feasible wherever there is sufficient current to work the herring properly. You can leave the spinner working down off the bottom for periods up to five minutes before stripping in the bait to make another cast. Blackmouth, except in the early morning or late evening, are inclined to be near bottom. And you must get the spinner down in order to attract them.

By this time it had become fully light and, using a dead spinner, one had time to relax and gaze around. Although it was a blustery day there were a dozen boats anchored near us. Three trollers were put-putting around with deeply trolled spoons and two hard-working moochers were rowing along the narrow section between us spinners and the shore.

Suddenly I notice the tip of my rod bob sharply twice. I gently take the rod off the gunwale, hold it up and carefully take in the slack. Then there is another jerk on the tip, I set firmly but not too hard. I feel the heavy jerking power on my line and then the tip of the rod is pulled into the water as the salmon takes off on a sudden fast dash. Then the line starts moving away from the boat, faster and faster, until it is screaming off the reel. The strike has been made and the salmon is making his bid for freedom.

There are 150 feet out, 200, and still the salmon runs. The nylon tests 12 pounds and the leader 6 pounds, so the fish must be handled with a velvet touch. Now 300 feet have melted away and the reel is still singing. But the salmon is slowing down and when it has taken out 400 feet it comes to the surface and swirls atop a wave beside one of the anchored boats.

Then I am able to retrieve line and the salmon comes in for a while rather easily. But it turns suddenly and again the reel sings and line melts away. This give and take goes on for 15 minutes before the fish breaks the surface near enough for us to see its silvery shape. As it sights the boat it makes another run, and it is five minutes more before we can get a net under a trim fat 15-pound blackmouth.

An angler close to shore is also playing a fish and all of the spinners are alert, hoping that a school of blackmouth is underneath us and on the feed. Most of the men are stripping busily now instead of using a dead spinner. They cast out with an easy swing of the rod and as the herring hits the water they give it a slight jerk to take it under. As it sinks they play out all the surplus line that their cast didn't carry. Usually the bait is cast into the pull of the tide so that it will be down before the line has straightened out near the boat.

I go to my dead spinner but Gus keeps on with his stripping. After an interval I see his back stiffen as he strips in with a faster tempo. I sense that he has had a soft strike and that he is trying to hook the softly nibbling salmon. He has pulled in half a dozen times, when his tip is pulled down and he has hung onto the fish.

He holds the tip up and watches anxiously as the loose line whips out of the bottom of the boat. But there aren't any kinks and now he is fighting the fish off the reel.

Gus' salmon makes a long run and then heads for the boat. He reels quickly and it surfaces, thrashes for a second or two and then sounds. It makes a short run but does not go far. Neither does it sound. Instead it makes short fast dashes and Gus is able to keep it fairly well under control. When he brings it to net we find it is a bright fresh-run dog salmon of about 12 pounds in weight.

This is evidently the piscatorial lunch hour and I sock onto another fish, a fast runner that has lots of pep but not much weight and proves to be only about six pounds when it comes in. Gus hooks another that he loses and then he hangs onto a beauty that dashes all over the place before he is able to get it near the boat. When we have lifted it in over the side after a lot of excitement it is the best fish of the day, a blackmouth close to the 20-pound mark.

By this time the tide has started a fast run-off aided by a stiff breeze, which combination makes it very difficult to keep the bait down. So we pull anchor and head for the float inside the harbor. We are short of a limit but have had a whale of a lot of fun and have enough tasty fresh salmon to feed several families.

Spinning-off-the-reel, although practiced by only a small group of anglers, appears to be an effective method when done by an experienced fisherman. This technique varies from the regular stripping in that the line is retrieved by taking it directly onto the reel instead of stripping it into the boat.

The bait is cast off the reel and then sufficient line is released to get the bait down to the bottom. In most cases the herring will be left to work in the current near the bottom, as with a dead spinner.

When taking in line directly onto the reel one should vary the speed and amount of line brought in at one time. This should be gauged so as to work the herring as if it were being stripped. One can reel easily and fairly slowly for a bit, hesitate, and then resume at the same rate. Or the reeling may alternate between fast and slow. One should learn to regulate this according to the flow of tide at the location.

As one has the reel under control at all times, the touch of a fish can easily be felt. One should therefore be able to hang onto a salmon whenever one feels a good strike.

Two locations where this type of spinning is customarily done is in the hole off Point No Point and at Baby Island out of Holmes Harbor on Whidbey Island.

The ideal type of spinning water is 75 to 100 feet in depth in locations where there are few abrupt tide changes or tide rips. However, one can strip well at depths down to 125 feet. Good stripping banks often lie on the edge of much deeper water. The feeding salmon will come out of the depths to seek food in the shallower water nearby. The fastest action usually comes either after dawn or when the tide is at a low or high slack.

Where the run-off becomes too strong, too heavy a lead is required to get down to make for good spinning. During a hard blow or if the waves are running high, spinners remain on shore. They cannot anchor safely or strip line effectively under such conditions.

Spinning Locations in Puget Sound. Although spinning may be done any time of the year there are two seasons when it is generally practiced. One is from December until May, when the best blackmouth fishing may be had. The second period is from August through October, when feeding and spawning silvers will be found scattered all over the Sound.

There are many well-known spots in the Sound where the spinning clan gathers during the winter. Right in Seattle's front yard, in both Elliott Bay, the City Harbor, and Shilshole Bay off Ballard, fine spinning may be found in December and January. Gig Harbor, Wollochet Bay and Port Angeles show their top spinning during the same months, with the latter noted for its large fish.

Off Everett Harbor, at McKees Beach and Onamac Point the black-mouth hit from January through March. Seal Rock, Quilcene Bay and Bald Point, all on Hood Canal, have their best season in March and April and, in the case of the last, into May. Off Orcas Island at East Sound, December through March is good.

Holmes Harbor on Whidbey Island has its season from March to May but results there have been spotty for some time. Anderson Island, once a "hot" spot, has about the same season, but it has fallen off greatly in the past five years.

Point No Point across from Whidbey is a year-round spinning spot which turns out good catches whenever the salmon are running through Admiralty Inlet.

There are many other locations where spinners make winter catches; some of them fairly well known and others patronized by only a few natives.

Chapter Four

MOOCHING FOR SALMON

Mooching, which is a combination of spinning and trolling, has been practiced in a limited way ever since salt-chuck anglers started cutting up spinners. But it has only been within the past ten years that it has risen to the point of general acceptance. At first this modified type of trolling was utilized only on feeding silvers and kings. But now it has been extended to include all types of salmon from the small salmon trout to the hefty mature kings.

A moocher is a salt water angler who uses the light sporty gear and hook-up of the spinner to troll for Pacific salmon. At first this type of trolling was used only in quiet waters, such as Elliott Bay, where there is very little tidal run. But now, except for fast narrow trolling channels such as are found off Hope Island, the moocher can take fish anywhere a spinner or troller can.

Origin of Mooching. Spinners in the old days often grew tired of being anchored in one spot, especially so when they failed to find fish. So they often pulled up their hooks and just drifted along with the tide, their spinners trailing along off the stern of the boat. As this method often produced a good catch of salmon, the inventive sort of angler rented a row boat and went out with the express purpose of trolling his spinner instead of casting it.

Two of the early-day proving grounds for these light-tackle anglers were in Seattle and Tacoma harbors. Here the local spinners helped to develop the technique of mooching that has now spread all up and down the Sound and up into British Columbia waters. And with the new group of mooching-with-a-motor advocates this style of trolling is now utilized in virtually every bit of the Sound and in the Strait.

Mooching in its simplest terms is trolling a cut spinner or plug-cut herring, at a slow rowing speed, down at the depth where the salmon are feeding. The herring is rowed along at the speed that will cause it to imitate a wounded herring as it is pulled through the water.

Exactly the same outfit that is used for spinning is used by the moocher. The two hook-ups are interchangeable. In fact an angler can spin for several hours and then spend the rest of the day trolling his bait.

The best type of mooching water will be a spot where salmon congregate and where there is no extreme run-off of tides. The bottom should be fairly clean and not too uneven, so that the bait may be trolled way down without being snagged continuously. Waters should not go down much deeper than 125 feet and anywhere the depth is between 75 and 100 feet is considered a fine mooching area. Among the salmon grounds best suited for the row-boat moochers outside of Seattle's harbors are Gig Harbor, Wollochet Bay, Dines Point, Baby Island, Port Angeles inside the Spit, McKees Beach and all along the shore of Camano Island; Everett Harbor, Seal Rock, Bald Point on Hood Canal, Possession Point and the mainland off Picnic Point.

Trolling the Spinner. The moocher hooks up in the same manner as the spinner and then slowly allows his bait to play out over the stern of his boat off the reel. Usually he will be alone. If he has started out for the early dawn fishing, he may begin by putting out only 40 to 60 feet of line. This will keep his spinner working near the surface where the salmon should be at that time of the day.

Then as day starts to break more line should be reeled off until the sinker bumps on the bottom. The angler may now row slowly along, keeping the bait well down. At times he may remain stationary, leaving a dead spinner to work just off the bottom. If the bait is not bothered by bottom fish such as cod or sole, the sinker should be kept bumping along, as the bigger fish will usually be found at that depth. But should these bottom fish become too troublesome the angler will have to get his bait to a higher level. When fishing familiar waters, it is well to try to troll the boat over and through the lie spots where salmon should be resting or where they have been taken in the past.

The angler can stop rowing for a bit, so as to allow the spinner to sink, and then speed up. This will vary the speed and action of the herring and bring it up through the water on an inclined plane. The angler should reel in his bait occasionally to check his spinner to see if it is working. The spinner should always be dragged alongside the boat to test its action each time the line is reeled in before it is allowed to sink into the trolling position.

Hooking and Playing a Fish. Many anglers sit on the butt, so as not to lose their rods on savage strikes, allowing the rod to extend over the stern at an angle. At times the salmon will hit with the power of a pile driver and one must grab the rod immediately and be ready to give the fish its head so that it can run as it desires. At other times the rod tip may simply jerk a couple of times. Then the angler must decide whether to set hard at once or perhaps wait for a harder strike. Sometimes rowing just a little faster after a nudge on the bait will help to put the fish on.

Most old-timers stand up in the boat to fight the fish. As they are men experienced in managing a small boat on salt water they retain their balance through practice. However, the "cracker" should not attempt this unless he is immune to the excitement of hooking a big fast fish, for he could very easily take a dive overboard during the thick of the fight.

Keep the rod tip up and, as with the spinning gear, allow the salmon to run and play itself out. However, always keep enough tension on the line so as to make the salmon work every minute. Should you hook a large king that sounds, do not get too impatient. Just wait a while and it should come up.

A trick often used by experts to bring up a sounding fish is to strip off several feet of line from the reel and then allow the slack to run out through the tip. This will permit the lead to drop down below the salmon and the fish will often swim upwards trying to get above the pull of the sinker.

If the fish does not come up try pumping up slowly then releasing fast and reeling in rapidly as the tip is lowered. This should regain line.

A long-handled net is the preferred landing gear and, as in spinning, a gaff is seldom used.

Mooching-with-a-Motor. While it is true that most of the salmon taken by moochers are blackmouth and silvers, more and more kings each year are boated by these light-tackle trollers. Even in the Salmon Derbies,

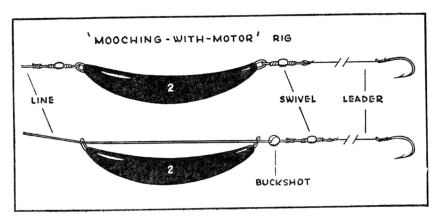

where the prize winners are usually taken on heavy gear, the moochers have broken into the magic circle.

In the last Ben Paris Salmon Derby, staged in September, 1946, Arnold Dunn boated the largest king, a 25-pound 6-ounce fish. He used mooching gear. Later that month, in the same year, in the Seattle *Times* City Salmon Derby, E. L. (Slim) Feathers won fourth place and an automobile by catching a 20-pound 12-ounce king on a mooched plug-cut herring. The largest king salmon to be taken in Elliott Bay on mooching gear was boated in 1944 by Mrs. Jackie Dahl. She hung onto a 40½-pound king on a 6-pound-test leader and battled it for an hour and a quarter before landing the lunker.

A new variation of this type of trolling developed recently is called mooching-with-a-motor. This type of fishing may be done almost anywhere in the Sound whenever the big kings are to be found. A small group of anglers are trolling the length of the Sound with motors and cut spinners from Neah Bay to Possession Point and their method appears to be attracting followers rapidly.

The gear follows closely that used by spinners. However, many of these moochers use a tubular steel or beryllium copper rod instead of the split bamboo. The reel should be large enough to spool at least 900 feet of 6- or 8-pound-test single filament nylon. The leader may be only 5 feet long, usually 6- or 8-pound test, with hooks either 3/0 or 4/0 Mustad preferred. The spinner should be cut on a 60° slant instead of the usual 30°

so that it can be trolled faster and at the same time have a tighter tail action.

The customary manner of attaching the sinker is the same as used with the spinning hook-up. However a new "kink" that is becoming popular varies this somewhat. You take the common oval flat spinning sinker, removing the swivel. Twist the ring at each end of the lead at a right angle and bring it over the straight edge of the sinker and flatten it a very little. The top figure in the drawing (page 219) shows the hook-up of a conventional sinker and the bottom figure this mooching hook-up.

Now thread the line through the pinched rings on the sinker and then tie the end of the line onto the seven-bead swivel on the end of the leader with a regulation figure-eight knot. Then in order to prevent the sinker from slipping down onto the leader, bite a number 4 buckshot onto the line just above the leader swivel. This will allow the sinker to slide back and forth on the line so that there will not be a savage jolt on the light leader when a king jerks against the lead. Throttle the motor down to about the same speed as used with a plug.

Trolling depths will depend on the fishing grounds. At Neah Bay or Sekiu it is well to troll at ranges of 30 to 70 feet, according to location. At Elliott Bay you can go down to 70 or 120 feet. In the Canal off Seal Rock you may have to reach down even to 200 to 225 feet.

After the fish strikes allow the salmon to run as it wills. If it keeps on going you may have to chase it with the motor. When mooching in congested areas it is well to open up the motor as soon as the king is hooked and then try to keep it on a short line. Salmon will usually head offshore and with a chinook around 35 pounds on a line it may take a wide-open five-horse motor to keep up with it when it decides to run. If there are other trollers nearby, it is well to circle so as to keep your boat between them and your fish.

Too much line out may result in a tangle and a lost fish. The secret of taking kings on light tackle is to keep them on as short a line as possible so as to try to prevent them from sounding. Do not hurry your fish. A "half-century" chinook is likely to break off the minute you start to do some "horsing." Two chinooks going more the 50 pounds were boated off the Strait in August of 1948 on nylon leaders testing only 10 pounds. That takes superlative skill as well as a generous portion of help from Lady Luck herself.

Chapter Five

BOATING THE LEAPING COHOE

Of the five species of Pacific salmon, the silver, or cohoe, is the "family fish" of the year-round anglers of this Puget Sound country. It is present in these inland waters virtually the year round—with a short slack period only during the mid-winter months of December and January.

During the spring months the young silvers, locally known as salmon trout, are caught in great numbers. They roam up and down the shores of the Sound, and family groups have little difficulty taking their limit of six of these tasty youngsters that run in size from 14 to 18 inches. These are the 20- to 24-month fish that are putting on weight before they either run out into the waters of the Pacific or wait to go up their home rivers.

Then through the summer months, feeding silvers that run from 2 to 5 pounds in weight also cruise these inland waters. Their numbers vary; some years the small salmon trout form the bulk of the summer catch. Then, as in 1948, the larger silvers spread out all over the Sound, and are taken readily on a troll or by spinners.

By August, the virile, fat, mature cohoes, on their way to their natal streams, enter the Sound by the same passageways on the Strait of Juan de Fuca utilized by the chinooks. And from this period until into November they provide fast, furious, exhilarating sport over their numerous feeding grounds. Coming into October they school up off the estuaries of their home rivers, waiting for a rise in water to pull them into the stream itself.

A Comparison of the Chinook and Cohoe as Sport Fish. While the lordly chinook may be the main entree on the anglers' bill of fare, the cohoe is the dessert—a tangy dish with an exhilarating flavor.

The chinooks, from the sportsman's viewpoint, are the powerhouses, the ten-ton trucks, the flying fortresses of the salmon family; but the cohoes on the other hand are the acrobats, the speedy jeeps, the jet-propelled pursuit planes.

A king hits solid and its run starts a relentless whirring of the reel. It can't be snubbed but must be given its head until it decides to stop.

The silver, on the other hand, hits like a summer-run steelhead; and on light tackle it melts line off the reel in a lightning dash. It fights near the top, almost always coming out of the water in one high leap after another. It will scoot along, just broaching the surface, then swim directly at the boat and as suddenly turn to scamper away like a frightened colt. When it finally sights the boat it puts up a thrashing, twisting struggle before it can be brought to net.

Silvers hit much the same type of lures that take kings or any of the other salmon. The two main exceptions are the gang trolls or "ford fenders" hook-ups utilized for the small immatures, and the use of flies for the feeding or spawning mature silvers.

Virtually all immature salmon after reaching the legal size of 12 inches look very much alike to the average angler. In fact very few sportsmen ever attempt to distinguish between them, simply lumping them all together under the name "salmon trout."

Young fingerling salmon, except the humpbacks, show parr marks like our coastal trout and when both occur together in salt water they are hard to differentiate. As they increase in size the salmon take on the silvery salt water hue of their species. However, when silvers and young kings are found together they look much alike. The king may have more spots along its back and the silver should, as its name implies, be completely dressed in a coat of gleaming aluminum.

The early spring trolling for young salmon is concerned mainly with the cohoe. These fish school up along various sections of the Sound and attract large numbers of anglers. Any type of rod may be used that will handle a set of trolling spoons. Usually a good-sized hook is baited with angleworms and attached with a short leader back of the spoons. The young salmon are attracted by the flash of the revolving spoons and hook themselves on the baited hook. Although little lead is used the hook-up is too heavy to afford much, if any, real sport on the small fish. However, these small salmon are so tasty that they attract many anglers who take them mainly as a toothsome food item.

During recent years many conservationists have questioned the wisdom of permitting such fishing, even though it may provide pleasure to family groups of unskilled anglers. They feel that it is only common sense to allow the salmon to grow until they have reached the "fighting" size that appeals to a sportsman's prowess. This growth is rapid, as the salmon have the bountiful food of the sea to gorge upon.

If only these immatures could be protected for six months or more, they would grow amazingly and become a worthy foe on light tackle. A silver that weighs 1¼ pounds in February for instance could grow to 3 pounds by May, to about 4 pounds by June, and then shoot up to 10 pounds by late September.

Spinning for Silvers. The next stage that silvers are taken by the sportsman is during the summer when these salmon are in the 2- to 5-pound class. These are wonderfully active fish, just coming into their prime—feeding voraciously in order to put on weight and store up oil for their coming spawning time.

While these cohoes will hit a trolled spoon or a dodger and herring, the most satisfying method of taking them is with spinning gear. The same technique as employed in stripping for winter blackmouth is customary. A rod with a light springy tip is preferred and single-filament nylon line with a 4- to 6-pound-test leader is the usual outfit.

The silvers at this time are found at varying depths. When they are near the bottom the same methods that work on blackmouth will be effective. Either plug herring or cut spinners may be utilized. During the summer when the large herring that cut into spinners are hard to obtain the small herring either whole or plug cut will prove satisfactory.

Silvers will often cruise back and forth over an area following the bait. At other times they will be near the surface and it is then that an anchored "spinner" will have fast and furious action. He will often hook a fish as his spinner is going down and sometimes as soon as it strikes the water.

Although not large, these cohoes are sporty foes for the spinning gang. They are fast runners and leapers and if not well hooked can shake loose easily. When the silvers are in, an experienced stripper fishing through a change of tide should hook into a dozen or so fish and be able to net his limit of six. These will probably be an assortment of sizes, from a couple of pounds up to six, all of them ranking high as a food item. A sportsman who has never tasted salmon except out of a can is due for a pleasant surprise when he sinks his teeth into a browned silver steak, juicy and tender, that only that morning had been "swimming meat" out in the Sound.

Often in late summer, spinners will hit into a mixed creel of silvers and blackmouth which will be found feeding together in locations such as Possession or Point No Point.

Catching the Mature Silver. Although silvers are present in the Sound most of the year it is only the dyed-in-the-wool salt-chuck angler who pursues them during the spring and summer. During the chinook runs when most anglers have "king fever" the silvers are pretty much neglected everywhere. But by late August, when the vanguard of the spawning cohoes have entered the Sound, until November when they are ascending their home rivers—the silver fishermen come into their own.

Now is the time when everyone goes silver fishing. It isn't a question of hanging onto a lunker chinook; of trying to boat a larger salmon than you have ever taken before. Instead it is the season to get out before the high winds of winter come along, and participate in the fast-moving action that accrues when you tie into a prancing acrobat: the energetic cohoe.

This is the season when the silvers are moving into the Sound in tremendous schools—spreading over the quiet inner waters to split up finally and then wait outside their appointed estuaries. Some of them may still be feeding salmon; they have left the ocean still taking on food as they are not yet quite fully prime for the spawning trial ahead.

These cohoes will wait at spots where there are herring and candle fish, eating and traveling with the bait. In late August they will average 4 to 8 pounds; and will take any type of lure that has the twisting flash of a small herring.

The trollers do well now and the dodger-and-herring is a common hook-up used everywhere from Sekiu to Elliott Bay. Others use jigger spoons and the pearl wobbler—a spoon fashioned of mother of pearl, with a red spot, which is a proven taker.

The Highly Prized "Hook nose." About the middle of September and then extending into November the spawners arrive. These are husky, prime, fully matured salmon, going up to 8-12-16 and occasionally to 20 pounds of dancing energy. This is the run of silvers from which the famous "hook nose" are taken.

A Cohoe Caught on a Regulation Fly Outfit

The silver or cohoe, the jumper of the salmon family, is a sporty fish to boat on any type of gear, but when an angler takes one on a cohoe fly, he is indulging in one of the most exciting, heart-thumping kinds of fishing to be found in the Pacific Northwest. The silver shown here is a prime salmon of about eight pounds. Note the cohoe fly, a double hooker, placed near the pectoral fin.

The waters off Tatoosh Island at the entrance of the Strait of Juan de Fuca are the mecca for the cohoe-on-a-fly anglers. Early in the season, which extends from July into September, the feeding silvers school up two to four miles outside of Tatoosh. Then later on they will be found inside the island off the Whistle Buoy or Duncan Rock. In September the cohoes move into the strait and start their migration toward Puget Sound.

The majority of silver anglers use regulation casting gear. A glass rod with a flexible tip is customary—using a small reel that can be set on free spool. The reel is filled with 12 to 15-pound monofilament. No weight of any kind is used. The fly is let out 20 to 40 feet behind the boat and trolled right on the surface. The fly is working best when it throws off a small rooster tail as it skips along. It may go under occasionally but it should be on the surface most of the time.

When hooked, the silvers will make a long, very fast run. They may leap at the end of the dash. They may make a sudden turn and swim toward the boat; then you must reel like mad to keep a tight line. They may come into the air in a flashing leap right off the stern and then swerve right under the boat. They act like a fish berserk and keep the angler at top tension until the fish is netted.

Young Fisherman with His 178-pound Halibut

The Strait of Juan de Fuca turns out the largest halibut boated on sports gear in Washington waters. The record halibut, one weighing 207 pounds, was caught in September, 1966, by Willy Perrenoud, fishing off Tatoosh Island. It measured 6 feet 2 inches in length.

Agate and Crescent Beach, which turns out kings and silvers in season, also has the best halibut hole in Washington. Each year monster halibut are caught, many weighing 100 pounds or more. The record for the area is the one shown here, a 178-pounder that was caught in 1965 by 12-year-old Bernard Barnes.

From Tatoosh Island east to Port Angeles, the Strait of Juan de Fuca is one of the best-liked salt chuck areas for the small-craft fisherman. During the season from May into September, small boats may safely ply all the inside waters for salmon or bottom fish. During the summer, anglers will find kicker boats available at the resorts at Neah Bay, Sekiu, Agate and Crescent Beach, and Port Angeles.

Many salmon anglers own their own outboard cruisers which they haul by trailer to the fishing grounds. There are many launching sites all along the strait. In addition, all boathouses provide launching ramps, and many of the public launching areas include camp grounds.

Two Fly-caught Shad from the Columbia

Shad fishing is a new sport in Washington and Oregon waters. This salt-water migrant is a terrific fighter on light tackle. It will hit flies or small spinners. It runs and twists with speed and power. When hooked it dives like a chinook. It must be played with skill and a light touch and cannot be stopped when it takes off on a steep, deep run.

The shad—which was introduced from the east coast into the Sacramento and Columbia rivers in the span of years between 1870 and 1880—has really taken hold in the Columbia River watershed. About 1.5 million shad enter the river annually, and the count of shad going over Bonneville Dam averages about half a million a year. Just below Bonneville, on either side of the river, shad may be taken by casting off the bank. The fish bunch up right at the angler's feet inside the turbulence created by the dam's tail race.

There is no limit on shad and when the fish are hitting an angler can take them by the score. In the accompanying photo of Columbia shad, the larger fish is the female.

The Author with a Catch of Shad

These shad were taken in the Columbia River off the mouth of the Washougal. The shad held is a female. You will note that it looks like a world-record herring. It attains its power by swinging its wide girth against the force of the current. Its mouth is without teeth and its scales are enormous for the size of the fish.

Almost any type of spinner will take shad. It must, however, be on the tiny side. An effective dressing of a fly consists of hook—six or four; tail—wine-colored hackle fibers; body—rear half, gold tinsel, front half, a ball of fluorescent wool yarn; no hackle or wings.

All male salmon as they approach their spawning time develop their upper jaw into a hook that turns down to meet a less-pronounced beak on the lower jaw. As they ascend their rivers and approach their spawning redds, this hook nose becomes more pronounced until occasionally it may turn down to completely close the mouth.

From a biological viewpoint, in salt water a hook nose is always a male no matter of what species of salmon it belongs to. Biologists of the State Department of Fisheries state that a hook nose in salt water must be a male of that species on its spawning migration. A female silver salmon virtually never shows a hooked nose in the salt chuck and about one out of 50 develops this type of jaw when it is on the spawning bed and at no other time.

The male silver is more likely to develop such a hook nose in the Sound than the larger king and often the larger buck silvers over 10 pounds show this development. Sportsmen speak of them as "hook noses," leaving off the silver part altogether. Old-time anglers were rather explicit in designating as a hook nose only the matured buck silver not the larger kings.

But in recent years, many of the newer fishermen have become accustomed to calling all large silvers "hook nose" regardless of sex. When a report comes down from up-Sound that the "hook nose" are in, at present this usually means that a run of fully matured cohoes have reached that location.

Trolling Lures and Boats. These large silvers are generally taken on dodger and herring, with mooching gear placing second and spoons and plugs a poor third. At times the silvers may be well down and it will take the flash of a large piece of metal to attract them. The dodger is particularly effective when the cohoes have ceased feeding and are waiting off a river mouth for a rise in water.

As it is extremely difficult to obtain any exact figures as to the effectiveness of various lures, I am again turning to the statistics as compiled by the Seattle *Times* in connection with its salmon derbies. These are exact counts as they are made at the time the fish were caught and noted by the boat-house operators. This table shows the lures which accounted for the qualifying salmon, silvers only, in both the 1947 and 1948 Silver Derbies.

Lures	Dodger Herring	Mooching	Plugs	Spoons	Spinning	Flies	Grand total
1947	1,163	302	66	17	13	15	1,576
1948	728	243	55	8	10	8	1,052
1949	531	209	36	3	9	2	790

In examining these counts it is important to remember that the great majority of these silvers were fully mature fish that were waiting in either Elliott or Shilshole Bays preparing to ascend their home rivers. Those from Elliott Bay will enter the Duwamish River to spawn in the Green River and its tributaries. Those out of Shilshole Bay will go through the Lake Washington Ship Canal to spawn in the various tributaries of Lakes Washington and Sammamish.

However, silvers that have just entered the Sound from the ocean or others that are still feeding would probably change the effectiveness of the various lures, undoubtedly bringing up the count on the fly.

When the silvers have arrived in the Sound they remain off designated spots for a period and these waters on holidays almost develop traffic tangles. Every resort boat in the vicinity will be engaged days ahead. Fishermen with powerful outboard motors will kick across long stretches of open water thinking little of 4- to 12-mile trips.

Various types of small craft called "kicker boats" have been developed here in Puget Sound that serve as ideal trolling boats for these inland waters. Some of the more popular boats have been made by Reinell, Lowback, and Franklin. They usually have semi-V bottoms, and are 14 to 16 feet long with a five-foot beam. They are almost flat in the stern, giving the fisherman a steady stance when he is stripping.

These boats are extremely seaworthy, handle well when caught in a blow, and steer easily when the outboard is throttled down. Most anglers use an outboard for silver trolling, as the lure is worked at a faster speed than when mooching with bait for kings. The smaller rowboats are utilized mainly by moochers who fish in the quiet protected waters such as those found in Elliott Bay.

Small cruisers of all types as well as craft up to the larger yacht class will mingle with the kicker boats when the silvers are hitting. Three to four lines will be trolled off the stern of a throttled-down cruiser, with the dodger-and-herring or spoon lures most commonly used. In such places the boats may be so congested that lines cannot help but become tangled occasionally. However this does not happen too often, particularly if each angler watches his pathway carefully. But anglers are gregarious, and when a fisherman hooks into a salmon he will quickly find himself surrounded by other boats that have crowded in hoping to hit a school of striking fish.

While the flasher, or larger spoon, appears to be the most effective lure for silvers during their spawning run, the feeding cohoes will respond to lighter tackle. The two most popular means of taking these fish are by spinning with herring or trolling a fly.

Spinning Locations for Cohoes. The spinning technique has been fully explained and although the description dealt mainly with its use in taking blackmouth, it is equally good for silvers. During the winter and early spring, the bulk of the spinner's catch will be blackmouth. But as the silvers increase in size after May, the strippers begin to hook the very active one- to two-pounders.

The waters just off the mainland from Seattle to Mukilteo, and the hole off Possession Point are two favored locations for these fish. Then during the summer, these silvers may be located in many areas all over the Sound. Spinners are able to make a one-day leisurely trip and, if they locate the fish, strip in a limit of these fine eating salmon in short order.

Then as the first vanguard of the ocean migrants come into Puget Sound, the tempo of the fishing picks up. Runs of silvers come in off Cape Flattery and later, of a sudden, appear in large numbers up and down the Sound. This is the time that the salt-chuck fishermen find the peak of their salmon harvest. As August merges into September there are kings off most of the estuaries and feeding silvers ganged up at many of the herring and candle-fish bait grounds.

Although there are anglers who are so afflicted by "chinook fever" that they can't see any other type of fishing, a large segment of the sportsmen now go after the flashy silver. They will be busily occupied spinning, mooching, or fly trolling all through September and into October until the hunting seasons on upland birds and big game open up.

They will follow the silvers around Whidbey and Camano Islands, off the Tulalip Indian Reservation, the San Juan Islands, and the mainland off Dungeness and Point No Point. The "Glory Hole" by Point No Point off from the swift tidal runs will at times hold a mixture of silvers and blackmouth which are feeding on the candle fish spawning here.

Creating Cohoe Flies. As the bulk of the cohoes' diet, when they are schooling off an estuary, is candle fish and herring, attempts were made around 1930 and later to represent this bait fish as accurately as possible artificially. A colored polar bear streamer fly became almost the standard lure. Some Canadian and American anglers had their own ideas as to patterns, however, and had individual flies dressed for their own use every time they went fishing in Vancouver Island waters.

To give an idea of the intensive study carried on with regard to these flies, I will give in some detail the experiments carried out by Letcher Lambuth of Seattle in 1936.

He constructed a tank in the basement of his house, of one cubic foot capacity, with a mirror bottom and glass sides. Covering the top of the tank with a tin cone, he placed a 200-watt electric light bulb inside the tank and closed the bottom with a green gelatin filter which simulated underwater illumination. The tank was then filled with salt water containing sufficient plankton to give the water the same optical values as that in which the cohoes would normally feed. This salt water was obtained on a cloudy day when the plankton were near the surface. Candle fish were then placed in this aerated tank.

To the human eye, under normal conditions, a candle fish is a small slender fish with a gray back, a pale green median line and a white belly. But when the room was plunged into darkness and the filtered light was turned on over the tank, the candle fish underwent a remarkable change in color. Now its back became an iridescent gray, its median line a carmine stripe, and the belly an iridescent white.

Letcher had previously prepared a good color range of dyed polar bear fur and by tying samples of it onto a hook he could lower this hook into the tank with a long tweezer to match the various shades of bear hair with the living candle fish. Thus, by various trials, a fly was finally evolved that matched the color of the candle fish very closely.

The exact dressing of this fly as now recommended by Letcher is as follows: A number 2/o to 3/o extra long shank hook is used, and the body of the fly is formed by winding the hook with flat silver tinsel. There is no hackle and the wings of the fly represent the fish itself. The white belly of the fish is imitated by three layers made up of natural white, pale green, and pale blue polar bear fur. A center layer of carmine fur is added to represent the median line. The back is composed of two colors: a yellowish blue green and a French blue (of a grayish tone) mixed and blended together.

A large generous head is necessary to hold the polar bear fur securely in place and this is finished off with blue thread. A coat of Duco may be applied to the head to give it protection as well as luster.

The polar bear fur must be tied in with great care as its consistency is so wiry and slippery that it tends to loosen up when cast. A good plan is to tie in one layer of hair and then soak it at the head with head cement or lacquer before applying the next layer of hair, which should in turn be followed by more cement. The tinsel body may also be lacquered so as to prevent its tarnishing in salt water.

This fly should be dressed so that the hair used to form the wings is at least 2½ to 3½ inches long. The shorter fly is best for casting and the longer one better when trolled.

In a later experiment, using the same tank, Letcher produced a representation of the common herring which is now almost universally used as a bait for salmon in the Puget Sound area. The salt water herring is a gleaming silvery fish when taken out of the water in daylight, but under the filtered light its color was transformed into an illusive tone very difficult to imitate.

Letcher evolved a pattern that had a silver tinsel body tied flat on the hook. The wings again were in three layers. The belly or bottom layer was natural white with a touch of green. The second layer was a gunmetal gray for the median line. The back was a full rich green with a few strands of olive green for topping.

These two patterns were intended to be fished over feeding cohoes. They represented the bait that the salmon were pursuing and under the right conditions should take fish.

Since then, as more anglers went into salmon fly fishing, and more fly tiers have become interested in the sport, a plethora of cohoe fly patterns have come onto the market. Most of these are not bait imitations but are attractor flies. They are various combinations of white, red, blue, or green polar bear with tinsel or wool bodies. When used on spawning silvers that are waiting off an estuary they can be exceedingly effective.

It must be remembered that these salmon have been gorged on food and their vitality is boosted up to the nth degree. They are at the apex of their life cycle and are pugnacious fish, full of fight and curiosity. When they are in the mood they will strike on impulse at any flashy lure set before them. In these circumstances any attractor pattern of fly will be a taker.

Such flies are usually dressed with bushy wings four to six inches long—preferably of polar bear fur. They are not intended to be cast but are always trolled. In the Puget Sound waters at the present time they are almost universally used with the addition of a spinner ahead of the fly.

Cohoe Fly Tackle. Even with the feeding silvers off Vancouver Island, the greater percentage of the catch is made on a trolled fly and not a cast one. For this type of fishing a fly rod from 9½ to 10½ feet long is preferred. Some like the easier-casting, soft-action rods, while others prefer to work with a stiff-action rod that will shoot a torpedo-head line with ease. The rods over 10 feet in length will cast and handle the bushy, large cohoe flies with facility compared to the labor necessary to cast such a fly with a nine-footer.

The longer, heavier rod is the more practical one for salmon. When two men are fishing from the same boat it is hardly fair or sporting for one angler to use a rod so light that it will take him more than an hour to handle a 12-pound silver. The longer rod enables one to give the butt to a heavy fish. It helps to stop dogging and sulking and adds rather than detracts from the thrill and excitement of the battle. A terminal tippet may be made light enough to give the salmon all the leeway desired in handling and landing the catch.

The rod should have a matching line that it can handle and cast efficiently. With the softer rods, B double-taper should fit the 10-foot length and an A or AA for the 10½-footer. With the stiffer rods of these lengths one would probably require torpedo lines in A or AA.

The fly reel should be of extra large size—one that can hold at least 100 yards of backing. The leader may be either 7½ or 9 feet with a terminal tippet of 8/5 or 6/5. A tapered leader, either gut or nylon, will turn the fly over better than a straight single-weight cast.

Trolling and Casting the Fly. When trolling the fly, one usually fishes with an outboard motor throttled down to a slow speed. The fly may simply be trolled as a lure directly behind the wake of the motor on about 35 to 60 feet of line. However, many anglers prefer to give their fly some added type of action. An effective method of producing this action is to manipulate the trolled fly. This may be accomplished by stripping in the line with irregular jerks, and carefully coiling it on the seat so that it may run out freely should a fish take during the stripping. The fly may be brought in for 25 to 30 feet and then allowed to drift back to the end of the line that is out. This stripping should be done slowly and then quickly, and will usually produce more strikes than if the trolled fly is left to its own devices.

Should the angler happen to be fishing with little competition from other fishermen, a good plan is to cut off the motor and cast from the drifting boat. Allow the boat to drift down through the feeding fish. Cast straight out to the side of the boat and allow the fly to swing to the stern until it reaches the limit of the line in use. Allow it to rest there for a short period, then strip it in and make another cast as before. If the silvers are feeding near the surface, they are prone to follow the fly, pushing a small bow wave ahead of them.

Whenever this happens the angler is on tenterhooks. The salmon swims along with its nose only an inch or so back of the fly. It may strike at any instant or it may follow the lure almost up to the boat and then swim away underneath. The angler must continue to impart action to his fly, never knowing whether he should speed up, strip slowly, or allow the lure to drift back. Silvers, like most fish, are not consistent in their feeding habits and the angler must trust to luck that he is doing the right thing.

When a salmon takes such a fly, it usually hits with a downward lunge, and the angler should not set the hook before the fish has turned onto the fly.

At times silvers will chase herring or candle fish to the surface and cause the small fish to dimple the water as if it were raining. A cast fly among the silvers who are slashing into the frightened bait will often be good for a "follow" or perhaps a hooked fish.

Kelp beds along a bar or in the shallower water appear to harbor bait and silvers will often be found in numbers among the long rope-like roots of the kelp. Row the boat slowly by the kelp and cast along its edge, stripping the fly slowly. Silvers will usually hit a fly presented in this manner as a trout does: quickly without fuss or warning.

The herring or candle fish are plankton feeders and will follow their food as it ranges through the water. Plankton abhors sunlight, and on brilliant sunny days it will go deep trying to escape the light. The herring will follow it down and at such times the silvers will be feeding at some depth. But in the early morning or late afternoon, the plankton comes to the surface, bringing the small bait fish with it, and the silvers should be cruising just below. This is when the trolled fly becomes a very efficient lure.

Dates for Best Cohoe Fly Fishing. Although predictions as to the best fishing periods are notoriously unreliable, a check of the Northwest waters indicates that the silver fishing is at its best under normal conditions at approximately the same time each year.

Off Campbell River the fly angler should find good sport from September 1st to 10th. Cowichan Bay usually comes through with its top fishing between October 5th and 15th. The Nimpkish—once one of the premier locations for both kings and silvers, but now greatly depleted—is much earlier, with the cohoes showing there about August 1st.

Coming down into American waters, the feeding grounds around Orcas Island in the San Juans will be at their best the latter part of July usually from the 20th to the 30th. Then into Puget Sound, the mature silvers appear off the south end of Whidbey Island around September 1st, and successive runs will hold up until October 1st. During the same month, silvers will be cruising all through the waters off Whidbey, the south end of Camano, and off Mission Bar and the Tulalip Indian Reservation. All of these spots offer sport with the fly much of which has not yet been exploited.

During some years, the silvers linger in Elliott and Shilshole Bays near Seattle until the latter part of October and will take a trolled fly there at that time in the same manner as they do further north.

Early Fishing with the Fly in Puget Sound Waters. Although anglers have been using the fly on cohoes in British Columbian waters for the past 20 years, the silvers south of the border have been virtually neglected. Why that is, it is hard to know. They are the same fish and they school up alike in feeding areas and river estuaries during the fall each season. But when the angler wanted to take a silver on a fly he invariably planned a vacation to Vancouver Island, passing up the Sound which at times was teeming with the leaping cohoes.

It is true that during the interim there have been the occasional curious American anglers who tried their flies on the Yankee silvers. Some of them enjoyed good fishing but the idea never took hold with the general public. Some of this fishing was done off Orcas Island and some off the north shore of Whidbey.

There was a flurry of fly anglers, from 1939 to 1941, who worked the fly in Elliott Bay when the silver run was on. They fished the British Columbian patterns amid the welter of derby fishermen who were trolling with heavier gear. In fact, during this period, several gold buttons were awarded by the Washington Fly Fishing Club for big silvers taken on the fly in the Bay. Then the war intervened and interest died out.

The Development of American "Cohoe-on-a-Fly" Fishing. American anglers have taken a rather different slant on cohoe fishing than their brethren in British Columbia. Trolling a fly as a lure proved so unexpectedly successful that it was immediately adopted by nearly everyone, with little thought given to combining it with regulation fly tackle.

At first, some anglers merely hooked the fly onto their regular mooching rods and trolled it like a spoon. Others hung it behind a dodger, and a few trolled it with lead as they would a cut spinner. But in almost all cases they used a small spinner ahead of the fly.

This spinner is usually of the Indiana type which revolves on a wire shaft with an eye at one end. The leader is attached to this eye with the opposite end hooked into the eye of the fly. These spinners range in sizes from 1 up to 3, with a few going larger than the size of a penny. Silver was preferred with the silver and brass "inside" second in popularity.

But as appreciation of the fly grew, anglers began to realize that this lure was ideally suited for trolling with a fly rod. So a heavy type of fly rod in either bamboo or metal (glass or copper) or a light spinning rod came more or less into standard use. This was combined with a bait-casting reel with two to three hundred yards of single monofilament nylon line testing 6 to 15 pounds. Leaders were invariably nylon varying from 6 to 8 pounds in strength.

The attractor patterns of flies now offered for sale have not become standardized. They vary all over the color range of red, white, green, blue, orange, or black, with each fly tier allowing his imagination to run riot in creating new designs. In size, they vary from 3 to 6 inches long and are dressed with hair wings (dyed polar bear, impala or bucktail) and either silver tinsel or red, green or orange wool or chenille bodies.

The fact that all of these haphazardly conceived lures take fish at times indicates that the salmon are striking primarily through impulse, anger or just orneryness and not because they think that they are hitting a herring or a candle fish.

Future Possibilities for the Fly in Salt Water. Taking the Pacific salmon on the fly is now only in its primary stage of development. Twenty years ago there was only a small band of fly anglers who tried for the cohoe in the salt chuck—today their group is numbered by the thousands. In the Puget Sound country the fly lure took like wildfire in the summer of 1948 and all indications point to a greater popularity for this type of fishing in succeeding seasons.

Although the trend in the Sound has been away from the strictly orthodox fly outfit that permits a cast fly and toward a trolling outfit, there promise to be further developments in the future along both lines. In the better-known fishing grounds, where anglers congregate in great numbers during a run, a trolled fly lure is by far the most effective.

But in the less-publicized locations where there are not too many boats, outboards or cruisers to put the fish down, the cast or the worked fly can produce marvelous sport. There are hundreds of such spots scattered around the Sound from Seattle to Port Angeles and up into the San Juans. Many of these are not accessible by resort boat but they enable the exploring cruiser-and-dinghy angler to find almost virgin cohoe fishing.

It has been proved many times that any of the Pacific salmon will take a fly. This does not necessarily mean that an angler can hope to catch a king salmon consistently on regulation fly gear. But he can adapt his tackle by the addition of a large-capacity casting reel, 1000 feet of line and a slight weight so that he can troll his fly down to where the chinooks are without abandoning the light fly rod. The lead may be attached so that it will be dropped free on the strike and he can fight his fish without that hindrance.

Blackmouth or young kings are boated often by the spinner and fly angler off Whidbey Island during the silver runs. This would indicate that these feeding kings are interested in a trolled fly.

The next step for the inventive, curious fly tier is to devise a feathered lure that may be used in place of a cut spinner for the large group of winter spinning and mooching enthusiasts. The field is wide open for this development. Good fresh herring for cut spinners are becoming harder to secure every season. An artificial spinner that worked would be received with open arms by every winter angler who freezes his fingers cutting up spinners during the blackmouth season.

INDEX

Abernathy Creek, 125-126
Alaska, rainbow fishing in, 97-100
Alaska Mary Ann, 51-52
Albion River, 153
Allouette Rivers, 120
Alsea River, 148-149
Angeline Lake, 37
Angling techniques, 198-200
    (*See also* Spinning; Trolling)
Apple Lake, 38
Ash River, 120
Asotin Creek, 126
Attractor fly patterns, 166, **232**

Bait, 32-33, 167
    for trolling, 22
Bear River, 126, 153-**154**
Beardsley trout, 6, 38
Big Qualicum River, 120
Big River, 154
Black gnat bucktail fly pattern, 55
Black O'Lindsay fly pattern, 51, 166
Blackmouth, 233
    spinning for, 201-215
Blue Lake, 36, 38
Blue upright fly pattern, 52
Boat drifting on Skagit, 80-81
Boat fishing, 79-80
Bogachiel River, 76-78, 137-138
Bonneville Dam, 85-86
Boyle spoon and worm, 11
Brad's brat fly pattern, 54, 91,
    96-97, 111, 165
Brats, 46
British Columbia, cohoe fly fishing
    in, 231-232
    Kamloops trout of, 22-24
    steelhead rivers of, 120-124
Brook trout, 8, 31
Brooks River, 97-98
Brown trout, 8
Brunette Creek, 120
Bucktail royal coachman fly
    pattern, 53
Bumping River, 37, 38
Byrne Lake, 37

Calawah River, 76, 137, 138
California, steelhead rivers in,
    118-119, 153-156
Campbell River, 120

Candlefish fly, 56
Canyon Creek, 126
Capilano River, 120
Carbon River, 126
Carey Special fly pattern, 13, 46,
    47, 51
    mooched, 23
Carot Nymph fly pattern, 46, 47, 50
Casting, fly, 230-231
    a run, 104-108
    spinner, 211
Casting lure for salmon, 199-200
Casting technique for steelheads,
    67, 73
Caycuse Creek, 120
Cedar River, 126
Cheakaamus River, 120
Chehalis River, 119, **121**, **126**
Chelan Lake, 6, 37
Chemainus River, **121**
Chetco River, 149
Chetwood Lake, 37
China River, 121
Chinook, 172, 173, 220
    and cohoe, comparison of, 222-223
    feeding grounds of, 181
    ocean migration of, 180-181
Cispus River, 127
Clallam River, 127
Clearwater River, 127
Cloquallum Creek, 1̃27
Cohoe flies, 56
    creation of, 227-229
    double hook, 56
Cohoe fly fishing, best, dates for, 231
Cohoe fly tackle, 229
Cohoe-on-a-fly fishing, American,
    development of, 232
Cohoes, 173-175
    boating of, 221-233
    mature, catching of, 224
    spinning for, 201-215, 223-224
    spinning locations for, 226-227
Columbia River, 127
    lower tributaries of, 199
    sport fishing in, 198-199
Conway, Dan, 43
Conway Special fly, 44, 53, 162, 166
Coos River, 149
Copper Lake, 8, 37
Coquahalla River, **121**

234